Salesforce Platform App Builder Certification Guide

A beginner's guide to building apps on the Salesforce Platform and passing the Salesforce Platform App Builder exam

Paul Goodey

BIRMINGHAM—MUMBAI

Salesforce Platform App Builder Certification Guide

Commissioning Editor: Richa Tripathi
Acquisition Editor: Denim Pinto
Senior Editor: Rohit Singh
Content Development Editor: Tiksha Lad
Technical Editor: Gaurav Gala
Copy Editor: Safis Editing
Project Coordinator: Francy Puthiry
Proofreader: Safis Editing
Indexer: Tejal Daruwale Soni
Production Designer: Jyoti Chauhan

First published: November 2020

Production reference: 1111120

Published by Packt Publishing Ltd.
Livery Place
35 Livery Street
Birmingham
B3 2PB, UK.

ISBN 978-1-80020-643-4

www.packt.com

Dedicated to mulligatawny, Nettlestone, good frogs, Pag cheese,
and amazing days in the spring.

Packt.com

Subscribe to our online digital library for full access to over 7,000 books and videos, as well as industry leading tools to help you plan your personal development and advance your career. For more information, please visit our website.

Why subscribe?

- Spend less time learning and more time coding with practical eBooks and Videos from over 4,000 industry professionals

- Improve your learning with Skill Plans built especially for you

- Get a free eBook or video every month

- Fully searchable for easy access to vital information

- Copy and paste, print, and bookmark content

Did you know that Packt offers eBook versions of every book published, with PDF and ePub files available? You can upgrade to the eBook version at packt.com and as a print book customer, you are entitled to a discount on the eBook copy. Get in touch with us at customercare@packtpub.com for more details.

At www.packt.com, you can also read a collection of free technical articles, sign up for a range of free newsletters, and receive exclusive discounts and offers on Packt books and eBooks.

Contributors

About the author

Paul Goodey, author of *Salesforce CRM Admin Cookbook* and *Salesforce CRM – The Definitive Admin Handbook* by Packt Publishing, has over 25 years' experience developing web technology solutions for companies of all sizes across a variety of industries, and has been building solutions with Salesforce CRM since 2006. While working with the Salesforce Lightning Platform, he has enjoyed working as a developer, business analyst, solutions architect, and system administrator to provide solutions for both in-house and consultancy-based end users. Based in the UK, near London, his professional qualifications include Salesforce Certified Administrator, and he is a keen and active member of Salesforce's administrator and developer online communities.

Writing this book has been a privilege, and I have thoroughly enjoyed working on the chapters. I am very lucky to have such amazing friends and family who have provided so much support, endless cups of tea, and encouragement, without which I would not have been able to complete my part of this endeavor. I would like to thank you for purchasing the book, the good folks at Salesforce for providing such a great product, and the team at Packt who have successfully orchestrated the completed work.

About the reviewer

Ashwini Sukumaran is a certified Salesforce Administrator and Platform App Builder. She has 10 years of experience and has worked with companies such as Genpact, IDC, and Symantec. She is currently based in Houston, working for an investment company as a Salesforce administrator. She is also working towards achieving the Salesforce Certified Application Architect Certificate.

I would like to thank my mother, Latha Manjusha; my late father, Sukumaran Nair; my brother, Abhilash; and my husband, Vijayraghavan Nair, for their constant encouragement and support. Without them, I would not have made it to where I am today. I am immensely thankful to them and appreciate all that they have done for me.

Packt is searching for authors like you

If you're interested in becoming an author for Packt, please visit `authors.packtpub.com` and apply today. We have worked with thousands of developers and tech professionals, just like you, to help them share their insight with the global tech community. You can make a general application, apply for a specific hot topic that we are recruiting an author for, or submit your own idea.

Table of Contents

2

Designing and Building a Data Model

3

Importing and Exporting Data

Section 2:
Behind the Scenes

4

Securing Access to Data

5

Setting Up the User Interface

6

Implementing Business Logic

7

Building Business Process Automation

8

Generating Data Analytics with Reports and Dashboards

Section 3:
A Step Closer to the Exam

9
Configuring the Mobile Features

10
Understanding the Social Features

11

Managing the App Building Process

12

Studying for the Certified Platform App Builder Exam

Other Books You May Enjoy

Index

Preface

As an industry-leading **software as a service** (**SAAS**) cloud application, the Salesforce Lightning Platform helps organizations of all sizes to manage customer interactions and improve business processes. The platform greatly enhances sales, marketing, and custom service operational performance and provides your business with an innovative and robust cloud computing system.

Salesforce Platform App Builder Certification Guide provides a step-by-step set of instructions and information that enables you to declaratively build apps and unleash the power of the Lightning Platform. This practical guide provides details that cover the topics in the Platform App Builder exam, which are presented with clear and comprehensive steps along with detailed screenshots, use cases, and practical examples.

Who this book is for

This book is aimed at beginner Lightning Platform developers who want to learn how to build apps on the Salesforce Platform or pass the Salesforce Platform App Builder exam. This book is also designed for experienced Salesforce administrators and existing Lightning Platform developers who are currently developing on the platform programmatically with code, and who want to learn more about the declarative, non-programmatic app building capabilities of the Salesforce Lightning Platform.

What this book covers

Chapter 1, Core Capabilities of the Lightning Platform, covers the Lightning Platform schema and core standard objects, looking at the boundaries of declarative app building compared to building apps programmatically, and describes the Salesforce AppExchange.

Chapter 2, Designing and Building a Data Model, explains how to design and build an appropriate data model and looks at field data types, relationship fields, and the impact of changing field type, along with a detailed look at the capabilities of Schema Builder.

Chapter 3, Importing and Exporting Data, looks at the utilities and features for importing and exporting data and describes how, with the use of external objects, data that does not reside in the Lightning Platform can be accessed within the platform.

Chapter 4, Securing Access to Data, shows you how to restrict and extend access to objects, fields, and records, and helps you to understand how, through the use of object-level permissions, organization-wide sharing defaults, and other sharing settings, appropriate access to records can be configured.

Chapter 5, Setting Up the User Interface, covers the declarative options to customize the Salesforce Lightning Experience user interface, where you will be shown how to configure and build functionality for custom buttons, links, and actions, as well as providing guidance for designing an appropriate user interface for a given scenario.

Chapter 6, Implementing Business Logic, describes how record types, formula fields, roll-up summary fields, and validation rules facilitate the control and presentation of values and the validation of business logic.

Chapter 7, Building Business Process Automation, looks at the features and capabilities for automating processes for given business requirements using workflow rules, Process Builder, and Flow, and how approval processes can be configured to automate the process of approving or rejecting records.

Chapter 8, Generating Data Analytics with Reports and Dashboards, describes how to use the analytics features to create reports and dashboards and how standard reports can be built, as well as how to configure custom report types to allow standard report templates to be extended.

Chapter 9, Configuring the Mobile Features, shows you how the declarative features can be used to customize mobile apps and set the mobile user interface, along with the configuration of global and object-specific actions.

Chapter 10, Understanding the Social Features, shows you how the capabilities of the social networking features can be configured to satisfy various use cases for linking Lightning Platform records with social network profiles.

Chapter 11, Managing the App Building Process, covers application life cycle management and describes Salesforce environments, sandboxes, and how to use change sets and unmanaged packages to deploy changes.

Chapter 12, Studying for the Certified Platform App Builder Exam, describes the certified Platform App Builder exam and looks at resources, including training courses and Trailhead, that are available to prepare for the exam and offers insight into the types of questions, along with suggested approaches for planning, booking, and taking the exam.

To get the most out of this book

The prerequisite for this book is a computer with an internet connection and the latest version of one of these supported browsers: Google® Chrome™, Mozilla® Firefox®, Apple® Safari®, and Microsoft® Edge (Chromium). You will need either the Enterprise, Unlimited, Performance, or Developer edition of the Salesforce Lightning Platform, along with system administrator permission.

Download the color images

We also provide a PDF file that has color images of the screenshots/diagrams used in this book. You can download it here:

https://static.packt-cdn.com/downloads/9781800206434_ColorImages.pdf

Conventions used

There are a number of text conventions used throughout this book.

Code in text: Indicates code words in text, database table names, folder names, filenames, file extensions, pathnames, dummy URLs, user input, and Twitter handles. Here is an example: "For example, IF(TEXT(Country__c) = "Australia", "Kilometer"... rather than if(text(Country__c) = "Australia", "Kilometer"."

A block of code is set as follows:

```
OR(
  ISBLANK(Sales_Person__c),
  NOT(Sales_Person__r.IsActive)
)
```

Bold: Indicates a new term, an important word, or words that you see on screen. For example, words in menus or dialog boxes appear in the text like this. Here is an example: "Click on **Report Types** in the **Setup** menu."

> **Tips or important notes**
> Appear like this.

Get in touch

Feedback from our readers is always welcome.

General feedback: If you have questions about any aspect of this book, mention the book title in the subject of your message and email us at customercare@packtpub.com.

Errata: Although we have taken every care to ensure the accuracy of our content, mistakes do happen. If you have found a mistake in this book, we would be grateful if you would report this to us. Please visit www.packtpub.com/support/errata, selecting your book, clicking on the Errata Submission Form link, and entering the details.

Piracy: If you come across any illegal copies of our works in any form on the internet, we would be grateful if you would provide us with the location address or website name. Please contact us at copyright@packt.com with a link to the material.

If you are interested in becoming an author: If there is a topic that you have expertise in, and you are interested in either writing or contributing to a book, please visit authors.packtpub.com.

Reviews

Please leave a review. Once you have read and used this book, why not leave a review on the site that you purchased it from? Potential readers can then see and use your unbiased opinion to make purchase decisions, we at Packt can understand what you think about our products, and our authors can see your feedback on their book. Thank you!

For more information about Packt, please visit packt.com.

Section 1: Introduction to the Lightning Platform Core

This section of the book covers the core capabilities of the Lightning Platform that relate to the essential knowledge required to understand the platform, how to build a data model for it, and how to import and export data.

This section consists of the following chapters:

- *Chapter 1, Core Capabilities of the Lightning Platform*
- *Chapter 2, Designing and Building a Data Model*
- *Chapter 3, Importing and Exporting Data*

1
Core Capabilities of the Lightning Platform

In this chapter, we will review the core capabilities of the Lightning Platform and test our knowledge of the Salesforce Fundamentals skillset, which is one of the primary objectives of the Salesforce App Builder Certification exam.

We will look at what makes up the Salesforce Lightning Platform and look at the concepts of the cloud, SaaS, multitenancy, and metadata-driven development.

There may be some sections in this chapter that you wish to skip if you have experience with Salesforce. However, it is hoped that these fundamental concepts will provide both a useful summary for experienced Salesforce app builders as well as key information for those that are new to Salesforce.

You will understand the capabilities of the standard Salesforce objects and the core Salesforce CRM schema and discover where the capabilities and boundaries lie when building apps with declarative and programmatic methods.

You will also learn about Salesforce AppExchange, which provides additional functionality that extends the core functionality.

Finally, you will be presented with a number of questions that test your knowledge of the core capabilities of the Lightning Platform that are covered in this chapter.

In this chapter, we will cover the following:

- Exam objectives: Salesforce Fundamentals
- What is the Salesforce Lightning Platform?
- Standard Salesforce CRM objects
- Customization options within the Lightning Platform
- Salesforce AppExchange
- Questions to test your knowledge

Exam objectives – Salesforce Fundamentals

The knowledge and skills that app builders are expected to demonstrate in order to pass the Salesforce Fundamentals section of the Certified Platform App Builder exam are as follows:

- Describe the capabilities of the core CRM objects in the Salesforce schema.
- Given a scenario, identify the boundaries of declarative customization and the use cases for programmatic customization.
- Identify common scenarios for extending an org using AppExchange.

> **Reference: Salesforce Certified Platform App Builder Exam Guide**
>
> This guide is published by Salesforce and can be referenced at `https://trailhead.salesforce.com/help?article=Salesforce-Certified-Platform-App-Builder-Exam-Guide`.

In the Salesforce Certified Platform App Builder Exam Guide the total number of questions is given as well as, a percentage break-down for each of the objectives, and an indication of the number of features/functions that can be expected in each of the objectives.

By analyzing these objectives, percentages, and question counts, we can determine the likely number of questions that will appear in the exam and for the Salesforce Fundamentals objective.

> **Salesforce Fundamentals: Total number of exam questions**
> There are likely to be 5 questions in total. This is calculated as 8% of the 60 total exam questions, which is 4.8 or 5 questions.

Using these figures for the Salesforce Fundamentals objective and the number of items that are likely to be assessed, we can determine that there would be **1-2 questions** for each of the following concepts:

- The capabilities of the core CRM objects in the Salesforce schema

- Where the boundaries lie between declarative and programmatic customization

- How and when to use AppExchange

Now, let's look at what is meant by the Salesforce Lightning Platform.

Understanding the Salesforce Lightning Platform

Now that we know about the skills and knowledge that are expected for passing the Certified Platform App Builder exam, let's seek to answer the question *what is the Salesforce Lightning Platform?* The Salesforce Lightning Platform is a cloud service that uses the **Software-as-a-Service** (**SaaS**) licensing and delivery model, and it has continued to evolve since its incarnation in 1999.

When it was first launched, the Salesforce Lightning Platform delivered services to empower Salesforce management within the limited realm of a **customer relationship management** (**CRM**) application. However, Salesforce disrupted the traditional software vendors of the day by introducing upgradeable, scaleable, feature-rich solutions for managing the sales process from lead to won deal and beyond within their initial CRM products.

The difference between the Salesforce Lightning Platform and other CRM software at the time was that not only did the CRM application contain standard CRM features but the features and functionality were continually enhanced and upgraded without the need for customers to install updates themselves. This ability of the platform to provide regular updates was achieved due to the multitenancy architecture of the Salesforce Lightning Platform. Let's discuss more about multitenancy.

Sharing system resources by using multitenancy

The multitenency architecture of the Lightning Platform provides a single instance of a database that is accessed by multiple organizations, or tenants. This is similar to multiple tenants sharing resources in an apartment block such as water, electricity, gas, and so on.

Multitenency allows economics of scale where the resource and maintenance overheads are shared by all those that are being serviced. Within the multitenency architecture, when used for a single instance of the Lightning Platform database, all of the data is managed for all customers and is stored in a single database schema. This allows Salesforce to update only one application and have the changes distributed for all customers, resulting in three major functional releases per year for spring, summer, and winter releases.

The single database schema, however, does not only store customers' data but it also stores the mechanisms for determining how the data is secured and how it is functionally used by each of the separate customers. The Lightning Platform ultimately controls the data storage and organization functionality for each customer to enable the customization of the core processes, and this is achieved by the use of metadata.

Building business solutions within a metadata-driven development model

If you are not familiar with the Salesforce Lightning Platform, you could be forgiven for thinking that the architecture for the application simply uses a set of web pages connected to data storage (such as a relationship database) using a common industry database connection. This, however, is not the reality, and instead, the Salesforce Lightning Platform uses metadata to expose a system built from an abstracted database with associated user interfaces.

Salesforce realized at the outset when designing its platform that businesses have unique business processes and challenges, and two organizations are rarely the same. As a result, Salesforce developed the Lightning Platform with a metadata-driven development model in mind so that it could be customized by its customers.

The features and functionalities of any given app for any given customer within the Lightning Platform are defined by the collection of metadata for that app, partitioned and stored securely in the core database.

The benefits of the metadata-driven development model mean app builders, developers, and system administrators don't need to worry about connecting to data or spending time analyzing data access scalability or performane; instead, they can concentrate on building business solutions. Hence, application build productivity is increased. More importantly, the metadata-driven development approach provides app builders with the facilities to build apps, pages, and business processes without any code development.

Since the platform is multitenant and paid for by a SaaS licensing and delivery model, there has to be some kind of limit on the amount of metadata, data storage, and usage, otherwise one customer might use far too much of the available resources at the expense of another customer. As a result, there are some limits that are fixed and cannot be amended and others that are able to be increased for an additional cost. Hence, organizations can choose to pay for an edition that will offer them the most appropriate set of features for the price they are willing to pay. There are the following editions: Essentials, Professional, Enterprise, and Unlimited.

Within the Lightning Platform, data such as files and records can be stored. The record storage mechanism uses structures known as objects. Let's look at the features and capabilities of Salesforce objects.

Looking at the features and capabilities of Salesforce objects

Objects in the Salesforce Lightning Platform are used for the storage of record data and also have built-in user interface mechanisms to enable users to interact with record data. Salesforce objects are key concepts that you will need to understand as an app builder and will most likely be included in the exam.

There are standard objects and custom objects in the Lightning Platform. Standard objects are provided out of the box by Salesforce and will be present when you first sign up and create your instance. Custom objects are objects that you can create to extend the standard functionality, where the need for a specific type of record data or process is not catered for by the provided set of objects.

Standard and custom objects are similar in nature to a database table and have properties that include fields, records, relationships, and tabs. Fields are a similar concept to a database column. Records are a similar concept to a database row. Relationships enable the association of data with other objects. Tabs are the user-interface elements used to display the underlying object data.

Salesforce provides standard objects known as the core CRM objects with which to store data records and enable your organization's business processes for customer relationship management. When you initially sign up for a new Salesforce instance, standard objects such as Lead, Account, Contact, and Opportunity are provided out of the box. Let's now learn about the standard Salesforce CRM objects.

Learning about the standard Salesforce CRM objects

At the core of the Salesforce Lightning Platform is the ability to create CRM solutions that manage the sales process with solutions for marketing, sales, and service. The CRM application has evolved over the years since its first introduction in 1999; however, at the heart of the platform are features and functionality that help businesses, large and small, to manage the sales process from lead to won deal and beyond.

Let's look at the standard Salesforce CRM objects in the Salesforce CRM. At this point, I'd like to invite you to log in to Salesforce and take a look at the home page, click on the setup link, and generally have a click around the CRM objects. If you do not have access to Salesforce or wish to create a new Salesforce instance, you can sign up for a free Developer Edition account.

Log in to your Salesforce instance or create a free Salesforce Developer Edition account by carrying out the following steps:

1. Navigate to the web URL https://developer.salesforce.com/.

2. Click on the **Sign Up** button on the page.

3. Enter your details into the **Sign Up** form.

4. Click on the **Sign me up** button.

5. You should then receive a *Welcome to Salesforce* email.

6. Finally, click on the **Verify Account** link in the *Welcome to Salesforce* email and you will have created your new Salesforce Developer Edition account.

Knowing about the standard Salesforce CRM objects and understanding where customization is required is key to the knowledge required for an app builder. In the Salesforce Certified Platform App Builder Exam Guide, the total number of questions that will appear for standard Salesforce CRM objects as part of the Salesforce Fundamentals objective is as follows:

Salesforce Fundamentals: *"Describe the capabilities of the core CRM objects in the Salesforce schema"*

There are likely to be 1 or 2 questions in total. This is calculated as 8% of the 60 total exam questions, which is 4.8 or 5 questions and 3 features/functions in the Salesforce Fundamentals objective.

At the core of the Salesforce Lightning Platform is the ability to easily deliver solutions for CRM. Standard objects and functionality go hand in hand. You can also create custom objects and customize functionality, which will be covered in *Chapter 2, Designing and Building a Data Model*.

There is lots to know about the core functionality that makes up the core objects and there is functionality that is in-built within processes, such as lead conversion. The capabilities of the Salesforce CRM enable the processing of marketing campaigns and leads through to accounts, contacts, and opportunities, and finally onto service cases, as shown in the following diagram:

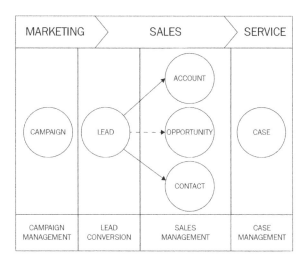

Figure 1.1 – Core object and business flow diagram

Let's look at the following feature areas and at the core concepts that are essential to understand before attempting to sit the exam: campaign and lead management; account, opportunity, and contact management; and case management.

The core features of marketing within the Salesforce CRM enable marketing professionals to manage and automate marketing campaigns in conjunction with lead development alongside the sales team. Within the marketing features, the following core CRM objects and capabilities are provided out of the box:

- The Campaign object
- The Lead object
- Lead conversion

We will first look at the features and capabilities of the Campaign object.

The Campaign object

The Campaign object provides features and functionality for the management of campaigns. Campaigns are marketing initiatives to target prospects and existing customers and include activities such as traditional conference and trade shows, print advertising, and direct mailings. Campaigns are also in the form of digital media, online advertising, and email targeting. The Campaign object facilitates the features and functions for campaign management and has links to the lead, as well as any opportunities that have been influenced by the campaign. The campaign management feature in the Salesforce CRM allows marketing users to manage and track outbound marketing activities. These can be direct mail, roadshows, online or print advertising, email, or other types of marketing initiatives.

The essential concepts, features, and built-in processes for the Campaign object include the following:

- **Marketing User checkbox**: Users must have **Marketing User** checked on their user record to use campaigns:
- **Campaign Members**: Contacts and leads can be associated with campaigns as campaign members.
- **Campaign Influence**: This is used to measure the effectiveness of campaigns by determining how the associated leads and opportunities have resulted in sales.
- **Campaign Effectiveness**: The effectiveness of a campaign can be analyzed using either the statistics on the campaign record or by running campaign reports. Standard reports are provided out of the box to analyze the effectiveness of the campaign, such as the Campaign ROI Analysis Report, the Campaign Revenue Report, and so on.

Let's look at the features and capabilities of the Lead object.

The Lead object

The Lead object provides the business with processes and structure for lead management. Leads are prospects or potential opportunities and are accessed in the Salesforce CRM from the **Leads** tab. They are sources of potential deals that usually need more qualification. They may be visitors to your website who have requested information, respondents to marketing campaigns, trade show visitors, and so on.

Leads are stored and managed independently in core objects such as **Account**, **Contact**, and **Opportunity** records, which are covered later in this section. However, Lead records can optionally be converted into an account, contact, and (at times optionally) an opportunity. If person accounts are activated (covered later in this section) and there is no value set for the account name, then the Lead record is converted to a person account and an opportunity.

The essential concepts, features, and built-in processes for the Lead object include the following:

- **Lead Process**: Establishing a lead business process involves implementing the steps and field values that are to be recorded by the sales and marketing teams during the lead life cycle. The lead process allows you to specify the Lead Status for lead records.

- **Web-to-Lead**: This enables leads to be directly entered into your Salesforce org from a public-facing website. This feature is used to generate **HTML** (**HyperText Markup Language**) code, which can then be incorporated into the required web page.

- **Web-to-Lead Auto-Response Rules**: Auto-response rules provide a mechanism to automatically respond to an individual after they have filled out a web lead form. The auto-response rules can contain logic to determine which email template and what content to send, which you can customize.

- **Lead Queue**: Queues can be thought of as a storage location to group records together. For leads, the lead queue is usually organized by geographic region or business function. Lead records remain in the queue until they are assigned or have been accepted by a user. Users who have been included as part of the queue can access and accept the records by clicking on a button labeled **Accept**.

- **Lead Assignment Rules**: Lead assignment rules determine how leads are automatically assigned to users or a queue. They contain rule entries, which are predefined business rules that determine the lead routing. Although you can create multiple rules, only one rule can be active at any one time.

Next, we will discuss lead conversion.

Lead conversion

Lead qualification depends on your business process, which usually involves the marketing and sales teams agreeing on the lead process, and when leads are qualified, users can convert the Lead record into an Opportunity record (the Opportunity object is covered later in this section).

When Lead records are converted, certain key information within the Lead record is mapped to the Salesforce CRM objects' accounts, contacts, and optionally the Opportunity records. Users can click on the **Convert** button on a Lead record, which presents the **Convert Lead** page.

The **Convert Lead** page allows the following:

- Choose to either create a new Account record or choose an existing Account record.
- Choose to either create a new Contact record or choose an existing Contact record.
- Choose to either create a new Opportunity record or choose an existing Opportunity record, or with the selection of the checkbox **Don't create an opportunity upon conversion** to not create an Opportunity record.

If you choose the existing Account and/or Contact records, only empty fields on the account and/or contact will be updated with the information from the Lead record. The fields on the existing Account and/or Contact records do not get overwritten.

Converted Lead records are set to read-only

Converted Lead records are set to read-only during lead conversion; however, as a system administrator, you can view converted Lead records. You can also provide users with permission to view and edit them, if necessary, by assigning them the **View and Edit Converted Leads** permission on their profile or within a permission set.

After the Lead record has been converted, the following values are set:

- The company name from the lead becomes the account name.
- The lead name from the lead becomes the contact name.
- The opportunity and contact are associated with the account.
- Any campaigns related to the lead are associated with the opportunity.

> **Person accounts lead conversion**
>
> If person accounts, which are covered later in this section, are activated and there is no value set for the company name, then the Lead record is converted to a person account and an opportunity.

The core features of sales within the Salesforce CRM enable marketing professionals to manage and automate marketing campaigns in conjunction with lead development alongside the sales team. Within the sales features, the following core CRM objects and capabilities are provided out of the box: Account or Person Account, Contact, Opportunity, and Case.

We will now look at the features and capabilities of the Account object.

The Account object

The Account object enables the management of company information for the organizations that your organization is involved with. Accounts may be considered as business accounts from a **Business-to-Business (B2B)** perspective and are usually the company records stored within the Salesforce CRM application.

Account records are also the primary mechanism used within the Salesforce CRM for the organization of records. Accounts are used within the record sharing and ownership hierarchy and are the parent object for other standard objects, such as contacts, opportunities, and cases. This is important to know when considering what permission security settings are needed to allow users to access record information. In this respect, record-level security controls and the sharing model for these child objects may be set as **Controlled by Parent**, which means they inherit their permission from the Account settings. This will be covered in more detail in *Chapter 4, Securing Access to Data*.

The essential concepts, features, and built-in processes for the standard Account object include the following:

- **Account Hierarchy**: By associating an Account record in the standard **Parent Account** field, a hierarchy of accounts can be established.

- **View Account Hierarchy**: This feature enables users to see the full association of parent and child Account records within the account hierarchy.

- **Account Teams**: This feature enables the granting of access to Account records for specific users who work on the same account. The feature can be used by users that are the owner of the Account record (or users that are above them in the role hierarchy and system administrators). This feature is disabled by default and there can only be one Account team but with multiple roles.

- **Account Merge**: This feature enables up to three **Account** records to be merged together in a wizard-style dialog. B2B accounts and **Business-to-Consumer (B2C)** person accounts cannot be merged with each other.

Salesforce provides another variety of account called a person account, which allows organizations with a B2C business model to manage relationships with individuals.

Let's look at the capabilities of the Person Account object.

The Person Account object

The **Person Account** object is used in the context of a B2C business model and provides a very similar set of features and fields to the standard Account object; however, Person Accounts have some differences.

> **Person Account object architecture**
> The Person Account object comprises both an Account object and a Contact object. There is an increased data storage requirement to house both these records per person.

The essential concepts, features, and built-in processes for the Person Account object include the following:

- **No Account Hierarchy**: There is no **Parent Account** field for person accounts, hence the hierarchy of accounts can be established and viewed.

- **Account Merge**: This feature enables up to three account records to be merged together in a wizard-style dialog. B2B accounts and B2C person accounts cannot be merged with each other.

We will now look at the capabilities of the Contact object.

The Contact object

The Contact object enables the management of contact information. Contacts are the individuals that your users want to keep in touch with. For the sales team, this is likely to be people such as purchasers and key decision-makers. For the marketing team, this may include the CEOs and CFOs and other influencers. For support, contacts could be any of the users of the product or service that your organization provides.

The essential concepts, features, and built-in processes for the Contact object include the following:

- Contacts to multiple accounts
- Contact hierarchy
- Private contacts
- Merge contacts

Let's look at the features and capabilities of the Opportunity object.

The Opportunity object

The Opportunity object enables the management of sales information. An Opportunity represents a financial transaction, deal, or a pledge between a customer or benefactor and a company or charity. For nonprofits, this could be donations and for business enterprises, this could be products and services.

Opportunity records are processed using a business sales process with predefined sales stages that typically advance to a final stage of either closed/lost or closed/won, where a closed/won opportunity represents a successful sale or paid donation. Opportunity records can either be generated from lead conversion or can be entered manually by the sales team.

The essential concepts, features, and built-in processes for the Opportunity object include the following:

- Sales team
- Opportunity splits
- Forecasting

Within the service features, the following Case object and capabilities are provided out of the box.

The Case object

The Case object enables the management of customer issues, feedback, incidents, or questions associated with the products and services that your organization is involved with. Organizations can use Cases to automate and manage requests for service and support by existing customers such as complaints, requests to return faulty merchandise, or requests from prospective contacts to provide information about products and services.

Case records can be manually entered from the **Cases** tab by users after, say, a phone call or email to or from a customer, and there are various features that support the automation of Cases within the Salesforce CRM and are associated with Contact records and/or Account records.

Case records can be created manually by users accessing the **Cases** tab, along with automated methods that allow external individuals to create Cases using web forms or email.

The essential concepts, features, and built-in processes for the Case object include the following:

- **Web-to-Case**: This feature enables customers to submit Case records online.
- **Email-to-Case**: This feature enables Case records to be automatically created when an email is sent to pre-configured email addresses.
- **Auto-Response Rules**: This feature allows the sending of an email to respond when Cases have been received in the Salesforce Lightning Platform.
- **Case Queues**: Cases are either manually assigned or they can be automatically assigned to Case queues (or to users) using assignment rules.
- **Assignment Rules**: Only one case assignment rule can be active at any one time, and each rule can contain multiple criteria up to a maximum of 25 criteria. Cases can be automatically assigned to users or queues using assignment rules.
- **Escalation Rules**: Automatically escalates unresolved Cases after a specified period of time.

So far, we have looked at the standard process automation that is available out of the box for standard objects. However, as briefly mentioned earlier in this chapter, Salesforce provides options to enhance the business process and modify the CRM application instance to meet specific business requirements for your organization.

We will now look at the features in the Salesforce Lightning Platform that enable app builders to customize the platform and build custom objects.

Customizing the Lightning Platform

Understanding when the standard Salesforce CRM processes and out of the box features are not appropriate or not sufficient to meet given requirements and require customization is key to the knowledge required for an app builder.

In the Salesforce Certified Platform App Builder Exam Guide, the total number of questions that will appear for customizing the Lightning Platform as part of the Salesforce Fundamentals objective is as follows:

> **Salesforce Fundamentals:** *"Given a scenario, identify the boundaries of declarative customization and the use cases for programmatic customization"*
>
> There are likely to be 1 or 2 questions in total. This is calculated as 8% of the 60 total exam questions, which is 4.8 or 5 questions and 3 features/functions in the Salesforce Fundamentals objective.

We will now look at the following concepts and considerations for customizing the Lightning Platform:

- Programmatic customization
- Declarative customization
- Process Builder action types
- The Workflow and Approvals action types
- General use cases for programmatic customization

Let's look at the features and capabilities for programmatic customization in the Lightning Platform.

Programmatic customization

The good news, if you do not enjoy being tested on coding skills, is that the Salesforce Certified Platform App Builder exam contains no questions on how to write code using programmatic customization.

While you will not be expected to know how to program or be given any questions on writing code, you are expected to have an understanding of how code can be used in the Salesforce Lightning Platform. You must have an awareness of what code options exist in the Salesforce Lightning Platform, and this is particularly important when app builders are faced with a need to build or implement the most appropriate solution.

The programmatic options for customizing the Salesforce Lightning Platform include the following:

- **Apex Code**: Apex is an object-oriented programming language that executes on the Salesforce Lightning Platform. Similar to Java, the Apex programming language allows the building of functionality that executes transaction control statements within the server.

- **Apex Triggers**: Apex triggers are used to create custom actions that execute before or after events such as record creation, record update, and record deletes, and are used when there is no user input.

- **Visualforce Pages**: Visualforce pages comprise sets of tags that connect to the server and render back to the web user interface. The tags are associated with standard or custom controllers that are used to connect to the database.

- **Lightning Components**: Lightning components are available in two programming models. Firstly, there is the Aura Components programming model, and secondly, there is **Lightning Web Components** (**LWC**), which uses a lightweight framework with JavaScript and HTML.

The advantages of using programmatic customization include the following:

- Flexibility
- Reusability
- User interface complexity
- Integration

While there are benefits, there are also disadvantages, such as the following:

- Additional testing requirements
- Higher development costs
- A potential lack of scalability
- Less responsiveness to change
- Additional risk when deploying changes
- A lack of availability of developer skills

Having outlined the options for code and the advantages and disadvantages, we will now outline the options for declarative customization.

Declarative customization

There are several terms you may be aware of that are used to describe declarative customization. Some of those terms are **Clicks not Code**, **Point and Click**, **Drag and Drop**, **Click v Code**, and **No Code Development**.

What these terms mean with respect to the Salesforce Lightning Platform is that they allow solutions to be built by individuals without the need to write code.

Let's look at the options for building apps using declarative development. We will look in far more detail at building solutions using declarative development tools in *Chapter 7, Building Business Process Automation*.

The declarative options for customizing the Salesforce Lightning Platform include the following:

- **Process Builder**: Process Builder is a workflow automation tool that allows you to automate business processes and uses a user-friendly visual interface with point-and-click features. The tool supports the building of multiple rules with associated criteria and actions in a single process where actions are fired when new or updated records meet the specified criteria. Process Builder starts when either a record is created or edited, Process Builder is called by another process, or a platform event message is fired.

- **Flow**: Flow is a workflow automation tool that allows you to automate business process screen wizards or complex background processes that use extensive branching logic.

  Like Process Builder, flows are created using Flow Builder, a user-friendly visual interface with point-and-click features. Flows can be either screen flows with a user interface or autolaunched flows that do not have a screen.

- **Approvals**: Approval processes allow the configuration of steps that are used to approve or reject records that have been submitted for approval. Approval processes include entry criteria and designated uses that must be met to allow approval during the steps. In addition, approval processes allow the creation of actions that are triggered as a record is submitted, approved, rejected, or recalled.

- **Workflow**: Workflow rules initiate workflow actions when specified conditions (or criteria) have been met. Workflow actions can be set to execute immediately or can be set using the time-dependent feature that results in the workflow actions being executed at a future date.

> **Automation and editions**
>
> At the time of writing, Process Builder and Flow are available in the following editions: Essentials, Professional, Enterprise, Performance, Unlimited, and Developer. Approvals and Workflow are available in the following editions: Enterprise, Performance, Unlimited, and Developer.
>
> Reference: `https://help.salesforce.com/articleView?id=process_which_tool.htm`

Now let's look at the type of actions that can be performed in Process Builder.

Process Builder action types

In Process Builder, the following actions types can be performed:

- **Apex**: Apex actions invoke an Apex class with an invocable method.
- **Create a Record**: Creates a record – actions allow you to create a record of any supported type.
- **Email Alerts**: Email alert actions use an email template that is used to populate the email details that are sent to specified recipients that can be either Salesforce CRM users or external email recipients.
- **Flows**: Flow actions enable the triggering of an auto-launched flow.
- **Post to Chatter**: This action enables the creation of a Chatter Post.
- **Processes**: These actions enable the invocation of a different process.
- **Quick Actions**: Quick actions are used to invoke an action.
- **Quip**: This action initiates a Quip integration. Quip for Salesforce provides a collaborative document and chat integration within Salesforce. Quip actions are available if you have Quip for Salesforce integration.
- **Send Custom Notifications**: This action sends custom notifications, which are used to notify users when important events occur.
- **Submit for Approval**: This action enables the automatic submission of an approval process.
- **Update Records**: This action enables the update of any related record.

Now let's look at the type of actions that can be carried out in flows.

Flow action types

The process automation actions that can be configured in Flow are separated into two areas: namely Flow Elements and Flow Core Actions. Flow Elements allow the following types of automation to be carried out:

- **Apex Action**: Apex actions invoke an Apex class with an invocable method.
- **Subflow**: This action enables the triggering of another flow.
- **Create Records**: This action enables the creation of either one or multiple records.
- **Get Records**: This action gets records based on specified criteria.
- **Delete Records**: This action deletes records using the record ID.
- **Update Records**: This action enables the update of any related record.
- **Email Alert**: Email alert actions use an email template that is used to populate the email details to be sent to specified recipients, which can be either Salesforce CRM users or external email recipients.
- **Core Action**: There are many types of core actions, such as Email Alerts, Submit for Approval, and so on, and these are listed in the next section.

Nested within the Flow Elements **Flow Core Action** options, the following types of actions can be performed:

- **Update Records**: This action enables the update of any related record.
- **Activate Session-Based Permission Set**: This action activates a session-based permission set for the user that is running the flow.
- **Deactivate Session-Based Permission Set**: This action deactivates a session-based permission set for the user that is running the flow.
- **Post to Chatter**: This action enables the creation of a Chatter Post.
- **Action**: Quick actions are used to invoke an action.
- **Send Custom Notification**: This action sends custom notifications, which are used to notify users when important events occur.
- **Email Alerts**: This action sends an email using a subject, body, and email recipients.
- **Submit for Approval**: This action enables the automatic submission of an approval process.

Now let's look at the type of actions that can be carried out in Workflow and approvals.

Workflow and approval action types

There are different Workflow and approval action types, which are listed here:

- **Email Alerts**: Email alerts actions use an email template that is used to populate the email details to be sent to specified recipients, which can be either Salesforce CRM users or external email recipients.

- **Field Updates**: Field update actions allow you to specify a field for update and set a new value for it. The field's update action depends on the data type of the field, where you can choose to apply a specific value, clear the field, or calculate a value according to criteria or a derived formula that you can specify.

- **Tasks**: Task actions enable the assignment of tasks to a user that you can specify. You would also specify the **Subject**, **Status**, **Priority**, and **Due Date** of the task. Tasks can be assigned on their own, but you can also combine them with an email alert to inform the user.

- **Send Action**: Send actions are used to automatically send email messages at the end of an approval process.

- **Outbound Messages**: This an action that can be activated by both workflows and approvals, which sends information to a web URL endpoint. The outbound message contains the data in specified fields in what is known as a SOAP message to the endpoint.

Having previously looked at the advantages and disadvantages of building solutions using code, we will now consider one of the often-difficult choices when working with the Lightning Platform, namely, when to use programmatic solutions and when to use declarative development.

In reality, in most Salesforce instances – certainly ones that have been customized over a reasonable period of time – there is no distinct separation between ones customized declaratively and ones that contain programmatic solutions. There tends to be a mix of both methods of customization both at the org level and also at the solution level.

We will now look at how we can assess the most appropriate method of customization for the types of requirements that app builders may encounter. Let's now identify the boundaries of declarative customization and the general use cases for programmatic customization.

General use cases for programmatic customization

As we learned previously in this chapter, Salesforce pioneered the ability to provide a platform that can be developed by using code and non-coded mechanisms. The platform allows an underlying architecture that supports business processing and data storage – metadata key building blocks needed are to build applications.

Although there are no hard and fast rules on when to use code, the specific use case and the resources available help to determine the best approach, and in other situations, there are some solutions that must be built with code as this is the only option.

Here are some general use cases for choosing programmatic solutions:

- Integration using the API to connect with other systems
- When highly complex user interfaces are required
- When large data volumes need to be batched and processed in the background
- When the out-of-the-box standard object features need to be extended
- When the out-of-the-box automation tools do not have the necessary actions

Here are some specific use cases where out-of-the-box automation tools lack the capability and that require a programmatic solution:

- When records need to be undeleted
- When multiple types of records need to be simultaneously created or updated
- When adding Apex to flows or Process Builder
- When adding Lightning components to flows

Often, adding Lightning components to flows or including Apex in Process Builder offers a far better solution than attempting to build a solution either entirely in code or entirely using declarative tools.

> **Avoid building complex flows**
>
> It is often better to avoid building complex flows that push the boundaries of the Flow Builder tool and are difficult to manage, and to instead use a programmatic solution.

Programmatic solutions such as Lightning components and apps can be sourced on Salesforce AppExchange, which we will now explore.

Exploring Salesforce AppExchange

Launched in 2006, Salesforce AppExchange is a business cloud marketplace provided by Salesforce and is integrated within the Salesforce Lightning Platform. Access to AppExchange can be gained via a website hosted by Salesforce and also from within the Salesforce CRM application.

There is an expectation that app builders will be familiar with what is available on AppExchange and what the use cases are for choosing to install solutions in an org from AppExchange, as noted in the Salesforce Certified Platform App Builder Exam Guide:

> **Salesforce Fundamentals:** *"Identify common scenarios for extending an org using the AppExchange"*
>
> There are likely to be 1 or 2 questions in total. This is calculated as 8% of the 60 total exam questions, which is 4.8 or 5 questions and 3 features/functions in the Salesforce Fundamentals objective.

There is a variety of solutions and services that are available on AppExchange that serve to extend the core functionality and features within Salesforce.

> **Note**
> Salesforce AppExchange can be accessed using the following URL: `https://appexchange.salesforce.com/`.

The solutions and services listed on AppExchange are provided by the Salesforce community of third-party developers and system integrators, as well as from Salesforce, and include **Apps**, **Components**, **Bolt Solutions**, **Lightning Data**, **Flow Solutions**, and **Consultants**, as shown in the following screenshot:

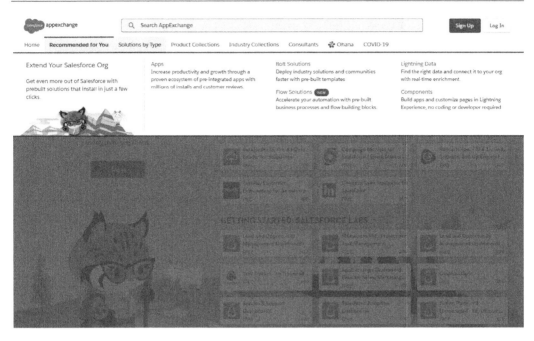

Figure 1.2 – Salesforce AppExchange

Solutions and services

At the time of writing, there are more than 5,000 solutions and at least 1,000 consulting services listed on the AppExchange marketplace.

Let's look at the types of solutions that are available on Salesforce AppExchange.

Apps

Apps contain prebuilt functionality that can be installed in your instance of Salesforce to extend the out-of-the-box features. An app contains items such as custom objects, tabs, code, components, and so on. Along with the listing for the app on AppExchange, there is a description of what it does, the items that it contains, and customer reviews.

In addition to the apps that are provided by the community of third-party developers and system integrators, many of the apps are provided by Salesforce through a team known as Force.com Labs. Apps are provided using various pricing models that are based on a price per user per month, a price per company per month, or are provided for free. In addition, some paid-for apps offer discounts for nonprofits.

Apps can range from highly complex, coded, feature-rich solutions with multiple screens to simple sets of dashboards or reports. Indeed, there are some instances where the full functionality of an app is not required and you just need a specific item of functionality to provide the solution, and this use case is where components can be used.

Components

Components are elements that may not function by themselves and are instead used as building blocks to build the overall solution. As an example, you may find Lightning components that automatically update records across a variety of object types given a particular scenario or automatically preset values on a record **Edit** page prior to saving a record, which are not out-of-the-box features in the Salesforce CRM.

There are two types of components:

- Components that are general-purpose and used for processing business logic, merging records, kicking processes, and so on

- Web components, which are designed for customizing the Lightning Experience user interface

An alternative to installing a complete app or building a custom solution with separate Lightning components is to install prebuilt declarative solutions that are available from AppExchange, called a flow solution.

Flow solutions

When building new flows, it is worth looking at AppExchange to check for existing flow solutions, which are often freely available, as it may not be appropriate to either re-invent the wheel and build or configure your own flow or install a less-flexible managed app package from AppExchange; this is where flow solutions can be used.

Flow solutions are prebuilt solutions that have been built by third-party developers and Salesforce to automate a business process, and there are two types of flow solutions:

- **Flow Actions**: These are standalone flows that perform a specified function and perform an action.

- **Flow Templates**: These are complete, end-to-end flow solutions that act as a starting point that you can save and customize to meet the business process requirements.

Another alternative to installing a complete app or building a custom solution is to work with a partner and install a prebuilt declarative solution that is available from AppExchange called a Bolt Solution.

Bolt Solutions

Bolt Solutions are solutions that have been built by third-party developers and system integrators that Salesforce customers would work with to complete their installation. The partners help customers to install and customize the solution to suit their needs. Sometimes organizations are faced with a particular industry or business standard requirement, which must be flexible, where there are industry experts at hand who can provide a declarative solution and customization guidance. In this scenario, it may not be appropriate to either re-invent the wheel and build or configure your own solution or install a less-flexible managed app package from AppExchange, and this is where Bolt Solutions can be used.

In addition to functional extensions to the Salesforce CRM, you can also find solutions that provide data enhancements for your Salesforce instances, and these are known as Lightning Data.

Lightning Data

You would use Lightning Data to make sure that the data in your Salesforce instance is in-sync and current with an external dataset from the given Lightning Data provider.

Lightning Data can be considered as special types of apps that use the services of a data connector to pull in external data to enrich the data stored in your Salesforce CRM instance. The data connector is part of an engine, called the Lightning Data Engine, that automatically connects your Salesforce instance and the third-party system and associated data feed.

Consultants

AppExchange also provides a listing of consultants that offer specialist Salesforce knowledge. Consultants are experts with proven Salesforce skills, able to provide guidance in various industry settings.

Installing an app from AppExchange

An app from the Salesforce AppExchange marketplace can be installed in your Salesforce CRM org by carrying out the following:

1. Click on the **Get It Now** button.

2. Select the location for the installation, where the options are to either **Install in production** or to **Install in sandbox first!**

3. Examine the package details showing what you are installing and where you are installing it.

4. Click on the checkbox labeled **I have read and agree to the terms and conditions** to confirm that you agree to proceed with the installation.

5. Click on the **Confirm and Install!** button to continue to the Salesforce login screen.

6. Log into the desired Salesforce org, ensuring that you log into your sandbox to test it before installing it in your **Production** org.

7. Choose the option to either install for **Admins Only**, for **All Users**, or for **Specific Profiles**.

8. Now click on the **Install** button.

9. Finally, perform any post-installation configuration.

There is some due diligence that you should be aware of and take the necessary measures for before and during the installation of a solution from AppExchange in your Salesforce instance.

AppExchange best practices

The following best practices should be applied when installing apps from the AppExchange marketplace website:

- Clarify that the specification for the app meets the requirements and assess any reviews and comments.

- Take a test drive, if available.

- Review all the components that are included in the package and be aware of any security issues concerning links and session IDs.

- Test the app in a sandbox before deploying to production.

- Try to enlist business support to own and validate the app before deploying to production.

- Consider undertaking a pilot deployment for selected users if the app is particularly complex.

- Communicate the app to the business prior to deployment and activation in production.

Questions to test your knowledge

We present five questions to verify your knowledge of the capabilities of the core CRM objects in the Salesforce schema, where the boundaries lie between declarative and programmatic customization, and how and when to use AppExchange. The answers can be found at the end of the chapter.

Question 1 – Lead conversion

The lead conversion feature results in which of the following objects being created? (Select one)

a) Account, Contact, Opportunity, and optionally a Campaign

b) Account, Contact, and optionally an Opportunity

c) Contact, Opportunity, and optionally an Account

d) Account, Opportunity, and optionally a Contact

Question 2 – Case automation

Which of the following statements are correct about Case automation? (Select one)

a) Case escalation rules allow Cases to be automatically routed to Queues only.

b) Case assignment rules allow Cases to be automatically routed to Queues only.

c) Case assignment rules allow Cases to be automatically routed to Queues and users.

d) There can be a maximum of 25 active Case assignment rules.

Question 3 – Customizing the Lightning Platform for marketing

The marketing director in your company has asked you to identify a solution that enables the sales team to convert certain types of leads. She wants the sales team to click a **Convert Lead** button but there should be no option to create new Accounts or Contacts (as these records always exist for these types of lead and are entered in fields on the Lead record by her marketing team). The lead conversion process should automatically create an Opportunity record.

How can this solution be built? (Select one)

a) Build a flow that gets the lead and executes the **Convert Lead Flow Element**, passing the appropriate Account and Contact information.

b) Build Apex code that gets the lead and executes the convert lead functionality, passing the appropriate Account and Contact information.

c) Build a process with Process Builder that invokes the convert lead action type, passing the appropriate Account and Contact information.

d) Explain to the marketing director that it is not possible to build this in the Lightning Platform.

Question 4 – Customizing the Lightning Platform for sales

The sales director in your company has asked you to identify a solution that forces the sales team to search for Account records before they are allowed to create new Accounts. He wants his sales team to click a **New** button but there should be a screen on which to enter the name of the account and search before allowing the salesperson to create a new Account.

How can this solution be built? (Select two)

a) Build an Apex trigger that searches for the Account record and creates a new record if one doesn't exist.

b) Build a flow that includes a screen to find the Account using the **Get Records Flow Element**, a **Decision**, and a **Create Records Flow Element**.

c) Build a process with Process Builder that invokes the **Find Duplicate Account** action type, passing the name of the Account.

d) Build a Lightning component that presents a search dialog and uses Apex to search for the account name and show matches before allowing access to the **New** account option.

Question 5 – Salesforce AppExchange

Which of the following solutions can be found on Salesforce AppExchange? (Select one)

a) Apps, Bolt Templates, Web Components

b) Apps, Components, Data Templates

c) Components, Flow Actions, Apps

d) Components, Flow Templates, Lightning Bolts

Here are the answers to the five questions to verify your knowledge of the capabilities of the core CRM objects in the Salesforce schema, where the boundaries lie between declarative and programmatic customization, and how and when to use AppExchange.

Answer 1 – Lead conversion

The answer is b) Account, Contact, and optionally an Opportunity

The following are not correct:

a) Account, Contact, Opportunity, and optionally a Campaign: Leads cannot be converted to a Campaign.

c) Contact, Opportunity, and optionally an Account: The Lead record must be converted to either a new or existing Account.

d) Account, Opportunity, and optionally a Contact: The Lead record must be converted to either a new or existing Contact.

Answer 2 – Case automation

The answer is c) Case assignment rules allow Cases to be automatically routed to Queues and users.

The following are not correct:

a) Case escalation rules allow Cases to be automatically routed to Queues only: Cases cannot be routed using escalation rules.

b) Case assignment rules allow Cases to be automatically routed to Queues only: Not only Queues but users can have Cases assigned to them using Case assignment rules.

d) There can be a maximum of 25 active Case assignment rules: Only one active Case assignment rule is permitted.

Answer 3 – Customizing the Lightning Platform for marketing

The answer is b) Build Apex code that gets the lead and executes the convert lead functionality, passing the appropriate Account and Contact information.

The following are not correct:

a) Build a flow that gets the lead and executes the **Convert Lead Flow Element**, passing the appropriate Account and Contact information: There is no **Convert Lead Flow Element** in Flow.

c) Build a process with Process Builder that invokes the **Convert Lead** action type, passing the appropriate Account and Contact information: There is no **Convert Lead** action type in Process Builder.

d) Explain to the marketing director that it is not possible to build this in the Lightning Platform: Where there is no declarative solution, consider Apex as it can be used when the out-of-the-box standard object features need to be extended.

Answer 4 – Customizing the Lightning Platform for sales

One correct answer is this:

b) Build a flow that includes a screen to find the Account using the **Get Records Flow Element**, a **Decision**, and a **Create Records Flow Element**.

The other is this:

d) Build a Lightning component that presents a search dialog and uses Apex to search for the account name and show matches before allowing access to the **New** account option.

The following are not correct:

a) Build an Apex trigger that searches for the Account record and creates a new record if one doesn't exist: An Apex trigger does not allow user input and so is not appropriate for this solution.

c) Build a process with Process Builder that invokes the **Find Duplicate Account** action type, passing the name of the Account: There is no **Find Duplicate Account** action type in Process Builder.

Answer 5 – Salesforce AppExchange

The answer is c) Components, Flow Actions, Apps

The following are not correct:

a) Apps, Bolt Templates, Web Components: There is no solution named Bolt Templates.

b) Apps, Components, Data Templates: There is no solution named Data Templates.

d) Components, Flow Templates, Lightning Bolts: There is no solution named Lightning Bolts.

Summary

Understanding the capabilities of the Lightning Platform is an important objective for all app builders, and you are now equipped with knowledge of the core Salesforce CRM objects and the capabilities that exist for these core features and associated process automation.

Knowing where the capabilities and boundaries lie for the declarative building of solutions when compared with programmatic development is vital, and you have gained this knowledge to help you choose, design, and build your next solution.

In addition, we discovered how additional functionality or data is available from the AppExchange marketplace and you now know how to exploit the various options that are available for adding value to your Salesforce instance.

Finally, we posed questions to help clarify the key concepts and features that are required when tackling the Salesforce Fundamentals section of the App Builder Certification exam.

In the next chapter, *Chapter 2, Designing and Building a Data Model*, we will look at how to design and build a data model in the Salesforce CRM and learn about Schema Builder. We will discuss how field relationships are used and how their use affects record access. We will also look at field types and understand the impacts of changing field types.

2

Designing and Building a Data Model

This chapter looks at how to design and build a data model both conceptually and using the features in the Salesforce Lightning Platform.

Using an example scenario that describes business requirements for a data solution, the chapter looks at ways to determine an appropriate data model and identifies the types of data model relationships that exist and can be built in Salesforce. This is a common activity whenever tasked with designing a solution and an essential skill to be learned whenever apps are to be built within the Lightning Platform.

We will look at field types that are available when creating custom fields and understand the impacts of changing field types.

Using the Object Manager setup option and Schema Builder, you will learn how to create custom objects and fields and how Schema Builder can be used in the Lightning Platform to build and view a data model.

Finally, you will be presented with a number of questions about designing and building a data model, about custom field types, and the capabilities of Schema Builder when compared to creating custom objects using the Object Manager setup feature.

In this chapter, we will cover the following:

- Exam objectives – Data Modeling and Management
- How to design a data model
- Choosing the correct relationship types
- How to select the appropriate field type
- Considerations when changing the type of a custom field
- Schema Builder
- Questions to test your knowledge

Let's now look at the objectives of the App Builder Certification exam in the area of designing and building a data model.

Exam objectives – Data Modeling and Management

To pass the Data Modeling and Management section of the Certified Platform App Builder exam, app builders are expected to demonstrate knowledge of the following:

- Given a scenario, determine the appropriate data model.
- Describe the capabilities of the various relationship types and the implications of each on record access, the user interface, and reporting.
- Identify the considerations when changing a field's type.
- Given a set of requirements, identify the considerations and select the appropriate field type.
- Describe the capabilities and considerations of Schema Builder.
- Describe the options and considerations when importing and exporting data.
- Describe the capabilities of and use cases for external objects.

> **Reference: Salesforce Certified Platform App Builder Exam Guide**
>
> This guide is published by Salesforce and can be referenced at `https://trailhead.salesforce.com/help?article=Salesforce-Certified-Platform-App-Builder-Exam-Guide`.

In the Salesforce Certified Platform App Builder Exam Guide, the total number of questions is given, a percentage breakdown for each of the objectives, and an indication of the number of features/functions that can be expected in each of the objectives.

By analyzing these objectives, percentages, and question counts, we can determine the likely number of questions that will appear in the exam, and for the Data Modeling and Management objective this is as follows:

> **Data Modeling and Management: Total number of exam questions**
>
> There are likely to be 12 questions in total. This is calculated as 20% of 60 total exam questions.

Using these figures for the Data Modeling and Management objective and the number of items that are likely to be assessed, we can determine that there would be **1-2 questions** for each of the following concepts:

- Determining an appropriate data model
- Relationship types and considerations
- Selecting appropriate field types
- Considerations for changing field types
- Use cases of external objects
- Considerations of Schema Builder
- Considerations for importing and exporting data

In the following chapter, *Chapter 3, Importing and Exporting Data*, we will cover the concepts needed for importing and exporting data to and from Salesforce and we will also look at the use cases and capabilities of external objects.

Now, let's look at how we can determine an appropriate data model when building solutions for the Salesforce Lightning Platform.

Designing a data model

In this section, we will look at how to determine an appropriate data model when building apps in Salesforce, which is one of the core objectives of the Data Modeling and Management objective in the Certified Platform App Builder exam. In the exam, you can expect to be given a scenario in which you will be asked how to design a data model in the Salesforce Platform that satisfies the requirements set out in the scenario.

To help reinforce the skills and knowledge needed to create the data model, we'll do some practical work in Salesforce. So, if you do not have a Salesforce environment to carry this out in, create a free developer org as detailed in *Chapter 1, Core Capabilities of the Lightning Platform.*

Using an example scenario, we will now design a data model and look at the process of identifying the most appropriate design for the entities and relationships.

Example scenario – custom lead assignment

You will now be presented with an example scenario to help reinforce the understanding of designing and building a data model.

Scenario – custom lead assignment

The sales and marketing directors in your company have asked you to build a solution that enables members of the marketing team to manage the assignment of lead records in the organization. Leads are to be automatically assigned to a salesperson based on the organization's sales regions, which deal with multiple lead locations (currently by country or US state).

The directors want only the marketing team to be able to choose which member of the sales team is to be assigned the lead based on location (and in the future based on availability).

Only leads in approved and active locations are to be assigned, and when a lead is assigned to a salesperson, they are to be assigned a task to call the lead. The directors, therefore, require a flexible solution that allows future changes and allows the marketing team to change the assignment at any time.

Design a data model in Salesforce that satisfies these requirements.

Let's consider this scenario. It is complex and more complicated than some of the scenario-based questions that appear in Salesforce exams. Scenario-based questions such as these can be challenging and usually need a fair amount of time to analyze them before responding to the given questions.

In this question, we are asked to design a data model that satisfies these requirements. For the solution, we can rule out any out of the box features being able to meet the requirements and we will return to this scenario later in this book to see how the functional aspects can be built.

For this chapter, we will concentrate on the method to design a data model in Salesforce that satisfies these requirements, however, we do need to consider the aspects of the functionality in order to determine an appropriate data model.

The standard lead assignment rules, which we looked at in *Chapter 1, Core Capabilities of the Lightning Platform,* cannot be used as the marketing team does not have system administrator permissions to make the necessary changes to the lead assignment rules, which need the capability to be changed daily. Furthermore, it could be time-consuming to create complex rules for every country or US state, and associated salespersons. Companies may not want this maintained by the system administrator given that the marketing team wants to be able to update this allocation in a timely manner, hence the standard lead assignment rules are not an option.

We will build a custom solution for this requirement that enables the marketing team to self-serve and update the sales regions, locations, and the assignment of a lead to a salesperson. Conceptually, we could build this solution using declarative or programmatic methods that use the location information stored on the lead and query the sales region lead assignment data when records are created.

As mentioned, in later chapters, we will return to this scenario and describe how to build this using declarative features in the Salesforce Platform. For now, let's start to design the data model and identify the entities and relationships that satisfy the requirement.

Identifying the data model entities

In order to identify the most appropriate Salesforce objects and relationships to use for our solution, we start the data modeling by abstracting the core entities and relationships.

Data model entities can be used to represent either the data records or the attributes of data that are to be stored or processed. As a more concrete example, data model entities are either a single Salesforce object or a Salesforce field. The modeling, however, can also represent a set of combined Salesforce objects or fields that are related in some way.

The relationships between objects in Salesforce must be designed correctly too as they impact record accessibility and reporting requirements. We will cover the method for identifying relationship types later in this chapter and look at record accessibility in *Chapter 4, Securing Access to Data,* where we cover the various security mechanisms that enable data to be accessed.

When designing data model entities, a useful approach is to review the given requirements and pick out the nouns, such as team, record, country, and so on. They can help to identify which data and which objects are to be built.

Let's apply this approach and highlight the nouns for our given scenario.

The sales and marketing directors in your company have asked you to build a solution that enables **members of the marketing team** to manage the assignment of **lead records** in the organization. Leads are to be automatically assigned to **a salesperson** based on **the organization's sales regions**, which deal with multiple **lead locations** (currently by **country or US state**).

The directors want only the marketing team to be able to choose which **member of the sales team** is to be assigned the **lead** based on location (and in the future based on availability).

Only leads in approved and **active locations** are to be assigned and when a lead is assigned to a salesperson, they are to be assigned **a task** to call the lead. The directors, therefore, require a flexible solution that allows future changes and for the marketing team to change the assignment at any time.

The list of nouns, in order, for the custom lead assignment scenario are as follows:

- Members of the marketing team
- Lead records
- A salesperson
- The organization's sales regions
- Lead location (currently by country or US state)
- Member of the sales team
- Active locations
- A task

These nouns can represent data records or attributes of data to be stored or processed and can be modeled as separate or combined data model entities or entity attributes. This reveals the following five entities and entity attributes for the nouns:

- **User entity:** Members of the marketing team, a salesperson, and members of the sales team
- **Lead entity and entity attribute:** Lead records and lead location
- **Region entity:** The organization's sales regions
- **Location entity and attributes:** Country or US state and active locations
- **Task entity:** Task records

The lead, region, user, task, and location data model entities can be seen in the following diagram:

Figure 2.1 – Scenario data model entities

Now that we have identified the conceptual data model entities, we can now consider how to build the functionality in Salesforce using appropriate objects.

Translating the data model entities to Salesforce objects

To implement the data model entities that we have designed, we can use both standard Salesforce objects and custom objects. Standard and custom objects are similar in nature to a database table and have properties that include fields, records, relationships, and tabs. Tabs are the user interface elements used to display the underlying object data.

In the previous chapter, *Chapter 1, Core Capabilities of the Lightning Platform*, we looked at the standard objects that are provided out of the box with Salesforce. Here, common business objects such as Account, Contact, Lead, and Opportunity are all standard objects as well as User for the individuals accessing and using the Lightning Platform.

Let's see how we can translate the data model entity to Salesforce objects:

- **User entity**: Standard User object.

- **Lead entity**: Standard Lead object and custom fields to include the country and/or US state. Lead records can be created by users or from the Web-to-Lead feature, so we need to ensure that the country or US state is mandatory when the lead record is created in order to automatically assign it to a sales team member.

- **Region entity**: Custom object to be created to store the organization's sales regions. We could use this for all of the company's business unit regions, such as the service team, instead of restricting them for use by sales and marketing. Hence, we can give this custom object the more generic name of Region.

- **Location entity**: Custom object to be created to store country and/or US state and include the active status. We can call this custom object Location.

- **Task entity**: Standard Task object.

For the Lead, User, and Task entities, the standard objects Lead, User, and Task can be used. Although we are yet to determine the scope for these objects at this stage and will ascertain the fields based on the functional and non-functional requirements in more detail, we know that they could be extended with custom fields and certain relationships as required.

For the Region and Location entities, there are no standard objects, so we would create custom objects with appropriate fields and relationships as required. We could have called this object Sales Region but giving this custom object the more generic name of Region allows it to be used by other departments or further extended.

Now that we have identified the Salesforce custom objects, let's use the Object Manager setup feature and create them.

Creating custom objects using Object Manager

We will now create the Region and Location custom objects using Object Manager. To create a custom object carry out the following steps:

1. Navigate to **Setup** and then search for **Object Manager** in the **Quick Find** search box located at the top of the **Setup** menu on the left sidebar.

2. Navigate to the **New Custom Object** setup screen by clicking **Object Manager |**
   Create | Custom Object.

Now complete the following details in the sections of the **New Custom Object** setup page:

1. **Custom Object Information**:

   Label: Region | Plural Label: Regions

   Starts with vowel sound: Not Checked

   Description: Platform App Builder Certification Guide, Custom Lead Assignment Scenario, Region Custom Object

   Object Name: Region (automatically set when Label is entered)

   Context-Sensitive Help Setting: (do not set)

   Content Name: (do not set)

2. **Enter Record Name Label and Format**:

   Record Name: Region Name (automatically set when Label is entered)

   Data Type: Text (default picklist selection)

3. **Optional Features**:

   Allow Reports: Checked

   Allow Activities: Checked

   Available for Customer Portal: Unchecked

   Track Field History: Checked

   Allow in Chatter Groups: Checked

4. **Object Classification**:

   Allow Sharing: Checked

   Allow Bulk API Access: Checked

   Allow Streaming API Access: Checked

5. **Deployment Status**: (do not set)

   In Development

   Deployed: Selected (default option)

   Search Status:

   Allow Search: Checked

6. **Object Creation Options** (Available only when custom object is first created):

   Add Notes and Attachments related list to default page layout: Unchecked

   Launch New Custom Tab Wizard after saving this custom object: Checked (this will present the New Custom Tab Wizard after the new custom object is saved).

7. Click on **Save** to continue with the creation of the new custom object.

   In the resulting New Custom Object Tab Wizard, complete the following details:

8. **Enter the Details**:

   Object: Region (automatically set)

   Tab Style: Choose a Tab Style (in our scenario, we have chosen **People**)

   Splash Page Custom Link: None (do not set)

   Description: Platform App Builder Certification Guide, Custom Lead Assignment Scenario, Region Tab

   Now click on **Next** to continue.

9. **Add to Profiles**:

   Apply one-tab visibility to all profiles: Default On (default option)

   Apply a different tab visibility for each profile (do not set)

   Click on **Next** to continue.

10. **Step 3. Add to Custom Apps**: (In this step we are prompted to **Choose the custom apps for which the new custom tab will be available**):

    Check the **Include Tab** at the top of the screen to deselect all custom apps.

    Choose **Sales (standard_LightningSales)**.

    Append tab to users' existing personal customizations: **Checked**

11. Finally, click on **Save** to complete the creation of the custom object and tab.

Having entered these details and saved the custom object, you will have created the **Region** custom object as shown in the following screenshot:

Figure 2.2 – Scenario Salesforce Region custom object

Now let's create another custom object, this time for the **Location**.

Using the same approach, we'll create the Location object with a tab but as the location details are to be maintained by system administrators, we need to restrict the permissions and only make it available for the specified profile, **System Administrator**. We will create it using the same method but with these tab permission differences:

1. **Custom Object Information**:

   Label: Location | Plural Label: Locations

   Starts with vowel sound: **Not Checked**

   Object Name: Location (automatically set when Label is entered)

   Description: Platform App Builder Certification Guide, Custom Lead Assignment Scenario, Location Custom Object

   Context-Sensitive Help Setting: (do not set)

   Content Name: (do not set)

2. **Enter Record Name Label and Format**:

   Record Name: Location Name (automatically set when Label is entered)

   Data Type: Text (default picklist selection)

3.   **Optional Features**:

Allow Reports: Checked

Allow Activities: Checked

Available for Customer Portal: Unchecked

Track Field History: Checked

Allow in Chatter Groups: Checked

4.   **Object Classification**:

Allow Sharing: Checked

Allow Bulk API Access: Checked

Allow Streaming API Access: Checked

5.   **Deployment Status**: (do not set)

In Development

Deployed: Selected (default option)

6.   **Search Status**:

Allow Search: Checked

7.   **Object Creation Options**: (available only when a custom object is first created):

Add Notes and Attachments related list to default page layout: Unchecked.

Launch New Custom Tab Wizard after saving this custom object: Checked (this will present the New Custom Tab Wizard after the new custom object is saved).

8.   Click on **Save** to continue with the creation of the new Location custom object.

In the resulting **New Custom Object Tab** wizard, complete the following details:

1. Enter the **Details**:

    Object: **Location** (automatically set)

    Tab Style: Choose a Tab Style (in our scenario, we have chosen **Globe**)

    Splash Page Custom Link: None (do not set)

    Description: **Platform App Builder Certification Guide, Custom Lead Assignment Scenario, Location Tab**

    Now click on **Next** to continue.

2. **Add to Profiles**:

    Apply one-tab visibility to all profiles: Tab Hidden

    Apply a different tab visibility for each profile: Chosen

    System Administrator: Default On

    All Other Profiles: Tab Hidden

    Click on **Next** to continue.

3. **Add to Custom Apps**: (In this step, we are prompted to **Choose the custom apps for which the new custom tab will be available**)

    Check the **Include Tab** at the top of the screen to deselect all custom apps.

    Choose **Sales (standard__LightningSales)**.

    Append tab to users' existing personal customizations: Checked

4. Finally, click on **Save** to complete the creation of the custom object and tab.

Now that we have identified and created the core custom objects, we can consider how the data records for the solution are to be related. When entering lead records, there needs to be a way to identify the salesperson based on the sales region. Here, there can be multiple locations within a sales region. In addition, the lead assignment process should be automatic when leads are created and always use the very latest sales region assignment information, which may be changed at any time by the marketing team.

Having considered the solution requirements and translated the entities and entity attributes to the core Salesforce objects, we can now identify the relationships between the objects and ultimately the way that data will need to be managed and accessed in accordance with the data modeling requirements.

Relationship types and considerations

Relationships enable the association of data with other objects. Before we start to design and build Salesforce relationships, let's look at generic relationship types and see how we could use them to associate the entities that we discovered earlier, in *Figure 1.1 – Scenario data model entities*:

- **One-to-one relationship:** An example of this type of relationship is where there is a list of prospects and a list of salespeople, but only one salesperson manages the prospect record and hence the prospect record is owned by only one salesperson.

- **One-to-many relationship:** An example of this type of relationship is where there is a list of prospects and a number of meetings to be set up with the prospects. This association allows there to be one prospect, but many meetings could be attended by the prospect.

- **Many-to-many relationship:** An example of this type of relationship is where there is a list of locations and a list of regions. A region contains multiple locations such as country and state and locations can be associated with more than one type of region, for example, a sales region, support region, and so on.

These relationships can be expressed using lines to join the entities and with our entity data modeling carried out earlier in the chapter, we can apply one-to-one, one-to-many, and many-to-many relationships to design the following entity-relationship diagram:

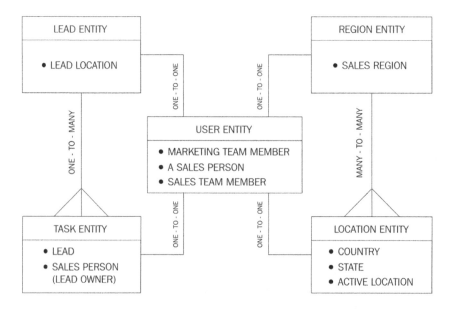

Figure 2.3 – Scenario data model entity relationship diagram

Let's consider the relationships between entities in more detail and see how the relationships can be modeled for Salesforce objects:

- **One-to-one relationship**: This depends on the requirements and can generally be modeled in Salesforce by adding the related entities as custom fields on the same object.

- **One-to-many relationship**: This can be modeled in Salesforce with either a lookup or a master-detail relationship.

- **Many-to-many relationship**: This can be modeled in Salesforce using a custom object, referred to as a junction object, along with two master-detail relationship fields. The master-detail relationship fields are created on the junction object and use the two objects that are to be given the many-to-many association as the master or parent association.

These relationships can be represented, for our scenario, in the following object-relationship diagram:

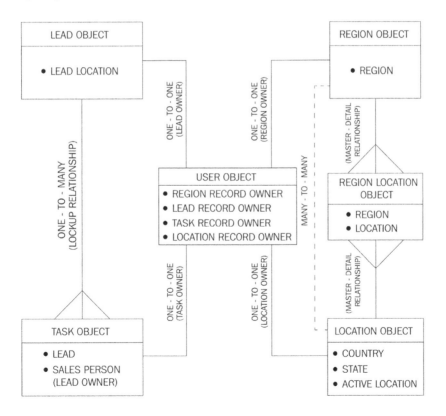

Figure 2.4 – Scenario Salesforce object relationship

Now that we have established the mechanism of relating objects in Salesforce, let's look at the Salesforce relationship types. Salesforce provides the following relationship types: lookup relationship, master-detail relationship, and hierarchical relationship.

The lookup relationship type

Using a lookup relationship enables two objects to be associated so that multiple records on one side of the relationship look up a single record. The multiple records are displayed in a related list on the associated record. This models a one-to-many relationship.

In our scenario and object relationship diagram shown in *Figure 2.4 – Scenario Salesforce object relationship*, the relationship between the two objects **Task** and **Lead** is a lookup relationship to model a one-to-many relationship.

Although the lookup relationship type enables two objects to be associated so that multiple records can be associated with a single record, it can also be used to simply relate two records together. This models a one-to-one relationship.

In our scenario and object-relationship diagram shown in *Figure 2.4 – Scenario Salesforce object relationship*, the relationship between the two objects **Task** and **User** is a lookup relationship to model a one-to-one relationship.

Lookup relationship types are used where the associated object records exist independently of each other and typically function on their own, therefore allowing the loosely coupled association of records. Lookup relationship types do not require a parent related field to be set when a child record is created and the child record security settings are configured separately to the parent. Lookup relationship fields can optionally be configured to prevent the deletion of the parent record when there are associated child records.

The master-detail relationship type

In a master-detail relationship, the detail, or child, related object does not typically function on its own. The detail records are tightly coupled and dependent on the master record. When creating child detail records, the master-detail relationship field is mandatory for all detail records, and whenever the master object record is deleted, all associated child detail records are deleted.

The master object in a master-detail relationship also controls the security settings for the detail object, which has implications for record access and the user interface, such as for any tab settings. Furthermore, the master control of the security settings for the detail object also impacts reports and dashboards, which will be covered in *Chapter 8, Generating Data Analytics with Reports and Dashboards*.

> **Master-detail relationship limits**
> Custom objects can have a maximum of two master-detail relationships.

The hierarchical relationship type

The hierarchical relationship type is only supported for the standard User object and uses a lookup relationship to associate two user records. An example use case for this type of relationship type is where a user can be assigned as the supervisor of another user.

Let's now continue building our scenario data model and create the junction object **Region Location** and the two master-detail relationships that enable the many-to-many relationship that meets the requirement to link **Region** records to **Location** records.

The many-to-many relationship type

As outlined previously, there is no "many-to-many relationship type" in Salesforce, as such. Instead, many-to-many relationship functionality can be achieved with the use of a custom object, known as a junction object.

The junction object is a custom object that uses two master-detail relationship fields. The two master-detail fields are created on the junction object, whereupon the first master-detail relationship fields that get created becomes the primary parent for the junction object. This means that the junction object inherits the security and tab settings from the primary master object.

Creating the junction object

For our given scenario, we are to model a many-to-many relationship to associate the **Region** and **Location** custom objects that we created earlier in this chapter.

Using the same approach that we used to create the custom objects for **Region** and **Location**, we'll create the junction object, which we'll call **Region Location**, however, we will not create a tab for the junction object as the records do not need to be accessed directly or independently created.

The **Region Location** junction object records are to be created from the parent records **Region** and **Location** pages and, since they need no independent identity or name, we'll set the **Data Type** option to **Auto-Number**.

Let's go ahead and create the **Region Location** custom object by carrying out the following steps:

1. Navigate to **Setup** and then search for `Object Manager` in the **Quick Find** search box located at the top of the **Setup** menu on the left sidebar.

2. Navigate to the **New Custom Object** setup screen by navigating to **Object Manager | Create | Custom Object**. Now complete the following details in the sections of the **New Custom Object** setup page:

3. **Custom Object Information**:

   Label: Region Location | Plural Label: Region Locations

   Starts with vowel sound: Not Checked

   Object Name: Region_Location (automatically set when Label is entered)

   Description: Platform App Builder Certification Guide, Custom Lead Assignment Scenario, Region Location Custom Object

   Context-Sensitive Help Setting: (do not set)

   Content Name: (do not set)

4. **Enter Record Name Label and Format**:

   Record Name: Region Location Name (automatically set when Label is entered)

   Data Type: Auto Number

   Display Format: RL-{00000}

   Starting Number: 1

5. **Optional Features**:

   Allow Reports: Checked

   Allow Activities: Checked

   Available for Customer Portal: Unchecked

   Track Field History: Checked

   Allow in Chatter Groups: Checked

6. **Object Classification**:

   Allow Sharing: Checked

   Allow Bulk API Access: Checked

   Allow Streaming API Access: Checked

7. **Deployment Status**: (do not set)

   In Development

   Deployed: **Selected** (default option)

8. **Search Status**:

   Allow Search: **Checked**

9. **Object Creation Options** (Available only when a custom object is first created):

   Add Notes and Attachments related list to default page layout: **Unchecked**

   Launch New Custom Tab Wizard after saving this custom object: **Unchecked**

10. Finally, click on **Save** to complete the creation of the new **Region Location** custom object.

The main difference between this junction object as compared to the two custom objects **Region** and **Location** that we created earlier is the choice of data type for **Record Name**. Here, we are setting the data type to **Auto Number**. Let's look at the effects and the associated settings when choosing the data type of the record name when creating custom objects.

Choosing the data type for the object record name

The data type for the record name can be either text or auto-number and if the chosen data type is **Text**, a value must be entered in the **Name** field whenever a record is created. If the chosen data type is **Auto Number**, the record **Name** field becomes a read-only value with new records being automatically set with an incremented number.

When creating custom objects and setting the record name data field to **Auto Number**, there are additional options to be set, which we will now look at.

Setting options for the Auto Number data type

When the **Data Type** field is set to **Auto Number**, an additional option is presented called **Display Format**. The **Display Format** option allows the user to choose the appearance of the **Auto Number** field. For example, RL-{00000} is a display format that produces a two-character text **RL** and a hyphen character - as a prefix to a number with leading zeros padded to five digits. Example data output would include RL-00001, RL-00002, RL-00003, and so on.

> **Auto Number incremented numbers**
>
> Records continue to be saved even when the number of records exceeds the length specified in **Display Format**. In our example, RL-{00000} numbers are incremented and eventually will reach RL-99999. At this point, any new record will still be saved but the automatically incremented number is set to RL-100000.

Along with the **Display Format** option, there is also the **Starting Number** option for **Auto Number** fields, which are automatically incremented when new records are created to enable the setting of the starting number for the incremental count, which can be set at any number and does not have to be set to start from 1.

We will now look at the setup option to create the two master-detail relationship fields for the junction object **Region Location**.

Creating relationship fields using Object Manager

Let's go ahead and create the primary master-detail relationship field on the **Region Location** custom object, which is associated with the **Region** custom object. This is done by following these steps:

1. Navigate to **Setup** and then search for `Object Manager` in the **Quick Find** search box located at the top of the **Setup** menu on the left sidebar.

2. On the **Object Manager** screen, search for `Region Location` in the **Quick Find** search box located at the top right of the page. Select the **Region Location** object and click on **Fields & Relationships**.

Now click on **New** and complete the following details in the sections of the **New Custom Field** setup page:

1. **Choose the field type:**

   Data Type: Master-Detail Relationship

   Now click on **Next** to continue.

2. **Choose the related object:**

   Related To: Region

   Click on **Next** to continue.

3. **Enter the label and name for the lookup field**:

   Field Label: **Region** (automatically set in step 3 – page load)

   Field Name: **Region** (automatically set in step 3 – page load)

   Description: **Platform App Builder Certification Guide, Custom Lead Assignment Scenario, Region Master-Detail Relationship**

   Help Text: (do not set)

   Child Relationship Name: **Region_Locations** (automatically set in step 3 – page load)

   Sharing Setting: **Read/Write: Allows users with at least Read/Write access to the Master record to create, edit, or delete related Detail records** (default option)

   Allow reparenting: (do not set)

   Lookup Filter: (do not set)

   Now click on **Next** to continue.

4. **Establish field-level security for reference field**:

   No option to set (visible for all profiles but controlled by master record)

   Click on **Next** to continue.

5. **Add reference field to Page Layouts**:

   No option to set (because this is a master-detail relationship, the field is required)

   Now click on **Next** to continue.

6. **Add custom related lists**:

   Related List Label: Region Locations (automatically set in step 6 – page load)

   Add Related List: Region Layout (keep checked as per default)

   Append related list to users' existing personal customizations: Checked (checked by default)

7. Finally, click on **Save** to complete the creation of the **Region** master-detail relationship.

Having entered these details and saved the custom field, you will have created the custom field as shown in the following screenshot:

Figure 2.5 – Scenario Salesforce Region Location master-detail relationship

Let's now create the secondary master-detail relationship field on the **Region Location** custom object, which is associated with the **Location** custom object. This is done with the help of the following steps:

1. Navigate to **Setup** and then search for `Object Manager` in the **Quick Find** search box located at the top of the **Setup** menu on the left sidebar.

2. On the **Object Manager** screen, search for **Region Location** in the **Quick Find** search box located at the top right of the page. Select the **Region Location** object and click on **Fields & Relationships**.

Now click on **New** and complete the following details in the sections of the **New Custom Field** setup page:

1. **Choose the field type**:

    Data Type: Master-Detail Relationship

    Now click on **Next** to continue.

2. **Choose the related object**:

    Related To: Location

    Click on **Next** to continue.

3. Enter the label and name for the lookup field:

   Field Label: **Location** (automatically set in step 3 – page load)

   Field Name: **Location** (automatically set in step 3 – page load)

   Description: **Platform App Builder Certification Guide, Custom Lead Assignment Scenario, Location Master-Detail Relationship**

   Help Text: (do not set)

   Child Relationship Name: **Region_Locations** (automatically set in step 3 – page load)

   Sharing Setting: **Read/Write: Allows users with at least Read/Write access to the Master record to create, edit, or delete related Detail records** (default option)

   Allow reparenting: (do not set)

   Lookup Filter: (do not set)

   Now click on **Next** to continue.

4. **Establish field-level security for reference field**:

   No option to set (visible for all profiles but controlled by the master record)

   Click on **Next** to continue.

5. **Add reference field to Page Layouts**:

   No option to set (because this is a master-detail relationship, the field is required)

   Now click on **Next** to continue.

6. **Add custom related lists**:

   Related List Label: **Region Locations** (automatically set in step 6 – page load)

   Add Related List: **Location Layout** (keep checked as per default)

   Append related list to users' existing personal customizations: **Checked** (checked by default)

7. Finally, click on **Save** to complete the creation of the **Location** master-detail relationship.

Having entered these details and saved the custom field, you will have created the custom field as shown in the following screenshot:

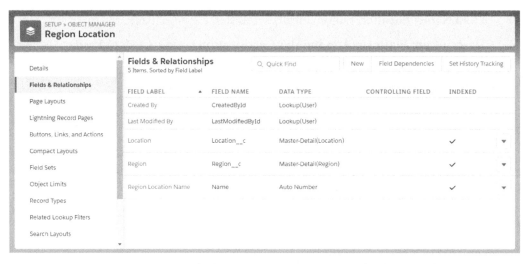

Figure 2.6 – Scenario Salesforce Region Location master-detail relationship

Having identified the model for the data entities and how records are to be associated, we can now consider how information is to be stored in the records. Here, we will look at the various custom field types and the capabilities and implications of them for all sections of the appropriate field types.

Selecting the appropriate field type

When given a set of requirements to create a data model, we need to identify the data that is to be stored and processed in order to ensure that the most appropriate custom field type is created.

There are many data types that can be chosen to ensure that the appropriate data is able to be stored using custom fields. Custom fields are unique to your business needs and can not only be added and amended but also deleted. Custom fields can be created on standard objects and custom objects.

When creating custom fields, you have the option to specify the field-level security and also, depending upon the type of field, some options to set the user interface and appearance of the field record. The first step when creating custom fields is to select the data type for the field, and the sections that describe the data types that are available are as follows:

- **Auto Number**: An **Auto Number** field is used to automatically generate a unique number for saved records. The number is automatically incremented by the platform and as such is a read-only field. This data type allows a maximum length of 30 characters, whereby 20 characters are used for additional text that you can set for either a prefix or a suffix; for example, RL-12345.

- **Checkbox**: A **Checkbox** field is used for storing a value as either True or False and appears on the user interface as a checked or unchecked value. Note: some features in Salesforce do not use the values of True or False for this data type, such as the import wizards, which will be covered in *Chapter 3*, *Importing and Exporting Data*; the values are 1 for True values and 0 for False values.

- **Currency**: A **Currency** field is used for storing a monetary value. The Salesforce Platform adds currency codes, for example, USD, GBP, and so on, which are applied when viewing the data type value in a record.

- **Date**: A **Date** field is used to either choose a date from a pop-up calendar or to manually key in a date. The data is validated as a correct date before allowing the record to be saved and prevents non-logical dates, for example, 29 days for February in a non-leap year.

- **Date/Time**: A **Date/Time** field is used to either choose a date from a pop-up calendar or to manually key in a date and time. Similar to the **Date** field, the time part gives the option to add A.M. or P.M. for non-24-hour time settings.

- **Email**: An **Email** field is used for storing an email address. The data is validated as a correct email format before allowing the record to be saved.

- **Formula**: A **Formula** field is used to automatically calculate a value that is obtained from other fields or values stored within the Salesforce Platform. Formula fields are very powerful and flexible mechanisms that allow cross-object references to merge data from related records.

- **Geolocation**: A **geolocation** field is used to show a location derived from a latitude and a longitude value.

- **Number**: The **Number** field is used for storing a number with or without a decimal place where the number of decimal places can be specified. The value is saved as a real number so if there are any leading zeros, they are removed when the record is saved.

- **Percent**: A **Percent** field in the Salesforce Platform is similar to a number field entered as a decimal. In addition, for the **Percent** field, the platform appends a percentage sign, for example, 50%, to the saved value.

- **Phone**: The **Phone** field is used for storing a telephone number. The Lightning Platform will attempt to change the number into a known telephone number format when saving for some locale settings. As an example, for English (United States) and English (Canada), a ten- or eleven-digit phone number that starts with one is automatically changed into the format (800) 555-1234. This data type allows a maximum length of 40 characters.

- **Picklist**: The **Picklist** field is used for storing a text value, which can be chosen from a predefined set of values. This data type provides optional settings that enforce the values that are saved when importing data. The **Picklist** field allows a maximum length of 255 characters and a total number of 1,000 values.

- **Picklist (Multi-Select)**: The **Picklist (Multi-Select)** field is used for storing one or more a text value(s), which can be chosen from a predefined set of values. This data type stores the chosen values as text with semi-colons to separate the individual picklist values and allows a maximum length of 255 characters for each picklist value and a total number of 500 values.

- **Roll-Up Summary**: The **Roll-up Summary** field is used to calculate and display summarized values of child related records. The **Roll-up Summary** field is only available on an object that serves as the master record when used with a master-detail relationship. These calculated values can be either the sum, minimum, or maximum value of the detail related records.

- **Text**: The **Text** field is used to store text values and can include alphanumeric and symbol characters. The maximum length of the text value is 255 characters.

- **Text Area**: The **Text Area** field is used to store alphanumeric characters, which are shown on separate lines on the page. The maximum length of the text value is 255 characters.

- **Text Area (Long)**: The **Text Area (Long)** field is used to store alphanumeric characters, which are shown on separate lines on the page. The maximum length of the text value is 131,072 characters and this data type allows the setting of a lower maximum length, which can be between 256 and 131,072 characters.

- **Text Area (Rich)**: The **Text Area (Rich)** field is used to store text that can be formatted and supports the embedding of images and web links. Formatting can be done using an embedded toolbar, which allows actions such as undo, redo, bolden, italicize, underline, and strike out text. The maximum length of the text value is 131,072 characters.

- **Text (Encrypted)**: The **Text (Encrypted)** field is used to store text values and can include alphanumeric and symbol characters. After saving, the text is encrypted using the **Advanced Encryption Standard (AES)** algorithm, which uses 128-bit master keys. The maximum length of the text value is 175 characters.

- **Time**: The **Time** field is used to store time without a date element. The time format allows the entry of hours, minutes, seconds, and milliseconds and is shown on the page with A.M. or P.M. to denote morning or afternoon.

- **URL**: The **URL** field is used to store a web link. The maximum length of the web link value is 255 characters. However, only the first 50 characters are shown on the page.

Creating custom fields using Object Manager

We will now create the following custom fields and specified field types for the **Location** custom object:

- **Country**: Picklist type
- **State**: Picklist type

> **State and Country picklists**
>
> Salesforce provides a feature that allows the universal setting of State and Country Picklists instead of creating object-specific text or picklist values. These are based on fully populated data that incorporates ISO-3166 standard values. The configuration of this feature is beyond the scope of the scenario that is covered in this book but more information can be obtained from `https://help.salesforce.com/articleView?id=admin_state_country_picklists_configure.htm`.

On the **Object Manager** screen, search for `Location` in the **Quick Find** search box located at the top right of the page. Select the **Location** object and click on **Fields & Relationships**.

Now click on **New** and complete the following details in the sections of the **New Custom Field** setup page:

1. **Choose the field type**:

   Data Type: Picklist

   Now click on **Next** to continue.

2. **Enter the details**:

   Field Label: Country

   Choose: **Enter values, with each value separated by a new line** and enter:

   ```
   Australia

   United Kingdom

   United States
   ```

   Display values alphabetically, not in the order entered: Checked

   Use first value as default value: Unchecked

   Restrict picklist to the values defined in the value set: Checked (checked by default)

   Field Name: Country (automatically set in *step 2* – page load)

   Description: Platform App Builder Certification Guide, Custom Lead Assignment Scenario, Country Picklist

   Help Text: (do not set)

   Required: Unchecked

   Default Value: (do not set)

   Now click on **Next** to continue.

3. **Establish field-level security for reference field**:

   Set Read-Only for All Internal Profiles except **System Administrator**

   Click on **Next** to continue.

4. **Step 4. Add to page layouts**:

   Add Field: Page Layout Name: Location Layout (checked)

5. Finally, click on **Save and New** to complete the creation of the **Country Picklist** custom field.

Having entered these details and saved the custom field, we'll now create the **State** custom field by completing the following details in the sections of the **New Custom Field** setup page:

6. Choose the field type:

    Data Type: Picklist

    Now click on **Next** to continue.

7. **Enter the details**:

    Field Label: **State**

    Choose: **Enter values, with each value separated by a new line** and enter:

    ```
    New South Wales

    Queensland

    San Francisco

    New York

    Texas
    ```

    Display values alphabetically, not in the order entered: Checked

    Use first value as default value: Unchecked

    Restrict picklist to the values defined in the value set: Checked (checked by default)

    Field Name: Country (automatically set in *step 2* – page load)

    Description: Platform App Builder Certification Guide, Custom Lead Assignment Scenario, State Picklist

    Help Text: (do not set)

    Required: Unchecked

    Default Value: (do not set)

    Now click on **Next** to continue.

8. **Establish field-level security for reference field**:

    Set Read-Only for All Internal Profiles except **System Administrator.**

    Click on **Next** to continue.

9. **Step 4. Add to page layouts**:

    Add Field: Page Layout Name: Location Layout (checked)

Finally, click on **Save** to complete the creation of the **State Picklist** custom field. You will have created the custom fields for **Country** and **State** on the Location object as shown in the following screenshot:

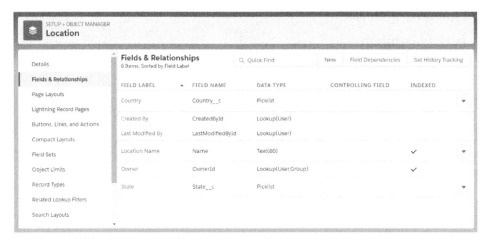

Figure 2.7 – Scenario Salesforce Location Country and State custom fields

Custom fields can be deleted and changed but there are some situations and combinations of data type changes that have some impacts, which we will now consider.

Considerations when changing the type of a custom field

Occasionally, after you have created custom fields in Salesforce, there is the need to change the field's type as the type of data that is to be stored needs to be changed. The reason for this change of data type could be because the initial requirements were not clear or because new discoveries about how the solution is used identify a more suitable field to be used.

Before attempting to change the data type of a field, you should carefully consider the effect that the change might have on the existing data and the impacts in general that may be experienced after the field's type has been changed. There are some situations and types of fields that are fully restricted and changing the data type of the field is not permitted.

There are some situations and types of fields where changes are permitted but have restrictions and have impacts on the stored data. These include the loss of data or system controls for what the field type can be changed to.

Let's look at the types of fields and situations that are fully restricted and do not allow the field type to be changed.

Situations and types of fields that are fully restricted

The following situations and types of fields are restricted and do not allow the type of field to be changed:

- **Lookup relationship**: The data type cannot be changed to a master-detail relationship if any existing records do not have a value within the lookup field.

- **Master-detail relationship**: The data type cannot be changed to a lookup relationship type if there is a **Roll-Up Summary** field on the master record.

- **Fields referenced in a Roll-Up Summary field**: When a field is referenced in a **Roll-Up Summary** field, it cannot be deleted.

- **Fields referenced in programmatic setup**: The data type of a custom field that is referenced by programmatic metadata such as Visualforce pages, Apex code, and Apex triggers cannot be changed.

- **Fields referenced in declarative setup**: The data type of a custom field that is referenced by declarative metadata such as processes or flows cannot be changed.

- **Fields referenced in Convert Lead mappings**: The data type of a custom field that is mapped as part of the lead conversion feature cannot be changed.

- **Formula**: Formula fields cannot be converted into another data type and existing custom fields cannot be converted into formula fields.

- **Text (Encrypted)**: Encrypted fields cannot be converted into another data type and existing custom fields cannot be converted into encrypted fields.

Situations and types of fields that have partial restrictions

We will now look at the types of fields and situations that permit the changing of type but have partial restrictions and have impacts on the stored data.

When changing to and from the following field types, there are things to consider:

- **Auto Number**: Changing to any other non-text data type results in the loss of data.

- **Checkbox**: Changing to any other data type from **Checkbox** results in a loss of data.

- **Currency**: Changing from any type to a **Number** field results in the loss of data.

- **Date**: Changing to **Date/Time** results in the loss of data.

- **Date/Time**: Changing to **Date** results in the loss of data.

- **Number**: Changing from any type to a **Number** field results in the loss of data.

- **Percent**: Changing from any type to a **Number** field results in the loss of data.

- **Picklist**: Changing to a multi-select picklist, the picklist values remain after changing to **Picklist (Multi-Select)**. However, if there are any records that contain a value that is not in the list of picklist values, these values are deleted. Changing to **Checkbox** results in the loss of data and you choose which of the picklist values is to be set on **Checkbox**, which is either a checked or unchecked value.

- **Picklist (Multi-Select)**: Changing to any other data type results in the loss of data.

- **Roll-Up Summary**: If there is a **Roll-Up Summary** field on an object, the master-detail relationship cannot be changed to a lookup relationship.

- **Text**: Changing to **Auto-Number** may result in the loss of data as Auto-number fields contain a maximum of 30 characters. Changing to **Picklist** results in the loss of data.

- **Text Area (Long)**: Changing to **Email**, **Phone**, **Text**, **Text Area**, or **URL** may result in the loss of data if the **Text Area (Long)** value is greater than 255 characters. Changing to any type except **Email**, **Phone**, **Text**, **Text Area**, or **URL** results in the loss of data.

- **Text Area (Rich)**: The **Text Area (Rich)** field can only be changed to a **Text Area (Long)** field. If there are any images or HTML code, they are deleted when **Text Area (Long)** is updated.

- **Fields with external ID**: Changing to a data type that does not support use as an **External ID** (such as **Text**, **Number**, or **Email**) results in the field losing its **External ID** setting.

Up to now, we have been using the Object Manager to create custom objects and fields, however, there is a feature in Salesforce called Schema Builder, which can also be used to create and carry out data modeling, as we will now cover.

Data modeling with Schema Builder

Schema Builder is a mechanism that is available out of the box that provides the facility to view the existing data model and create new custom objects, custom fields, and relationship types.

As an alternative to using the Object Manager, which we used earlier in this chapter, we can add objects and fields by dragging and dropping visual elements onto a schema screen. In addition, Schema Builder allows the viewing of standard objects and the creation of custom fields within standard objects.

The features and capabilities of Schema Builder enable the following:

- Creating and deleting custom objects

- Creating and deleting custom lookup and master-detail relationship fields

- Creating and deleting custom fields

- Viewing standard objects

- Viewing standard lookup and master-detail relationship fields

- Viewing standard fields

> **Custom fields not available**
>
> At the time of writing, Schema Builder does not allow the creation of the following custom field types: **Geolocation** and **Time**. All other field types can be created.

In addition to the types of object and field that can be accessed or manipulated, Schema Builder also provides the following features and has the following differences in comparison to using Object Manager:

- **Autosaving**: The data model is autosaved as you make changes to objects and fields.

- **Page Layouts**: Custom fields are not automatically added to page layouts and there is no option to add custom fields to page layouts immediately after creating them with Schema Builder. However, you can add them by accessing page layouts and adding custom fields afterward.

- **Tabs**: The tab selection screen option is not available and Tab selection does not automatically appear after you have created objects.

- **Field-Level Security**: Created fields are set to be visible and editable for all internal profiles.

- **Saved Data Model View**: When you exit Schema Builder, the settings and layout that you last worked with are stored and are seen when you next use the tool.

- **Auto Layout**: You can use the auto layout feature to reorganize the way that the data model appears on the Schema Builder page. When you first open up Schema Builder, you're likely to see all objects selected, which can appear somewhat complicated, but you can de-select all objects, apply filtered views, and select only the detail that is of interest.

We have created the core data model for our example scenario with the custom objects and some of the custom fields. It would be good to take a look at how the data model fulfills the requirements and reflects the entity relationship diagrams that we designed.

Creating custom fields using Schema Builder

Let's now use Schema Builder to see the data model for custom objects and fields and standard objects, and create the following new custom fields for the **Region** and **Location** custom objects:

- A **Sales Person** lookup on the **Region** custom object
- An active checkbox on the **Location** custom object

Let's now create the **Sales Person** lookup relationship field on the **Region** custom object and the **Active** checkbox field type on the **Location** custom object. This will be done with the following steps:

1. Navigate to **Setup** and then search for Schema Builder in the **Quick Find** search box located at the top of the **Setup** menu on the left sidebar.

2. After clicking on **Schema Builder** in the **Setup** menu on the left sidebar, the **Schema Builder** screen appears. When accessing for the first time, all objects are checked in the object selection area on the left-side panel. By selecting the objects that we have identified and created for our example scenario, we can generate a data model for **Lead**, **Task**, **User**, **Region**, **Region Location**, and **Location** as shown in the following screenshot:

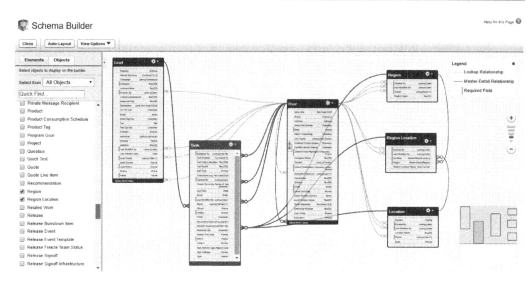

Figure 2.8 – Scenario Salesforce Schema Builder

3. Now let's create the **Sales Person** lookup relationship field on the **Region** custom object by clicking on the **Elements** tab and dragging the lookup item to the **Region** custom object as shown in the following screenshot:

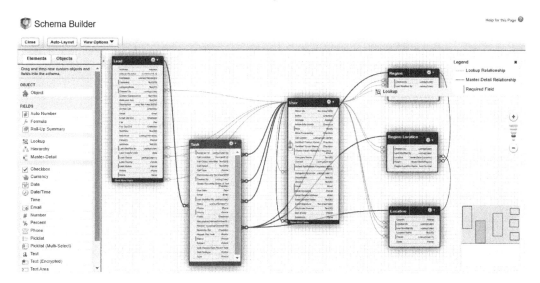

Figure 2.9 - Scenario Salesforce Schema Builder Sales Person lookup

4.   After dropping the item onto the **Region** custom object, complete the following on the **Create Lookup Field (Object: Region)** dialog screen:

Field Label: Sales Person

Field Name: Sales_Person (automatically set after **Field Label** value is entered)

Description: Platform App Builder Certification Guide, Custom Lead Assignment Scenario, Sales Person lookup

Help Text: (do not set)

Related To: User (selected from list of objects)

Child Relationship Name: Regions (automatically set after the **Related To** option is selected)

Related List Label: Regions (automatically set after the **Related To** option is selected)

5.   Finally, click on **Save** to complete the creation of the **Sales Person** lookup relationship field.

Now let's create the final new custom field for our scenario, which is the **Active** checkbox field type on the **Location** custom object by clicking on the **Elements** tab and dragging the **Checkbox** item onto the **Location** custom object.

After dropping the item onto the **Location** custom object, complete the following on the **Create Checkbox Field (Object: Location)** dialog screen:

- **Field Label: Active**
- **Field Name: Active** (automatically set after the **Field Label** value is entered)
- **Description: Platform App Builder Certification Guide, Custom Lead Assignment Scenario, Active checkbox**
- **Help Text**: (do not set)
- **Default Value**: Unchecked option (set by default)

Finally, click on **Save** to complete the creation of the **Active** checkbox field.

This concludes the exercise on creating the two custom fields: the **Sales Person** lookup relationship field on the **Region** custom object and the **Active** checkbox field type on the **Location** custom object using Schema Builder, and we can now view the completed data model as shown in the following screenshot:

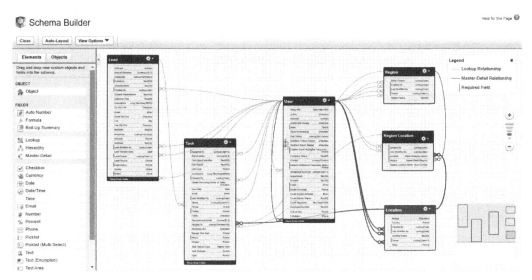

Figure 2.10 – Scenario Salesforce Schema Builder complete

Let's now see how we can use Schema Builder to view and modify custom objects and fields.

Modifying elements using Schema Builder

You can modify objects and fields within the data model view. Standard objects cannot be edited and must be accessed in the setup Object Manager. Custom objects can be modified by clicking the gear icon at the top right of the object to reveal a menu that presents the following options:

- **Hide Object on Canvas**
- **Edit Object Properties...**
- **Delete Object...**
- **View Object** (in new window)
- **View Page Layouts** (in new window)

These options are as shown in the following screenshot:

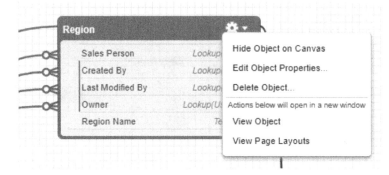

Figure 2.11 – Scenario Salesforce Schema Builder modifying an object

Standard fields cannot be edited and must be accessed in the setup for **Object Manager**. Custom fields can be modified by right-clicking on the field item whereupon menu options are presented:

- **View Field in New Window**
- **Edit Field Properties…**
- **Manage Field Permissions**
- **Delete Field…**

These options are as shown in the following screenshot:

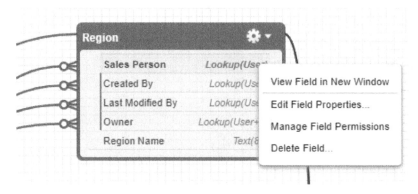

Figure 2.12 – Scenario Salesforce Schema Builder modifying a field

Let's now assess our understanding of how to design and build a data model using the features in the Salesforce Lightning Platform.

Questions to test your knowledge

We'll now present seven questions to help assess your knowledge of designing a data model in the Lightning Platform. There are questions about the choice of relationship types and appropriate field types when presented with a given scenario.

There are questions about the impacts of changing data types along with questions to test your knowledge of the capabilities of Schema Builder. The answers can be found at the end of the chapter.

Question 1 – Designing a data model

Your company has asked you to build an app for managing the equipment that is used in meeting rooms in the organization. There are many rooms and each room can have many pieces of equipment and equipment can be moved from room to room. How can you design the data model for this requirement? (Select one)

a) Create a Room custom object and custom fields on the Room object to store the equipment in use.

b) Create an Equipment custom object and a Room custom object along with a master-detail relationship from the Equipment object to the Room object.

c) Create an Equipment custom object and a Room custom object along with a junction object. Associate the objects to form a many-to-many relationship between the Equipment and Room custom objects.

d) Create an Equipment custom object and custom fields on the Equipment object to store the Room details.

Question 2 – The many-to-many relationship type

Which of the following statements is true about modeling a many-to-many relationship between Object X and Object Y in Salesforce? (Select one)

a) Create a junction object and create a master-detail relationship on Object X and a master-detail relationship on Object Y both associated with the junction object.

b) Create a junction object and a master-detail relationship on the junction object associated with Object X and a master-detail relationship on Object Y associated with the junction object.

c) Create a junction object and a master-detail relationship on the junction object associated with Object X and a master-detail relationship on the junction object associated with Object Y.

d) Create a junction object and a master-detail relationship on the junction object associated with Object Y and a master-detail relationship on Object X associated with the junction object.

Question 3 – The master-detail relationship type

Which of the following statements are true about the master-detail relationship type? (Select two)

a) A custom object can have a maximum of one master-detail relationship field and when the parent record is deleted, all child records are deleted.

b) A custom object can have a maximum of two master-detail relationship fields and a child record cannot be created without an associated parent record.

c) A custom object can have a maximum of two master-detail relationship fields and a child record can be created without an associated parent record.

d) A custom object can have a maximum of two master-detail relationship fields and when the parent record is deleted, all child records are deleted.

Question 4 – Changing relationship types

Which of the following statements are true about changing relationship types? (Select two)

a) A lookup relationship can always be changed to a master-detail relationship.

b) A lookup relationship cannot be changed to a master-detail relationship if any existing records do not have a value in the lookup field.

c) A master-detail relationship can always be changed to a lookup relationship.

d) A lookup relationship cannot be changed to a master-detail relationship if there is a **Roll-Up Summary** field on the parent record.

Question 5 – Changing a Picklist type to a Picklist (Multi-Select) type

Which of the following statements are true about changing a **Picklist** type to a **Picklist (Multi-Select)** type? (Select two)

a) A **Picklist** type cannot be changed to a **Picklist (Multi-Select)** type if there are existing records.

b) The picklist values remain after the field type has been changed.

c) Existing records that contain a value that is not in the list of picklist values remain after the field type has changed.

d) Existing records that contain a value that is not in the list of picklist values have the value removed after the field type has changed.

Question 6 – Using Schema Builder

Which of the following can be carried out using Schema Builder? (Select two)

a) Creating and editing custom objects

b) Creating and editing tabs for custom objects

c) Editing but not creating standard fields

d) Creating and editing custom fields

Question 7 – Capabilities of Schema Builder

Which of the following statements are true about the capabilities of Schema Builder? (Select two)

a) Objects can be created but not edited using Schema Builder.

b) The tab selection screen option is not available and tab selection does not automatically appear after you have created objects.

c) Created fields are set to be visible and editable for all internal and external profiles.

d) Created fields can be added to page layouts in Schema Builder after you have created them.

Here are the answers to the eight questions that were presented to help verify your knowledge of designing a data model in the Lightning Platform, knowing when to use particular field types, and the impacts of changing data types.

Answer 1 – Designing a data model

The answer is c) Create an Equipment custom object and a Room custom object along with a junction object. Associate the objects to form a many-to-many relationship between the Equipment and Room custom objects.

The following are not correct:

a) Create a Room custom object and custom fields on the Room object to store the equipment in use.

b) Create an Equipment custom object and a Room custom object along with a master-detail relationship from the Equipment object to the Room object: This provides a one-to-many relationship and not a many-to-many relationship.

d) Create an Equipment custom object and custom fields on the Equipment object to store the Room details: This provides a one-to-one relationship and not a many-to-many relationship.

Answer 2 – The many-to-many relationship type

The answer is c) Create a junction object and a master-detail relationship on the junction object associated with Object X and a master-detail relationship on the junction object associated with Object Y.

The following are not correct:

a) Create a junction object and create a master-detail relationship on Object X and a master-detail relationship on Object Y both associated with the junction object.

b) Create a junction object and a master-detail relationship on the junction object associated with Object X and a master-detail relationship on Object Y associated with the junction object.

d) Create a junction object and a master-detail relationship on the junction object associated with Object Y and a master-detail relationship on Object X associated with the junction object.

Answer 3 – The master-detail relationship type

The answers are b) and d):

b) A custom object can have a maximum of two master-detail relationship fields and a child record cannot be created without an associated parent record.

d) A custom object can have a maximum of two master-detail relationship fields and when the parent record is deleted, all child records are deleted.

The following are not correct:

a) A custom object can have a maximum of one master-detail relationship field and when the parent record is deleted, all child records are deleted.

c) A custom object can have a maximum of two master-detail relationship fields and a child record can be created without an associated parent record.

Answer 4 – Changing relationship types

The answers are b) and d):

b) A lookup relationship cannot be changed to a master-detail relationship if any existing records do not have a value in the lookup field.

d) A lookup relationship cannot be changed to a master-detail relationship if there is a **Roll-Up Summary** field on the parent record.

The following are not correct:

a) A lookup relationship can always be changed to a master-detail relationship: A lookup relationship cannot be changed to a master-detail relationship if any existing records do not have a value in the lookup field.

c) A master-detail relationship can always be changed to a lookup relationship: A master-detail relationship cannot be changed if there is a **Roll-Up Summary** field on the master record.

Answer 5 – Changing a Picklist type to a Picklist (Multi-Select) type

The answers are b) and d):

b) The picklist values remain after the field type has changed.

d) Existing records that contain a value that is not in the list of picklist values have the value removed after the field type has changed.

The following are not correct:

a) A **Picklist** type cannot be changed to a **Picklist (Multi-Select)** type if there are existing records.

c) Existing records that contain a value that is not in the list of picklist values remain after the field type has changed.

Answer 6 – Using Schema Builder

The answers are a) and d):

a) Creating and editing custom objects

d) Creating and editing custom fields

The following are not correct:

b) Creating and editing tabs for custom objects: Tabs cannot be created using Schema Builder.

c) Editing but not creating standard fields: Standard fields cannot be edited.

Answer 7 – Capabilities of Schema Builder

The answers are b) and c):

b) The **Tab selection** screen option is not available and **Tab selection** does not automatically appear after you have created objects.

c) Created fields are set to be visible and editable for all internal and external profiles.

The following are not correct:

a) Objects can be created but not edited using Schema Builder: Custom objects can be created and edited using Schema Builder.

d) Created fields can be added to page layouts in Schema Builder after you have created them: There is no capability to add fields to page layouts in Schema Builder; this must be done instead on the object's **Page Layout** screen.

Summary

In this chapter, we have looked at how to design and build a data model both conceptually and using features in the Salesforce Lightning Platform.

Learning how to design and build a data model both conceptually and using the features in the Salesforce Lightning Platform is necessary when building apps in the Salesforce Platform. Having gone through this chapter, you will have gained the knowledge to create custom objects and custom fields and looked at the ways to determine an appropriate data model.

This chapter will have equipped you with the skills to design data model relationships and understand the implications of changing field types. In addition, you will have gained the knowledge and skills to use the Object Manager setup option and Schema Builder to create custom objects and fields and understand how Schema Builder can be used in the Lightning Platform to build and view a data model.

Finally, you were presented with a number of questions to help clarify the key concepts and features that are required when tackling the Data Modeling and Management section of the App Builder Certification exam.

In the next chapter, *Chapter 3*, *Importing and Exporting Data*, we will continue to look at the exam objectives: this time, for Data Modeling and Management Use Cases of External Objects. Here, we will look at the options for importing and exporting data and external objects.

3
Importing and Exporting Data

In this chapter, you will learn about the features and capabilities that exist for importing data into the Lightning Platform.

When building and maintaining apps on the Lightning Platform, there are occasions when you, as an app builder, need to either import or export data. Importing data is necessary in order to load existing user-generated data and also to create system data that is used by apps. Exporting data is needed for data backups and integrations with other systems.

Within this chapter, you will discover the options that are available to import and export data to and from Salesforce.

You will also learn how external objects can be used in Salesforce to access external data that does not reside within the Salesforce Lightning Platform.

Finally, you will be presented with a number of questions about importing and exporting data and the capabilities of external objects.

In this chapter, we will cover the following topics:

- Exam objectives – Data modeling and management
- Importing and exporting data to and from the Lightning Platform

- Understanding the features and capabilities of external objects

- Questions to test your knowledge

Let's now revisit the objectives of the App Builder Certification exam in the area of data modeling and management, which we looked at in *Chapter 2, Designing and Building a Data Model*.

Exam objectives – Data modeling and management

To pass the *Data modeling and management* section of the Certified Platform App Builder exam, app builders are expected to demonstrate knowledge of the following data management topics:

- Describe the options and considerations when importing and exporting data

- Describe the capabilities of, and use cases for, external objects

---

Reference: Salesforce Certified Platform App Builder Exam Guide

This guide is published by Salesforce and can be referenced at `https://trailhead.salesforce.com/help?article=Salesforce-Certified-Platform-App-Builder-Exam-Guide`.

In the Salesforce Certified Platform App Builder Exam Guide, the total number of questions is given, along with a percentage breakdown for each of the objectives, and an indication of the number of features/functions that can be expected in each of the objectives.

By analyzing these objectives, percentages, and question counts, we can determine the likely number of questions that will appear in the exam and, in the case of the data modeling and management objective, this is as follows:

Data modeling and management: Total number of exam questions

There are likely to be 12 questions in total. This is calculated as 20% of 60 total exam questions.

As we saw earlier, using these figures for the data modeling and management objective and the number of items that are likely to be assessed, we can determine that there would be 1-2 questions for each of the following concepts:

- Determining an appropriate data model

- Relationship types and considerations

- Selecting appropriate field types

- Considerations for changing field types

- Use cases of external objects

- Considerations for the Schema Builder

- Considerations for importing and exporting data

We covered the data modeling aspects in *Chapter 2, Designing and Building a Data Model*, where we looked at how to design and build a data model.

In this chapter, we will complete the data management topics as specified for the exam and cover the concepts needed to import and export data to and from Salesforce and look at the use cases and capabilities of external objects.

Let's now look at the options and considerations for importing and exporting data within the Lightning Platform.

Importing and exporting data to and from the Lightning Platform

When building and maintaining apps on the Lightning Platform, there are occasions when you, as an app builder, need to either import or export data. Importing data is necessary to load existing user-generated data or to create system data that is used by apps.

User-generated data needs to be imported when you are migrating from an external data management system or from spreadsheets into Salesforce or are restructuring the data model in Salesforce. The type of data that is often imported includes account, opportunity, and contact records. User-generated data can also originate from lists of contacts or prospects, which a sales or marketing team would purchase, such as lists of new leads or contacts that are contained in marketing spreadsheets.

System data is records that are used to control or configure the apps that we build or are installed by third-party app providers. An example of system data includes the list of country codes and state information that we identified as a required dataset in our data modeling within the example scenario covered in *Chapter 2, Designing and Building a Data Model.*

In addition to the user-generated and system data, there is often the need to integrate external data management systems, which can be done by importing and exporting data between the different systems. This method of data integration uses an approach known as **ETL**, which involves the **Extraction**, **Transformation**, and **Loading** of data.

A typical file format that is used when importing and exporting data records between different data management systems is CSV, which is a system-independent format that enables the data records to be universally processed.

> **CSV file format**
>
> **CSV** is a system-independent format that is universally recognized and stands for **Comma Separated Values**, where the data records are differentiated from one another using the comma character ",".

The following options and features are available for the importing and exporting of data to and from the Lightning Platform:

- **Data Loader**: Importing and exporting data
- **Data Import Wizard**: Importing data
- **Data Export**: Exporting data

Let's now look at the features, capabilities, and considerations of **Data Loader**, which is used to import and export data.

Importing and exporting data using Data Loader

Data Loader is a standalone application that is provided by Salesforce to enable the importing and exporting of data to and from the Lightning Platform. In addition to importing and exporting data, Data Loader can also be used to delete data.

The Data Loader software is provided and supported by Salesforce at no additional cost, and since Data Loader is a standalone application and is not cloud-based, the software must be installed on your local computer.

The features and capabilities of Data Loader are as follows:

- A standalone client application that uses the Salesforce API to connect to the Lightning Platform.
- An interactive wizard-style interface that provides a drag-and-drop field mapping between the source and destination data fields.
- The ability to import, export, and delete records of all types, which includes standard and custom objects.
- The ability to import and export data files to a maximum of 5 million data records.
- The ability to import attachments.
- Data Loader does not support the export of attachments. Instead, Salesforce recommends using the Data Export feature described later in this chapter to export attachments.
- The generation of post-processing error and success log files in CSV format.
- The options to set the size of data batches and use of a Bulk API batch mechanism.
- Options to set US or European date formats and all time zones.
- Options to set the CSV import file record delimiters and file encoding.
- A built-in CSV file reader.

> **Data Loader operating system support**
>
> Data Loader is supported for use with the Microsoft Windows or macOS operating systems. To see the latest system requirements and considerations for installing Data Loader, visit the Salesforce Help article at `https://help.salesforce.com/articleView?id=installing_the_data_loader.htm`.

To start the installation of the Data Loader software, perform the following steps:

1. Navigate to **Setup** and then search for **Data Loader** in the **Quick Find** search box located at the top of the **Setup** menu on the left side bar.
2. Locate the **Data Loader** setup screen by clicking on **Data Loader**.

3.   Within the **Data Loader** setup screen, you can choose the installation download link for your operating system using either **Download Data Loader for Windows** or **Download Data Loader for Mac**, as shown in the following screenshot:

Figure 3.1 – Data Loader setup screen

In addition, for the Windows operating system only, the Data Loader client application includes a command-line interface to enable the automated importing and exporting of Salesforce data records.

Within the Data Loader setup screen shown in *Figure 3.1*, there are links to installation instructions for Windows and Mac.

> **Installation instructions for Windows and Mac**
>
> At the time of writing, the installation instructions for Windows and Mac are located at: `https://help.salesforce.com/articleView?id=loader_install_windows.htm` for Windows and `https://help.salesforce.com/articleView?id=loader_install_mac.htm` for Mac.

After you have installed the appropriate version of the Data Loader client application for your given operating system and invoked the program, the following menu screen appears:

Figure 3.2 – Data Loader menu screen

The operations that you can perform using Data Loader are as follows:

- **Insert**: This option allows you to create new records.

- **Update**: This option allows you to update existing records that are specified by a Salesforce unique identifier.

- **Upsert**: This option is a combination of insert and update, whereby existing records that are specified by a Salesforce unique identifier are updated and, if no record is present, a record is created.

- **Delete**: This option allows you to delete existing records that are specified by a Salesforce unique identifier. Please note that the deleted records are stored in the Recycle Bin for a limited period of time.

- **Hard Delete**: This option allows you to permanently delete records that have been deleted and are stored in the Recycle Bin.

- **Export**: This option allows you to extract data into a file with the saved data in CSV format.

- **Export All**: This option allows you to extract all data, including any deleted data that is located in the recycle bin, into a file with the saved data in CSV format.

Before accessing the Data Loader options, click on the **Settings** tab to check that all the necessary settings are correct before proceeding as shown in the following screenshot:

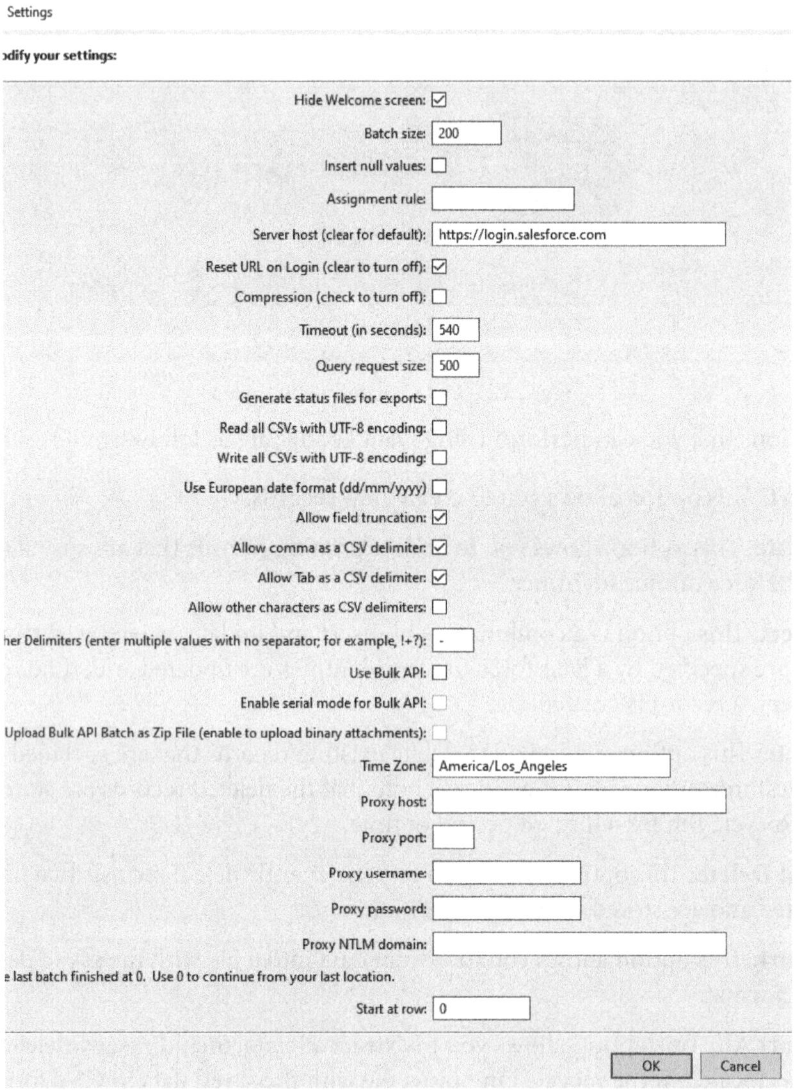

Figure 3.3 – Data Loader settings

Whenever making changes to Salesforce, it is usually good practice to test changes first in a sandbox environment, which is a copy of your production system. This is covered in more detail in *Chapter 11, Managing the App Building Process*. In addition to testing apps built in the Lightning Platform, you can also test the effects of importing data by first importing into a sandbox environment.

To test changes before importing into a production system, you can change the **Server host** value from the default production setting, which is `https://login.salesforce.com`, as shown in *Figure 3.3 – Data Loader Settings*. Change the value of the **Server host** setting to `https://test.salesforce.com` to import or export using a sandbox environment.

Let's now look at the options and capabilities of using the Data Import Wizard feature, which is used to import data.

Importing data using Data Import Wizard

Data Import Wizard is a feature that is available out of the box and provides the facility to import data for custom objects and some specified standard objects. Data Import Wizard can be used for importing data as an alternative to using Data Loader, which we looked at earlier in this chapter, but which cannot be used to export data.

The features and capabilities of Data Import Wizard are as follows:

- A standard out-of-the-box feature within the Lightning Platform that presents an interactive wizard-style interface for drag-and-drop field mapping between the source and destination data fields and opens in a full browser window.

- There is no requirement to download and install any software.

- The ability to import custom object records and the following standard objects: Contact, Account, Lead, Solution, and Campaign member status.

- The ability to import data files to a maximum of 50,000 data records.

- Duplicate prevention feature when importing records that can be associated with fields that contain specified keys, such as account name, account site, contact email address, or lead email address.

To help reinforce the skills and knowledge needed to import data using Data Import Wizard, we will now carry out some practical work in Salesforce. So, if you do not have a Salesforce environment to facilitate this, you can create a free developer org as detailed in *Chapter 1, Core Capabilities of the Lightning Platform*.

Using an example CSV file, we will now carry out the process of importing data using Data Import Wizard. The CSV files will be imported into the Location custom object that we created in *Chapter 2, Designing and Building a Data Model*, and we'll create it using comma-separated values.

To create a CSV file that can used to import the data in to Salesforce, copy and paste the following text into Notepad or an equivalent text editor:

```
Country,State,Active
Australia,New South Wales,1
Australia,Queensland,1
United Kingdom,,1
United States,San Francisco,1
United States,New York,1
United States,Texas,0
```

Now, save the file as `Location.txt`, which will show this text as follows:

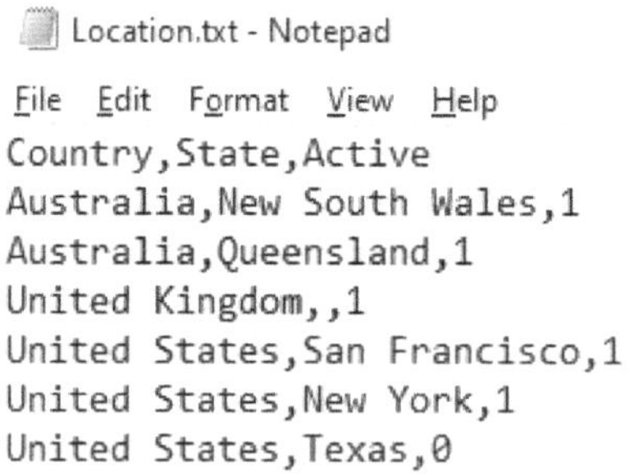

📄 Location.txt - Notepad

File Edit Format View Help

```
Country,State,Active
Australia,New South Wales,1
Australia,Queensland,1
United Kingdom,,1
United States,San Francisco,1
United States,New York,1
United States,Texas,0
```

Figure 3.4 – Data import location CSV file

As a recap about data types in Salesforce, we'll be importing the values into picklist type fields and a checkbox type field. The columns `Country__c` and `State__c` are picklist types, and the column `Active__c` is a checkbox type.

Checkbox values for importing data

Checkbox field types are used to store a value as either true or false, which appears on the user interface as a checked or unchecked value. However, when importing data, the values are 1 for true values and 0 for false values.

To import the location data using Data Import Wizard, perform the following steps:

1. Navigate to **Setup** and then search for **Data Import Wizard** in the **Quick Find** search box located at the top of the **Setup** menu on the left side of the tool bar.

2. Click on the **Data Import Wizard** option to reveal the **Data Import Wizard** page, as shown in the following screenshot:

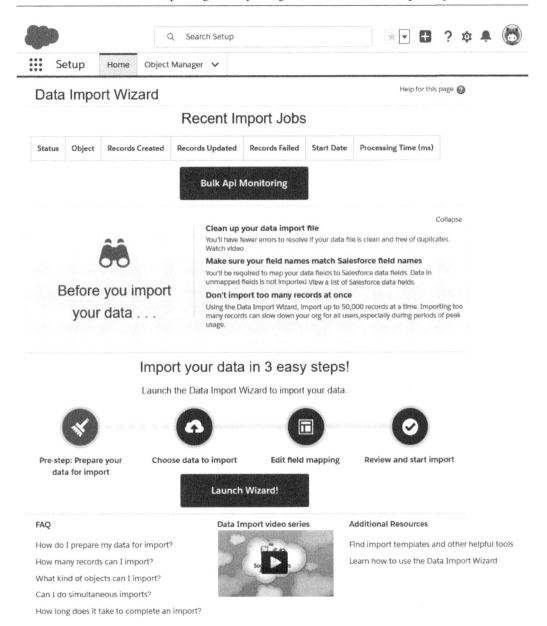

Figure 3.5 – Data Import Wizard launch screen

Within the **Data Import Wizard** screen, perform the following steps:

1. Click on **Launch Wizard!**.

2. Choose **Custom objects** in the **What kind of data are you importing?** section.

3. Scroll down and select the **Locations** object.

4. Choose **Add new records** in the **What do you want to do?** section.

5. Leave the following options unspecified:

   Match by: --None--

   Which User field in your file designates record owners? --None--

   Trigger workflow rules and processes for new and updated records: Unchecked.

6. Click on the CSV icon in the **Where is your data located?** section.

7. Click on **Choose File** and select the CSV file that you created in the steps for creating the `Location.txt` file.

8. Click on **Next**.

9. In the **Edit mapping** step, **Data Import Wizard** automatically maps the columns in the file to the fields in the Location custom object. However, you can also manually map the fields by clicking on **Change**, as shown in the following screenshot:

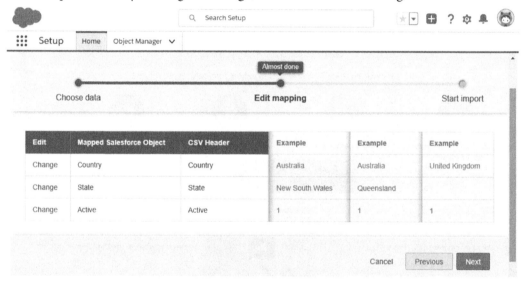

Figure 3.6 – Data Import Wizard screen almost done

10. Click on **Next**.

11. In the next screen, you can check the type of import and the number of mapped fields using the **Review & Start Import** screen and then click on **Start Import** to continue.

12. You will be presented with a confirmation that the import has started. Click on **OK** to view the import status in the **Bulk Data Load Jobs** page, as shown in the following screenshot:

Figure 3.7 – Bulk Data Load Jobs screen

In addition to the confirmation screen, you will receive an email with the email subject **Salesforce import of "Location.txt" has finished. 6 rows were processed**.

We will now look at the mechanism for exporting data using the Data Export facility.

Exporting data using Data Export

The Data Export facility is used to export data from within Salesforce. Data Export is an out-of-the-box feature within the Lightning Platform with the following key features and capabilities:

- **Types of export**: The exporting of files can be either scheduled or requested manually.

- **File format**: The data export comprises multiple files in CSV file format.

- **File format encoding**: You can select the file encoding mechanism to adjust the type of character encoding within the file to cater for different character sets.

- **Exporting of attachments**: Attachments can be added to the exported data.

- **Sandboxes**: The data export functionality does not support the exporting of data from sandboxes. The options to activate a data export are present in sandboxes. However, the export files are not actually generated and received.

- **Requesting Export Files**: Export files can be scheduled and generated automatically or requested manually.

- **Export files availability**: Export files are available for download for up to 48 hours after generation.

- **Formula and roll-up summary fields**: Data in formula and roll-up summary fields are not added to the exported data.

- **Recycle Bin data**: The data in the recycle bin is not added to the exported data.

Now, let's look at the mechanism for scheduling an export of data using the Data Export facility.

Scheduling an export of data using Data Export

The scheduling mechanism in Data Export allows the automated request for CSV export files to be scheduled.

The scheduled export can be set to be weekly for editions such as Enterprise Edition and Unlimited Edition, and monthly for Professional Edition and Developer Edition. When the export is complete, you will receive an email with a link to the data.

To schedule a data export, perform the following steps:

1. Navigate to **Setup** and then search for Data Export in the **Quick Find** search box located at the top of the **Setup** menu on the left side of the tool bar.

2. Click on **Data Export**.

3. Click on **Schedule Export** to navigate to the **Data Export setup**: **Schedule Data Export** screen.

In the **Data Export setup**: **Schedule Data Export** screen, perform the following steps:

1. **Export File Encoding**: Choose a file encoding option from the picklist.

2. **Include images, documents, and attachments**: Include by checking the checkbox.

3. **Include Salesforce Files and Salesforce CRM Content document versions**: Include by checking the checkbox.

4. **Replace carriage returns with spaces**: Include by checking the checkbox. This is checked by default.

5. **Schedule Data Export**: Choose the frequency using either **On day 1 of every month, On day 15 of every month**, and so on, or by choosing **1st Sunday of every month, 2nd Monday of every month**, and so on.

6. **Exported Data**: Include all data by checking the checkbox. This is checked by default but you can select specific data types, as shown in the following screenshot:

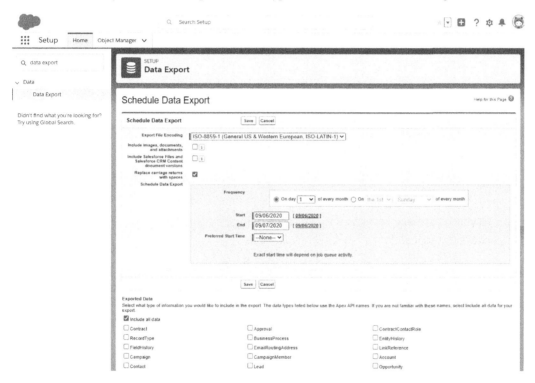

Figure 3.8 – Schedule Data Export screen

7. Finally, click on **Save**.

> **Data export delays**
>
> The Data Export extract and delivery system can get delayed by the processing capacity of the Lightning Platform. Here, the underlying queue of data export requests is dependent upon other system processes, which means that the target date for receiving export files is not always met.

We will now look at the steps for exporting data manually using the Data Export facility.

Manually exporting data using Data Export

The mechanism to manually request a data export allows the request for CSV export files to be activated without having to wait for a scheduled time.

To carry out a manual data export, perform the following steps:

1. Navigate to **Setup** and then search for Data Export in the **Quick Find** search box located at the top of the **Setup** menu on the left side of the tool bar.

2. Click on **Data Export**.

3. Click on **Export Now** to navigate to the Data Export setup: **Schedule Data Export** screen.

In the **Data Export setup**: **Weekly Export Service** or **Monthly Export Service** screens, perform the following steps:

1. **Export File Encoding**: Choose a file encoding option from the picklist.

2. **Include images, documents, and attachments**: Include by checking the checkbox.

3. **Include Salesforce Files and Salesforce CRM Content document versions**: Include by checking the checkbox.

4. **Replace carriage returns with spaces**: Include by checking the checkbox. This is checked by default.

5. **Exported Data**: Include all data by checking the checkbox. This is checked by default but you can select specific data types.

6. Finally, click on **Start Export**.

Let's now look at the capabilities and use cases of external objects.

Understanding the features and capabilities of external objects

We have learned about the options for importing and exporting data to and from the Lightning Platform and we have carried out some practical methods of importing or copying data into the Lightning Platform using the ETL processes of extract, transform, and load.

ETL processes generally produce copies of data in the Salesforce org, which are static references at the point of extraction and have the disadvantage that the data may not need to be permanently stored and, at some point in time, becomes out of date.

As an improvement to the integration of Salesforce and third-party systems, where data is always up to date, Salesforce provides a feature known as Salesforce Connect that uses external objects that represent the data tables and records that are located in external systems.

External objects are similar to custom objects, which we looked at in *Chapter 2, Designing and Building a Data Model*. Custom objects define the data model for data that is located within the Salesforce Lightning Platform, whereas external objects provide the data model for data that is stored externally and does not reside within the platform. Typical examples of external data include financial or sales order processing information.

Salesforce Connect is the framework that provides the integration of data between external objects in the Lightning Platform and external systems and allows the viewing, searching, and updating of data that is stored externally.

The framework and protocol used by external objects are as follows:

- **Salesforce Connect framework**: Uses Salesforce Connect adapters
- **Salesforce Connect adapters**: Uses the open data protocol

> **Open data protocol**
> Details of OData are available at `https://www.odata.org/`.

The features and capabilities of external objects are as follows:

- External objects can be referenced programmatically within Apex code and Salesforce APIs.
- External objects can be deployed using Metadata API, change sets, and packages.
- Each Salesforce instance can have a maximum of 100 external objects. External objects are not included in the total number of custom objects.
- External objects can be associated with other external objects and internal standard and custom objects using relationship fields.

We will now look at the types of relationships that can be associated with external objects.

Understanding relationship types of external objects

As we learned in *Chapter 2, Designing and Building a Data Model*, relationships enable the association of data with other objects.

For external objects, there are the following relationship fields:

- **Lookup**: Lookup relationship fields, when used with external objects, require the presence of an 18-character Salesforce ID on the external dataset. Only then can the lookup relationship be created on the external object. The lookup relationship is used to associate the child external object with a parent internal object that can either be a standard or a custom object.

- **Indirect Lookup**: Indirect lookup relationship fields are unique to external objects and use external ID fields on the parent record to associate the external data. **Indirect lookup** is created on the external object and is used to link the child external object to a parent internal object that can either be a standard or a custom object.

- **External Lookup**: External lookup relationship fields are created on standard, custom, or external objects and are used to link the child internal or external object to a parent external object.

The Salesforce Connect framework ensures that the data reflected within the external objects are synchronized with the external data. This method of synchronized access provides a real-time data connection to the data instead of a copy of the data. By not copying the data, there are no additional storage needs with which to store the copied data. Synchronized data access also means that there is no need for any additional processes or resources for exporting, importing, and managing processes for keeping the data in sync.

The main use case for external objects is to enable information that is stored in an external system to be accessed from within Salesforce Lightning Platform and to display or process that information within Salesforce. Other use cases for external objects include the following:

- **Real-time access**: This is when immediate and timely access is needed to dependent information, an example of which is to have payment information from an external financial system available to a salesperson while visiting a customer.

- **Large data volumes**: With large amounts of data, the volume of data and the time that it takes to process that data can become costly and, over time, can become a burden. Typically, external sales processing and support information can increase over time.

- **Small data volumes**: With small amounts of key information, the overhead of building integration and synchronization processes is not always cost-effective given that there is not much data to be associated. Organizations may opt to re-key this data, which may introduce incorrect data. Typical examples could include maintaining information for a selected number of key accounts from a separate marketing database.

Let's now check our understanding of the options available for importing and exporting data and the capabilities of external objects.

Questions to test your knowledge

We now present four questions to help assess your knowledge of the options and features for importing and exporting data and how external objects can be used in Salesforce to access external data that does not reside within the Lightning Platform. The answers can be found at the end of the chapter.

Question 1 – Importing data into the Lightning Platform

Your marketing manager has asked you to import over 500,000 lead records into the Lightning Platform. Which data import solution provided by Salesforce has the ability to meet this requirement? (Select one)

a) None. Only a third-party partner app available from the App Exchange

b) Data Import Wizard only

c) Data Loader only

d) Either Data Loader or Data Import Wizard

Question 2 – Importing and exporting data using Data Loader

Which of the following can be carried out using Data Loader? (Select two)

a) Importing and exporting data files up to a maximum of 5 million data records

b) Importing and exporting of attachments

c) Deleting custom object records and all types of standard objects

d) Deleting custom object records and some specified types of standard objects

Question 3 – Importing data using Data Import Wizard

Which of the following can be carried out using Data Import Wizard? (Select two)

a) Importing custom object records and all types of standard objects

b) Built-in duplicate prevention feature

c) Importing data files up to a maximum of 500,000 data records

d) Automatic field mapping between the source and destination data fields

Question 4 – External data access

Your service manager has asked whether the order data that exists in an external data management system can be accessed in real time in Salesforce. Which solution has the ability to meet this requirement? (Select one)

a) Either Data Loader or Data Import Wizard

b) Data Import Wizard only

c) Only the Data Loader command-line interface to enable automated importing and exporting

d) External objects

Here are the answers to the four questions that were presented to help verify your knowledge of designing a data model in the Lightning Platform, knowing when to use appropriate field types, and the impact of changing data types along with questions to test your knowledge of the Schema Builder.

Answer 1 – Importing data into the Lightning Platform

The answer is c) Only the Data Loader.

The following options are incorrect:

a) None. Only a third-party partner app available from the App Exchange

b) Data Import Wizard only

d) Either Data Loader or Data Import Wizard

Answer 2 – Importing and exporting data using Data Loader

The answers are a) Importing and exporting data files up to a maximum of 5 million data records, and c) Deleting custom object records and all types of standard objects.

The following options are incorrect:

b) Importing and exporting of attachments: Attachments can be imported, but not exported, using Data Loader.

d) Deleting custom object records and some specified types of standard objects: Custom object records and all types of standard objects can be deleted using Data Loader.

Answer 3 – Importing data using Data Import Wizard

The answers arc b) Built-in duplicate prevention feature, and d) Automatic field mapping between the source and destination data fields.

The following options are incorrect:

a) Importing custom object records and all types of standard objects

c) Importing data files up to a maximum of 500,000 data records

Answer 4 – External data access

The answer is d) External objects.

The following options are incorrect:

a) Either Data Loader or Data Import Wizard

b) Data Import Wizard only

c) Only the Data Loader command-line interface to enable automated importing and exporting

Summary

In this chapter, you have acquired knowledge of how to import data into the Lightning Platform. To understand the process of importing data, we carried out a practical task to import data using Data Import Wizard. You have also gained knowledge and an understanding of how data can be exported and the capabilities of the Data Export feature.

You learned about external objects and how they can be used within Salesforce Connect to provide real-time connectivity to data stored in Salesforce and external data management systems. You learned about the typical use cases of external objects and the benefits of synchronizing data. You gained an understanding of how external objects provide solutions that avoid the unnecessary copying of data, enabling real-time access and offering benefits for integrating both large and small data volumes.

In the next chapter, you will learn about the features and capabilities to restrict and extend access to objects, fields, and records. You will understand how, with the use of object-level permissions, organization-wide sharing defaults, and other sharing settings, appropriate access to records can be configured.

Section 2: Behind the Scenes

This section of the book provides detailed information about how to secure access to the data we generated in the previous section; how to configure the user interface, business logic, and data validation mechanisms while building process automation; and finally, how to generate data analytics using reports and dashboards.

This section has the following chapters:

- *Chapter 4, Securing Access to Data*
- *Chapter 5, Setting Up the User Interface*
- *Chapter 6, Implementing Business Logic*
- *Chapter 7, Building Business Process Automation*
- *Chapter 8, Generating Data Analytics with Reports and Dashboards*

4
Securing Access to Data

In this chapter, you will learn about the features and capabilities that exist in the Lightning platform to restrict and extend access to objects, fields, and records; and understand how data security in the platform is applied using a number of layers.

You will understand the key difference between object security, field-level security, and record sharing; and how, with the use of object-level permissions, organization-wide defaults, and sharing settings, appropriate access to records can be configured.

You will gain the knowledge to be able to view and create permission sets and profiles that serve to control object and field-level access and how and when to assign profiles and permission sets.

Finally, you will be presented with a number of questions about securing access to data using object, record, and field-level data access features and capabilities in the Lightning Platform.

In this chapter, we will cover the following topics:

- Exam objectives – Data Security
- Understanding the layers of data security in the Lightning Platform
- Learning about profiles and permission sets
- Setting up data access for objects and fields
- Controlling data access to records
- Summarizing data security capabilities in the Lightning Platform
- Questions to test your knowledge

Let's now look at the objectives of the App Builder certification exam that covers data security.

Exam objectives – Data Security

To pass the Data Security section of the certified platform App Builder exam, app builders are expected to demonstrate knowledge of the following:

1. Describe the features and capabilities available to restrict and extend object, record, and field access.
2. Given a set of business requirements, determine the appropriate sharing solution.

> **Reference: Salesforce Certified Platform App Builder Exam Guide**
>
> This guide is published by Salesforce and can be referenced at `https://trailhead.salesforce.com/help?article=Salesforce-Certified-Platform-App-Builder-Exam-Guide`.

In the Salesforce Certified Platform App Builder Exam Guide, the total number of questions is given, a percentage breakdown for each of the objectives, and an indication of the number of features/functions that can be expected in each of the objectives.

By analyzing these objectives, percentages, and question counts, we can determine the number of questions that will appear in the exam and for the Data Security objective, this is as follows:

> **Data Security: Total number of exam questions**
> There are likely to be 6 questions in total. This is calculated as 10% of 60 total exam questions.

Using these figures for the Data Security objective and the number of items that are likely to be assessed, we can determine that there will be 3 or 4 questions on features and capabilities available to restrict and extend object, record, and field access, and 3 or 4 questions on determining the appropriate sharing solution for a given set of business requirements.

To help reinforce the skills and knowledge needed to secure access to data, there is some practical work in Salesforce. So if you do not have a Salesforce environment to carry this out, create a free developer org as detailed in *Chapter 1, Core Capabilities of the Lightning Platform*. We will use the data model for our example scenario that we designed in *Chapter 2, Designing and Building a Data Model*, to demonstrate how to secure data access at the object, field, and record level.

Now, let's look at the layers of data security that exist and the features available to restrict and grant object access within the Salesforce Lightning Platform.

Understanding the layers of data security in the Lightning Platform

The Lightning Platform uses a layered data security model that incorporates the concept of applying the principle of least privilege security.

The **principle of least privilege** is a data security concept that stipulates that users should have the minimum amount of access to data required to carry out their use of the system. As an example, a user record that has been created for managing sales opportunity records should not automatically be provided with full access to marketing campaign records unless it is specifically required.

By using a layered data security model in the Lightning Platform, along with a flexible set of inter-related features that allow you to set the security at each level, data can be secured and only exposed to users that you have determined need it. The following diagram shows the data security levels and the general data security mechanisms that can be applied at an object, record, and field level:

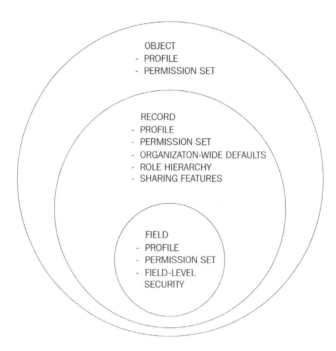

Figure 4.1 – Layers of data security

The overarching level of data security access is at the object level and can be set to allow or prevent users from creating, reading, updating, or deleting records for any given object. The features that are available in the Lightning Platform to control object-level access are **Profiles** and **Permission Sets**.

The next level of data access is applied at the record level and uses the concept of record visibility to determine whether users have access to records. Again, as with object-level security, the key data security mechanisms for record-level security are Profiles and Permission Sets, however, there are additional concepts for record access, which are **roles** and **sharing**.

Using roles and sharing, you can widen the level of data access using the in-built data access security model in the Lightning Platform. The data access security model enables you to control data access at the most precise level so you can allow specific users to view objects, but then prevent certain records associated with that object type from being accessed. The features that allow you to fine-tune record-level security include organization-wide defaults, roles, and sharing rules.

The lowest level of data access is field-level security. Field-level security can be set for each object and can be set to allow or prevent users from creating, reading, updating, or deleting values in fields for any given object. You can enforce a particular field to be read-only or further restrict access to prevent specific users from accessing it. This restriction of field access can be done even if the restricted user has full access to the associated object.

Understanding the difference between permission settings and roles

It is important to understand the difference between permission settings and roles as they are used to control very different aspects of data security within the Lightning Platform.

Permissions are granted with the use of Profiles and Permission Sets and are used to control the users' access to various resources. Users' permissions impact the following:

- The functions that the user is able to perform
- The types of data they can access
- The operations that can be carried out on that data

Roles are primarily used to control the visibility of specific datasets by using the role hierarchy. The combination of the record owner and the position of that record owner in the role hierarchy determines the record-level access for all other users.

The relationships between the user, profile, permission set, and role features in the Lightning Platform are shown in the following diagram:

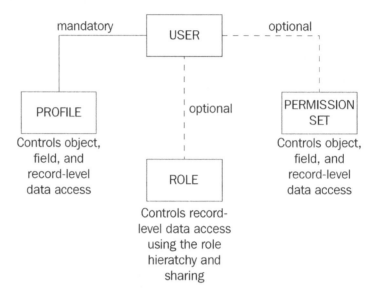

Figure 4.2 – User, profile, permission set, and role

Now that we've learned about the different layers of data security, let's move on to see how profiles and permission sets are used.

Learning about Profiles and Permission Sets

Profiles and Permission Sets are used to control and assign system and data access permissions to users in the Lightning Platform. Within the Profile or Permission Sets, there is a setting or collection of settings that are used to control what features and functions are available to them, along with the types of operations that can be carried out on data.

The difference between Profiles and Permission Sets is that Profiles are integral to the user's association with the system and data configuration with the Lightning Platform and users can be assigned to only one Profile. When creating new user records, the intended Profile that the user is to have must exist in order for the newly created user record's profile to be assigned. In contrast, the user record can be associated with multiple Permission Sets.

Generally, when setting up permissions for users, you should consider the use of profiles to grant the base-level system and data privileges that users of a particular function require and then add additional Permission Sets to grant further privileges as strictly necessary.

> **Assigning a single Profile or multiple Permission Sets to users**
>
> Users can be assigned a single profile only and optionally multiple permission sets.

Profiles can be used to not only provide additional access to systems or types of data at a broad level but they can also remove access to systems or types of data. Conversely, Permission Sets can only provide additional access for users that the Permission Set is assigned to. Typically, Profiles and Permission Sets are implemented in combination with each other whereupon the Profile provides the basic set of permissions that allows the core privileges and Permission Sets to be used to extend the permissions for selected users.

Now, let's look at the features and capabilities of Profiles.

Understanding the features and capabilities of Profiles

Profiles are used to control the system and app features and functionality that can be performed by users in the Lightning Platform. Along with the control of system and app functionality, Profiles are also used to determine the type and operations of data that can be accessed.

When assigning a Profile to a user, it needs to exist prior to any user records being created. This is to allow the assignment of the profile during the creation of the new user record logins.

There are standard profiles in the Lightning Platform that are provided out of the box and cover profiles such as system administrator, standard user, marketing user, solution manager, and so on.

Standard profiles cannot be edited but they can be cloned and then edited. There are also custom profiles that you can create that contain the desired collection of system and data access privileges for a given user's job role. Custom profiles can also be created by cloning existing standard or custom profiles and then tailoring the settings to fit the new type of profile.

Clone standard or custom profiles

You can clone standard and custom profiles. This offers two benefits: firstly, it is quicker to clone a profile than to create it from scratch, and secondly, standard profiles can get updated by Salesforce from time to time, which may cause the settings in a user's profile to change. When cloned as custom profiles, they are not likely to be automatically changed.

When creating Profiles, the permissions settings are grouped into either apps or system permissions and the type of permissions determine the privileges that the assigned users have when using the system and accessing data.

You assign a single profile to each user record and typically prior to creating the user you identify or clone, or create a new profile that reflects that user's job role, such as system administrator, sales representative, marketing profile, and so on.

Create profiles before creating users

When creating user records, you select a profile to assign to the user. It is therefore important that you have already created any profiles that are to be assigned to users prior to creating the user record.

Once you have created or cloned a new profile, you can assign it to multiple users, as necessary. The profile that you assign to a user can be changed, however, only one profile can ever be assigned to a given user at any given time.

The features and capabilities of Profiles are as follows:

- **Users must have a profile**: All users in the Lightning Platform must be assigned a profile and users can only be assigned one profile at any one time.

- **System, app, and data access**: Profiles determine what system and app functions, data access, and type of operations can be performed on that data by the assigned user.

- **Standard and custom profiles**: There are read-only standard out-of-the-box and custom profiles that you create for a tailored collection of system and data access privileges.

- **Profiles can be used to restrict access**: When system and data access privileges are excluded from a profile and the user is not assigned these privileges using a Permission Set, then access to these features for data is restricted for any users assigned the Profile.

Understanding the features and capabilities of Permission Sets

Permission Sets, in the same way as Profiles, are used to control the system and app features and the functionality that can be performed by users in the Lightning Platform. Again, as with Profiles, Permission Sets also determine the types of data and the operations that can be performed on that data.

The differences between Permission Sets and Profiles are that Permission Sets are used to extend a user's system or data access without the need to modify their profile. You can also assign multiple Permission Sets to a user as opposed to only having one Profile per user.

> **Permission Sets add privileges only**
>
> It is important to understand that if a user has a specific privilege that is added by their profile, the privilege cannot be removed by excluding that permission from an assigned Permission Set. Permission Sets can only be used to add extra privileges.

Unlike Profiles, there are no out-of-the-box Permission Sets and hence you must create them. Once created, you can edit them and they can also be cloned and edited.

When creating Permission Sets, the permissions settings are grouped into either app or system permissions and the type of permissions determine the privileges the assigned users have when using the system and accessing data.

The features and capabilities of Permission Sets are as follows:

- **Users can have multiple Permission Sets**: All users in the Lightning Platform must be assigned a profile and users can only be assigned one profile at any one time.

- **System, app, and data access**: Permission Sets determine system and app functions, data access, and the type of operations that can be performed on that data by the assigned user.

- **Permission Sets are used to extend access**: Permission Sets extend a user's system, app, or data access without the need to modify their profile.

In addition to these core features and capabilities of Permission Sets, the following features are on offer to extend the use of Permission Sets:

- **Permission Set Groups**: These enable you to build a combination of permissions that are made of several Permission Sets. They are useful to create an overall set of system, app, and data access permissions that a user's function might need to carry out their job within the Lightning Platform. They save time assigning all the separate Permission Sets to new users by requiring the single Permission Set Group to be assigned instead.

- **Muting Permission Sets**: This is used to exclude a set of permissions that is contained within a Permission Set Group. This is also used if the user that has been assigned the Permission Set Group should no longer have access to all the permissions that the Permission Set Group allows.

- **Session-Based Permission Sets**: These are used to provide system, app, and data access permissions only during the time that a session is valid. A use-case of Session-Based Permission Sets is for when you want to provide access for only a short period of time such as when an app connects to the Lightning Platform to retrieve information. For security, the app only requires access for the duration of the connection and the permissions are revoked when the app disconnects. Session-Based Permission Sets can be activated and deactivated by Lightning flows. Lightning flows are covered in *Chapter 7, Building Business Process Automation*.

Setting up data access for objects and fields

Profiles and Permission Sets can both be used to control the data access permissions for objects and fields for users in the Lightning Platform. Within Profile or Permission Sets, there is a setting or collection of settings that are used to specify the objects and fields along with the types of operations that can be carried out on the objects and fields.

Data access at the object level can be considered to be the bluntest method of controlling access to record data for a specific type of object. Object-level data access is set by granting the privileges in the Profile assigned to the user or by creating and assigning multiple Permission Sets.

Object-level data access forms an overarching level of data security access and determines whether users are able to create, read, edit, and delete records of the specified object type.

Configuring field-level data access allows a more granular setting of privileges so you can expose data records to users but restrict the user's access to specific fields within the object record. By applying field permissions, you can control whether the values for a specific field for an object can be created, read, edited, and deleted by users.

To help reinforce the skills and knowledge needed to set up data access for objects and fields, we will carry out some practical work in Salesforce. We will now show how you can set up data access for objects using Profiles and apply field-level data access known as field-level security using Permission Sets.

In *Chapter 2, Designing and Building a Data Model*, we looked at standard and custom objects and we showed how object-level permissions can be set up and assigned to specified profiles when creating new custom objects.

Let's consider the scenario that we looked at in *Chapter 2, Designing and Building a Data Model*, and at how we can use Profiles and Permission Sets to gain or restrict object and field-level access to one of the custom objects that we created: `Region`, `Region Location`, and `Location`.

These custom objects can be seen in a schema diagram that has been created using Schema Builder, which was described in *Chapter 2, Designing and Building a Data Model*, and can be seen in the following screenshot:

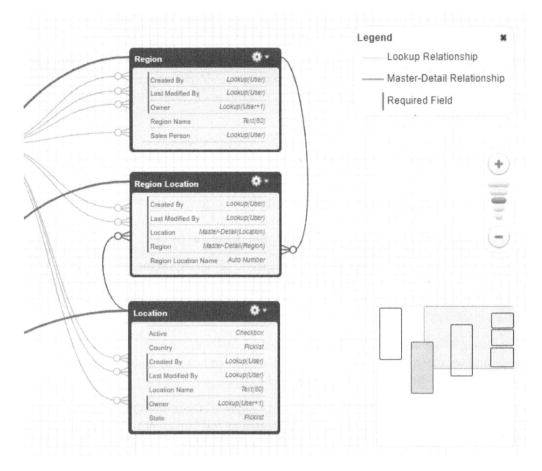

Figure 4.3 – Scenario custom objects

Let's look at the mechanisms that exist for setting object-level data access permissions.

Configuring data access for objects

In this section, we will now see how object-level permissions, which form an overarching level of data security access, enable users to create, read, edit, and delete records for the Region custom object that we created in *Chapter 2, Designing and Building a Data Model*.

We will consider the privileges and type of access that was required for the marketing team. Here, the level of access to the **Region** custom objects and the operations that can be carried out by the marketing team are set as shown in the following table:

Custom Object	Purpose of Access	Create	Read	Edit	Delete
Region	A marketing user can choose which salesperson is to be assigned leads within the Region custom object.	No	Yes	Yes	No

To meet this requirement, we must configure the object permissions for the marketing team and in this instance, we could use either Profiles or Permission Sets to set these object-level data access privileges. For this scenario, there is no right or wrong method and so, for the purposes of showing how to use Profiles, we will use the Profiles mechanism.

For this example, we will now apply the permissions using Profiles, so let's look at how to manage Profiles to control object access.

Cloning a standard Profile

In order to apply customized object permissions for the marketing team, we must use a custom marketing profile. There is a standard **Marketing User** profile, but only a few options can be changed on standard profiles as they are provided as a template from which to start for a base profile. When creating new objects, the object permissions cannot be modified using a standard profile. We will, therefore, clone the standard Marketing User Profile. To clone a Profile, carry out the following steps:

1. Navigate to **Setup** and then search for `Profiles` in the Quick Find search box located at the top of the **Setup** menu on the left sidebar.
2. Click on **Profiles** in the **Setup** menu.
3. Click on **Marketing User** on the **Profiles** setup screen.
4. Click on **Clone** in the top section of **the Profile Overview** setup screen.
5. Enter `Custom Marketing User` in the **Clone Profile** setup screen.

6. Finally, click on **Save** as shown in the following screenshot:

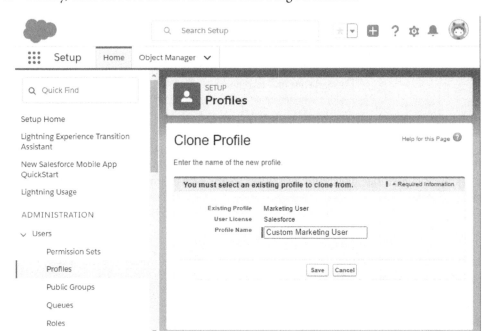

Figure 4.4– Cloned Profile

Configuring Profiles to control access

We will now configure the permissions for the Region custom objects in the Profile for the newly cloned custom **Marketing User**. To set the permissions, carry out the following steps:

1. Navigate to **Setup** and then search for `Profiles` in the Quick Find search box located at the top of the **Setup** menu on the left sidebar.

2. Click on **Profiles** in the **Setup** menu.

3. Click on **Custom Marketing User** on the **Profiles** setup screen.

4. Click on the **Object Settings in the App** section of the **Profile Overview** setup screen.

5. Click on **Regions** on the **Object Settings** setup screen.

6. Click on **Edit**.

7. Enable the following permissions: **Read**, **Edit**, and **View All**.

8. Finally, click on **Save** as shown in the following screenshot:

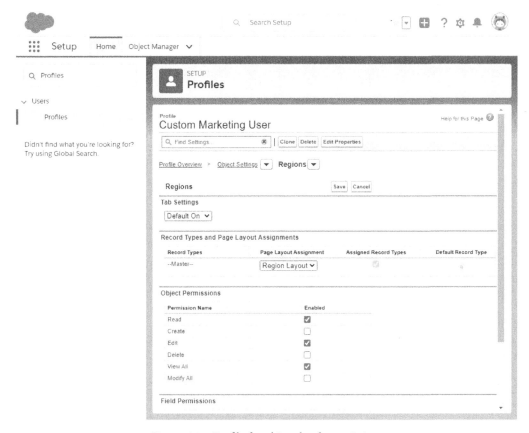

Figure 4.5 – Profile for object-level permissions

We will now look at how to configure field-level data access.

Configuring data access for fields

In this section, we will now see how field-level permissions enable users to create, read, edit, and delete values for fields within the Region custom object that we created in *Chapter 2*, *Designing and Building a Data Model*.

We will consider the privileges and type of access that was required for the marketing team. Here, the level of access to the **Sales Person** lookup custom field and the operations that can be carried out by the marketing team are set as shown in the following table:

Custom Field	Purpose of Access	Create	Read	Edit	Delete
Sales Person	A marketing user can choose which salesperson is to be assigned leads within the Region custom object.	Yes	Yes	Yes	Yes

To meet this requirement, we must configure the object permissions for the marketing team and in this instance, we could use either Profiles or Permission Sets to set these object-level data access privileges. For this scenario, there is no right or wrong method and so for the purposes of showing how to use Profiles, we will use the Profiles mechanism.

Field-level security provides the mechanism to protect certain fields from users that should not have access. This could be either due to sensitive information that is stored that should not be visible or because the field information is needed to perform some other function, such as in our example, allowing a restricted set of users from controlling who leads can be assigned to.

In the same way as object-level permissions, field-level data access is determined by Profiles and Permission Sets. Profiles allow you to add or restrict field-level security and Permission Sets allow you to extend field-level data access.

Creating Permission Sets to control access

We will now create a Permission Set for the purpose of granting the users in marketing the privileges of choosing the salesperson on the Region object. We could equally use Profiles to meet this requirement but we're using Permission Sets so that in the future, the ability to choose the salesperson on the Region object can be done by a non-marketing user profile if we so wish.

To create a new Permission Set, carry out the following steps:

1. Navigate to **Setup** and then search for `Permission Sets` in the Quick Find search box located at the top of the **Setup** menu on the left sidebar.

2. Click on **Permission Sets** in the **Setup** menu.

3. Click on **New** on the **Permission Sets** setup screen.

4. Enter the text `Region Set Sales Person` in the **Label** field.

5. The text **Region Set Sales Person** automatically appears in the **API Name** field.

6. Enter the text `This provides permission to set the Sales Person field on the Region custom object` in the **Description** field.

7. Click on **Object Settings** in the **App** section of the **Permission Set Overview** setup screen.

8. Click on **Regions** on the **Object Settings** setup screen.

9. Click on **Edit**.

10. Scroll down to the **Field Permissions** section of the page.

11. Enable the following permissions for the **Sales Person** field: **Read Access** and **Edit Access**.

12. Finally, click on **Save** as shown in the following screenshot:

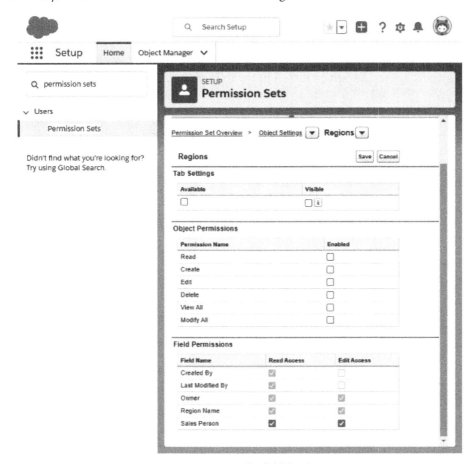

Figure 4.6 – Permission Set for field-level permissions

Now, let's see how to assign permission sets to users.

Assigning permission sets to users

Permission Sets can be assigned to one or multiple users in the Lightning Platform.

To assign permission settings, carry out the following:

1. Navigate to **Setup** and then search for `Permission Sets` in the Quick Find search box located at the top of the **Setup** menu on the left sidebar.

2. Click on **Permission Sets** in the **Setup** menu.

3. Select the required **Permission Set** in the list on the **Permission Sets** setup screen.

4. Click on **Manage Assignments** in the top section of the **Permission Sets** setup screen.

5. Click on **Add Assignments** in the top section of the **Permission Sets** setup screen.

6. Select one or more users on the **Assign Users** setup screen.

7. Finally, click on **Assign** as shown in the following screenshot:

Figure 4.7 – Assigning Permission Sets

Let's now look at the features and capabilities that exist in the Lightning Platform for controlling data security at the record level.

Controlling data access to records

After having looked at setting data security at the object level, which is the overarching level of access to data records, and at how the lowest access is set at the field level, you will now learn about how data access to actual records is applied at the record level.

The data access that is applied at the record level involves multiple types of access settings for records using the concept of record visibility to determine whether users have access to records. Record visibility is coupled with object-level security and the base level of data security is always applied using Profiles or Permission Sets.

To control data access to records and after having configured object-level access permissions, access settings for the actual records are carried out using organization-wide defaults, which specify which data records users are permitted to access.

In addition to the organization-wide defaults, the Lightning Platform security model has been designed in such a way that all records have an owner, which is a user – typically the user that has created the record. The user that is set as the owner of a record is granted full access to that particular record.

This concept of record ownership is important as it also means that access to records is also extended or restricted according to the user's position in a hierarchy, known as the **role hierarchy**. Here, the role hierarchy results in users that are above the record owner in the role hierarchy having access to all the records that are owned by any user at a lower level in the hierarchy.

In addition to the organization-wide defaults, a role hierarchy record can be shared between users automatically by sharing rules or other team associations and in certain conditions, records can be manually shared by the record owner.

The levels of record sharing in the Lightning Platform provide a flexible approach to ensuring the required users can access records starting with a base level of data access and increasing with the use of additional record-level access as shown in the following diagram:

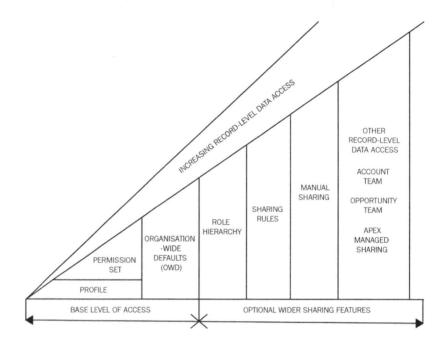

Figure 4.8 – Record-level data access

Record-level data access is applied in layers whereby access to the actual records is gained in an increasing order. After the permissions of the Profile or Permission Set are determined, the organization-wide defaults are then automatically calculated to either lock down the record-level access to the most restrictive or permit access.

In spite of a highly restrictive organization-wide lockdown default, access can still be granted with the use of other record-level security mechanisms, such as the role hierarchy or sharing rules to permit users to access the specified records.

The record-level data access privileges are evaluated using a combination of object-level, field-level, and eventually record-level permissions. However, if there is a conflict between the privilege that is set at the object level and the permissions a user would gain from record-level data access, then the most restrictive permission settings are applied. As an example, say you have created a Permission Set that gives delete access at the object level to a user but the record-level permissions do not include that particular record, then the user is unable to carry out the deletion of that record.

Let's look at the features and capabilities of record-level data access and at the ways in which record access can be provided to users in the Lightning Platform:

- **Record Ownership**: In the Lightning Platform, records are owned by users and by queues.

- **Organization-wide defaults**: These determine the basic record-level position for each of the object types and the operations that can be carried out on those records for users that are not the record owner.

- **Role hierarchy**: This determines the visibility that users have of records based on their ownership and position in the role hierarchy.

- **Sharing rules**: These defaults are used to automatically expand the record-level access that is provided by organization-wide defaults and enable the users or groups of users that have been included in the sharing rules to gain access to the records that they are not owners of or do not have access to.

- **Manual sharing**: This allows owners of a record to share it with users that are not automatically able to access the record.

- **Other sharing features**: The following additional sharing features exist in the Lightning Platform: **Account Teams**, **Opportunity Teams**, and Apex managed sharing. These options can be used either in combination with the previous record-level data access options or where these options do not provide the required access.

Let's look at how record ownership is a central mechanism for record-level data security.

Understanding record ownership

In the Lightning Platform, there are two types of record owners. Firstly, a user becomes the owner of a record when they create the record or have the record assigned to them. Secondly, there is the queue, which is a mechanism of allocating records before they are allocated to users.

Record owners have, by virtue of being the owner, privileges such as viewing, editing, transferring, sharing, changing ownership, and deleting records that they own providing that they are to perform these operations at the object level.

Let's look at how record-level data security in association with object-level security can make use of organization-wide settings.

Establishing organization-wide defaults

Organization-wide defaults serve to provide access to records to users that are not the owner of the record. In effect, organization-wide defaults can be considered as automatic provisioning of a default level of access to records for users in the Lightning Platform.

The organization-wide default levels of access ordered in level of access provision are as follows:

1. **Private**
2. **Public Read Only**
3. **Public Read/Write**

In addition, the following levels of access exist:

- **Controlled by Parent**: The Controlled by Parent access level determines the access based on the access level that the user has to the parent object for the records as part of a master-detail relationship.
- **Public Full Access**: The Public Full Access access level is available for campaign records only.
- **View Only**: The View Only access level is available for price book records only.

> **The Grant Access Using Hierarchies option**
>
> Within the options for setting organization-wide defaults for objects, the **Grant Access Using Hierarchies** option sees the record data that is owned by or accessible to a given user, made accessible to the users that are positioned higher in the role hierarchy. The **Grant Access Using Hierarchies** option is enabled by default for all objects, although the option can only be changed for custom objects and not for standard objects.

To assign the sharing settings for our custom Region object, carry out the following steps:

1. Navigate to **Setup** and then search for `Sharing Settings` in the Quick Find search box located at the top of the **Setup** menu on the left sidebar.
2. Click on **Sharing Settings** in the **Setup** menu.
3. Click on **Edit** in the **Organization-Wide Defaults** section.
4. Scroll down the **Setup** screen to the **Region** object.

5.   Set the **Default Internal Access** option for **Region** to **Public Read Only** as shown
in the following screenshot:

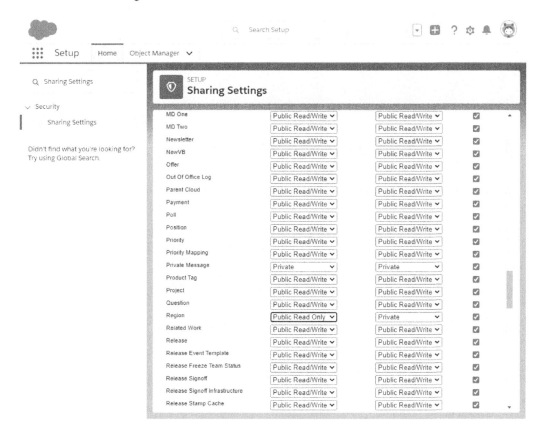

Figure 4.9 – Sharing settings

6.   Finally, click on **Save**.

Let's now look at how, with the use of the role hierarchy, we can widen access to records.

Defining the role hierarchy

After having specified the organization-wide defaults, you can provide wider access to
records using the role hierarchy. Users do not have to be part of a role hierarchy and the
roles mechanism is an optional setting but when users are added to the role hierarchy, the
access to the records they own is widened.

Managers are usually positioned above the users that report to them and are placed above the record owner in the role hierarchy. Being above a user in the role hierarchy provides that user with access to the records owned by the users at all lower levels in the role hierarchy.

Roles provide wider access to records

The role hierarchy provides wider access to records and gives users additional access to records; roles cannot restrict data access and can never restrict the record-level access provided by the organization-wide defaults.

Roles usually reflect a category of record ownership within the organization and do not need to be created to mirror the company organization chart as many specific job functions will likely need the same permissions for record access.

To view and configure the role hierarchy, carry out the following steps:

1. Navigate to **Setup** and then search for Roles in the Quick Find search box located at the top of the **Setup** menu on the left sidebar.

2. Click on **Roles** in the **Setup** menu.

3. Optionally, click on the **Set Up Roles** button and check the **Don't show this page again** checkbox (this is only required when you access the **Roles Setup** screens for the first time).

4. Select the **Show in tree view** in the hierarchy view selection on the right of the **Roles** setup screen. Other options are **Show in sorted list view** and **Show in list view**.

5. In the tree view, there are the options to **Collapse All** and **Expand All**. To show the full list of nodes in the role hierarchy, select the option to **Expand All** as shown in the following screenshot:

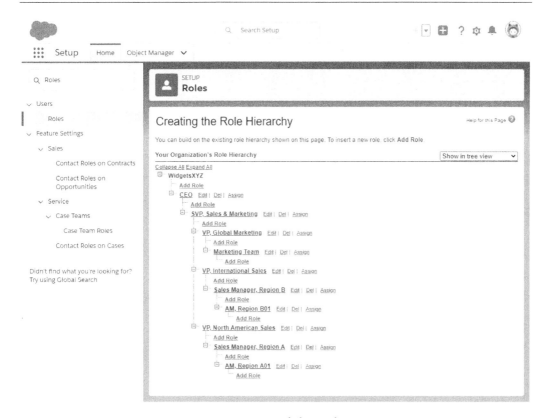

Figure 4.10 – Role hierarchy

Configuring sharing rules

After having specified the organization-wide defaults and optionally set the role hierarchy settings, you can provide wider access to records using sharing rules.

Sharing rules are used to automatically extend the data access that is provided by organization-wide defaults and allow specific users or groups of users to access records they would not have access to.

> **Sharing rules provide wider access to records**
>
> Sharing rules, like the role hierarchy, provide wider access to records and give users additional access to records; roles cannot restrict data access and can never restrict the record-level access provided by the organization-wide defaults.

To view and configure sharing rules, carry out the following steps:

1. Navigate to **Setup** and then search for `Sharing Settings` in the Quick Find search box located at the top of the **Setup** menu on the left sidebar.

2. Click on **Sharing Settings** in the **Setup** menu.

3. Scroll down the **Setup** screen to the **Sharing Rules** section as shown in the following screenshot:

Figure 4.11 – Sharing settings

Let's look at the options that are available to extend record-level data access using manual sharing.

Extending access using manual sharing

All the methods of record-level data access that we have looked at so far automatically derive the set of users to which to permit access.

These automated features are based on organization-wide default settings, the record owner, or calculated sharing rules, and may not always capture all the scenarios in working practice for when data access needs to be shared. This is where manual sharing has a part to play and provides owners of records with the capability to share specific records with
other users.

Each record owner can use a **Share** button on the page layout for the record to manually share specific records with the selected user.

Share button availability

At the time of writing, the **Share** button is not available in Lightning Experience. Users must temporarily switch to Classic to access the feature to manually share records.

For the latest information, see the following Salesforce article: `https://help.salesforce.com/articleView?id=000339349&type=1&mode=1`.

Let's now look at other features that provide a widening of record-level access in the Lightning Platform.

Widening record-level access using other sharing features

In addition to sharing rules and manual sharing, there are additional mechanisms in the Lightning Platform that can be used to share data records between users.

The following additional features allow the widening of record-level access:

- **Account Teams**: They allow users within that team to access the account record. The users are granted record-level access to the account record and some of its related records. Typically used when the organization-wide defaults on the account object are set to private and there is no other sharing rule.

- **Opportunity Teams**: These allow users within that team to access the opportunity record. Typically used when the organization-wide defaults on the opportunity object are set to private and there is no other sharing rule.

- **Apex managed sharing**: This is a feature that can be used by developers to programmatically share custom objects and is used when sharing rules and manual sharing cannot provide the sharing combinations or logic in your specific use case.

Let's now review and present a summary of the data security capabilities in the Lightning Platform.

Summarizing data security capabilities in the Lightning Platform

Data security in the Lightning Platform is performed using a set of layered features that allow or prevent users from creating, reading, updating, or deleting records for different datasets. This means users can be set up to only have access to the data that their job function stipulates.

Using permission sets and profiles, the overarching level of data security at the object level can be set along with the control of access at the field and record level.

To determine how users can be provided with access to record data, the various data security mechanisms that are available in the Lightning Platform are summarized in the following diagram:

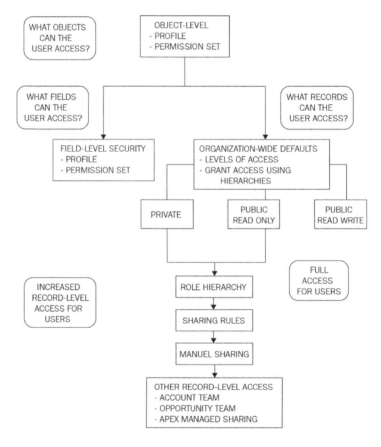

Figure 4.12 – Data access summary

Questions to test your knowledge

We now present six questions to help assess your knowledge of securing access to data in the Lightning Platform and the answers can be found at the end of the chapter.

We will present three questions to test your understanding of the features and capabilities available to restrict and extend object, record, and field access. We'll also pose three questions to help determine an appropriate sharing solution for a given set of business requirements.

Question 1 – Object permission settings

Which permission settings can be used to control the data access permissions for objects and determine whether users are able to create, read, edit, and delete records of the specified object type? (Select two)

  a) Organization-wide defaults

  b) Profiles

  c) Role hierarchy

  d) Permission Sets

Question 2 – Field permission settings

Your company has asked you to create a new custom field on the lead object to set the date and time when the lead record was automatically assigned to a salesperson. The requirement is that for all users that do not have either the sales or marketing profiles, this field should be hidden. How can this requirement be implemented? (Select one)

  a) Remove all access to the custom field using field-level security for the non-sales or marketing profiles.

  b) Create a permission set with all access removed for the custom field using field-level security and assign it to users without the sales or marketing profiles.

  c) Create a sharing rule with the level of access for the custom field set to **Hidden**, which then can be shared with all non-sales or marketing users.

  d) Set the organization-wide defaults to restrict access to the custom field for all non-sales or marketing users.

Question 3 – Granting other users access to records

A custom object exists in the Lightning Platform with the organization-wide defaults set to private. Your company has asked you to modify settings to allow record owners of this type of custom object to grant other users access to their records. How can this requirement be implemented? (Select one)

    a) No action is necessary because the **Grant other users access** button automatically appears whenever the organization-wide defaults are set to private.

    b) Enable the **Grant other users access** option in the security settings of the custom object.

    c) Add the **Share** button to the page layout for the custom object.

    d) No action is required because the **Share** button automatically appears whenever the organization-wide defaults are set to private.

Question 4 – Data access options for records

Your company has asked you to modify the data access options for lead records. The requirement is that system administrators are only permitted to delete leads and all other users are allowed to view and update leads. How can this requirement be implemented? (Select one)

    a) Create a sharing rule with the level of access set to **Read Only** based on the record owner whereby leads owned by all users in the role hierarchy are shared with all users in the role hierarchy. This will not prevent system administrators from deleting records as they are able to delete records by default.

    b) Remove the delete permission using the object permissions on the lead object for all profiles except the system administrator profile.

    c) Remove the **Delete** button from all lead page layouts and create new lead page layouts with a **Delete** button and associate them with the system administrator profile.

    d) Create a permission set and uncheck the delete permission using the object permissions on the lead object and assign them to all users except for users that have the system administrator profile.

Question 5 – Data access issues

Your company has asked you to review some legacy data access issues in a Lightning Platform org. You have spotted that there is a profile with read permission for a custom object and there is a sharing rule with edit access shared to the same profile. From your knowledge of data access, what actual access do the users with that profile have to the custom object? (Select two)

a) Edit access because of the sharing rule

b) Read access because of the profile object permissions

c) Read access because of the sharing rule

d) No edit access due to the profile object permissions

Question 6 – Limiting data access

Your company has asked you to create a new custom object called Equipment Booking that allows all marketing users and a few specific members of the sales team to book marketing equipment. There are two profiles, one for marketing, which has 50 active users, and one for sales, which has 500 active users. What is the most appropriate way to provide access? (Select one)

a) Modify the marketing and sales profiles to enable access to the custom object and create a permission set that restricts access to the custom object and assign it to all the members of the sales team that are not allowed to book marketing equipment.

b) Modify the marketing profile to enable access to the custom object and clone the sales profile, enable access to the custom object in the cloned sales profile, and assign the cloned sales profile to the few specific members of the sales team allowed to book marketing equipment.

c) Modify the marketing and sales profiles, enable access to the custom object for marketing and disable for sales, and create a permission set that enables access to the custom object and assign it to all the members of the sales team that are allowed to book marketing equipment.

d) Create sharing rules on the custom object: one for the marketing profile and one for the members of the sales team allowed to book marketing equipment.

Here are the answers to the six questions that were presented to help verify your knowledge of securing access to data in the Lightning Platform.

Answer 1 – Object permission settings

The answers are b) Profiles and d) Permission Sets.

The following are not correct:

a) Organization-wide defaults

c) Role hierarchy

Answer 2 – Field permission settings

The answer is a) Remove all access to the custom field using field-level security for the non-sales or marketing profiles.

The following are not correct:

b) Create a permission set with all access removed for the custom field using field-level security and assign to users without the sales or marketing profiles.

c) Create a sharing rule with the level of access for the custom field set to **Hidden**, which then can be shared with all non-sales or marketing users.

d) Set the organization-wide defaults to restrict access to the custom field for all non-sales or marketing users.

Answer 3 – Granting other users access to records

The answer is c) Add the **Share** button to the page layout for the custom object.

The following are not correct:

a) No action is necessary because the **Grant other users access** button automatically appears whenever the organization-wide defaults are set to private.

b) Enable the **Grant other users access** option in the security settings of the custom object.

d) No action is required because the sharing button automatically appears whenever the organization-wide defaults are set to private.

Answer 4 – Data access options for records

The answer is b) Remove the delete permission using the object permissions on the lead object for all profiles except the system administrator profile.

The following are not correct:

a) Create a sharing rule with the level of access set to **Read Only** based on the record owner whereby leads owned by all users in the role hierarchy are shared with all users in the role hierarchy. This will not prevent system administrators from deleting records as they are able to delete records by default.

c) Remove the **Delete** button from all lead page layouts and create new lead page layouts with a **Delete** button and associate them with the system administrator profile.

d) Create a permission set and uncheck the delete permission using the object permissions on the lead object and assign it to all users except for users that have the system administrator profile.

Answer 5 – Data access issues

The answers are b) Read access because of the profile object permissions and d) No edit access due to the profile object permissions.

The following are not correct:

a) Edit access because of the sharing rule

c) Read access because of the sharing rule

Answer 6 – Limiting data access

The answer is c) Modify the marketing and sales profiles, enable access to the custom object for marketing and disable for sales, and create a permission set that enables access to the custom object and assign it to all the members of the sales team that are allowed to book marketing equipment.

The following are not correct:

a) Modify the marketing and sales profiles to enable access to the custom object and create a permission set that restricts access to the custom object and assign it to all the members of the sales team that are not allowed to book marketing equipment.

b) Modify the marketing profile to enable access to the custom object and clone the sales profile, enable access to the custom object in the cloned sales profile, and assign the cloned sales profile to the few specific members of the sales team allowed to book marketing equipment.

d) Create sharing rules on the custom object: one for the marketing profile and one for the members of the sales team allowed to book marketing equipment.

Summary

In this chapter, you have gained knowledge about how to restrict and extend access to objects, fields, and records and understand how data security in the Lightning platform is applied using a number of layers.

You have learned about the key differences between object security, field-level security, and record sharing and how, with the use of object-level permissions, organization-wide defaults, and sharing settings, appropriate access to records can be configured.

You discovered the mechanisms for viewing and creating profiles and permission sets to control object and field access and how and when to assign profiles and permission sets. Learning about the different security options that are available will equip you with the necessary skills and confidence to configure and build secure apps in the Lightning Platform.

In the next chapter, you will learn about the features and capabilities to configure and build the functionality for custom buttons, links, and actions. You will be presented with the declarative options that are available for using Lightning components plus how to design appropriate user interfaces.

5

Setting Up the User Interface

In this chapter, you will learn about the features and capabilities that exist in the Lightning platform to customize the user interface.

You will gain the knowledge required to configure custom buttons, links, and actions, and you will understand about the declarative options that are available for building Lightning Pages and using Lightning components within Salesforce.

You will learn about designing an appropriate user interface when presented with various scenarios, and you will discover how different configuration options exists for various use cases.

Finally, you will be presented with a number of questions about the ways to customize the user interface and configure custom buttons, links, and actions, along with the declarative options with Lightning components in the Lightning Platform.

In this chapter, we will cover the following topics:

- Exam objectives – User interface
- Learning about the user interface options
- Customizing buttons, links, and actions
- Using declarative options with Lightning components
- Determining appropriate user interface designs
- Questions to test your knowledge

Let's now look at the objectives of the App Builder Certification exam that cover the user interface in the Lightning Platform.

Exam objectives – User interface

To pass the **User interface** section of the Certified Platform App Builder exam, app builders are expected to be able to carry out the following:

1. Describe the user interface customization options.

2. Describe the capabilities of, and use cases for, custom buttons, links, and actions.

3. Describe the declarative options available for incorporating Lightning Components in an application.

4. Given a scenario, determine the appropriate user interface design.

Reference – Salesforce Certified Platform App Builder Exam Guide

This guide is published by Salesforce and can be referenced at `https://trailhead.salesforce.com/help?article=Salesforce-Certified-Platform-App-Builder-Exam-Guide`.

In the Salesforce Certified Platform App Builder Exam Guide, the total number of questions is given, along with a percentage breakdown for each of the objectives, and an indication of the number of features/functions that can be expected in each of the objectives.

By analyzing these objectives, percentages, and question counts, we can determine the likely number of questions that will appear in the exam and, for the user interface objective, this is as follows:

User interface – Total number of exam questions

There are likely to be 8 or 9 questions in total. This is calculated as 14% of 60 total exam questions, which equates to 8.4.

Using these totals for the user interface objective and the number of items that are likely to be assessed, an approximate number of questions for each objective is as follows:

- **User interface options**: Two questions

- **Customizing buttons, links, and actions**: Two questions

- **Using declarative options with Lightning components**: Two or three questions

- **Determining appropriate user interface designs**: Two questions

To help reinforce the skills and knowledge required to set up the user interface, there is some practical work for you to do in Salesforce. So, if you do not have a Salesforce environment in which to carry this out, create a free developer org as detailed in *Chapter 1, Core Capabilities of the Lightning Platform*.

We will use the example scenarios that we covered in *Chapter 2, Designing and Building a Data Model*, to demonstrate how to incorporate Lightning Components using the Lightning App Builder.

Now, let's look at the options for setting up the user interface within the Salesforce Lightning Platform.

Learning about the user interface options

One of the benefits of the Lightning Platform is the capability to customize it so that it is tailored to the way that users access it.

The Lightning Platform provides features and functionality that allow customization at various levels, which, in turn, allow not only programmatic solutions, but also declarative solutions requiring no coding knowledge and these declarative features enable the user interface to be customized.

The user interface for the Lightning Platform has evolved over time and there have been several styles or themes added and different models used for the way that the user interface elements have been rendered. The current theme in the Lightning Platform uses the User Interface API, which is a framework that is used to retrieve data and metadata from within the platform and this is known as **Lightning Experience**. There are also older themes that use a different mechanism for retrieving data and metadata and rendering screens, known as **Salesforce Classic**.

Salesforce provides support for different browsers and devices that is dependent on which theme you are using, which we will explore now.

Supported browsers and devices

The support that is provided by Salesforce for browsers and devices differs according to the type of user interface that you are using. In the Lightning Platform, there are two different user interface themes, namely Salesforce Classic, which was first introduced in 2010, and the more recent interface, known as Lightning Experience.

In fact, there is an older classic version known as **Salesforce Classic 2005**, but we'll not be discussing that as it is unlikely that you are using the Classic 2005 theme.

The following browsers are supported by Salesforce for use with Salesforce Classic:

- Google Chrome™, latest version
- Microsoft® Internet Explorer®, version 11
- Microsoft® Edge (non-Chromium), latest (supported until December 31, 2020)
- Mozilla® Firefox®, latest version
- Apple® Safari®, latest version

The following browsers are supported by Salesforce for use with Lightning Experience:

- Google Chrome™, latest version
- Microsoft® Internet Explorer®, version 11 (supported until December 31, 2020)
- Microsoft® Edge (non-Chromium), latest (supported until December 31, 2020)

- Microsoft® Edge (Chromium), latest version

- Mozilla® Firefox®, latest version

- Apple® Safari®, latest version

> **Lightning Platform-supported browsers and devices**
>
> At the time of writing, there are considered to be two user interface themes. These themes are known as Lightning Experience and Salesforce Classic. The supported browsers and devices vary depending on which theme you are using.
>
> For the latest information on supported browsers and devices for the theme that you are using, refer to the following Salesforce Help page: `https://help.salesforce.com/articleView?id=getstart_browser_overview.htm&type=5`

Let's now look at the mechanisms and options that are available for you to change the appearance and features that are available to users within the Lightning Platform.

Configuring the user interface settings

The Lightning Platform provides the capability for you to change the appearance and enable or disable various features by configuring the user interface options. Most of the options apply to both the Lightning Experience and the Salesforce Classic themes, although there are some user interface options that are only applicable within either the Lightning Experience or Salesforce Classic theme.

We will outline the various **User Interface** settings and identify which theme they are applicable for. Using the Lightning theme, the list of settings is as shown in the following screenshot:

Figure 5.1 – User Interface options

Generally, these user interface settings are applicable for both the Lightning Experience and Salesforce Classic user interface themes. Where the setting is not applicable to either Lightning Experience or Salesforce Classic, or there is a difference in behavior, this is duly noted. Let's now look at the main **User Interface** settings, as shown in the following screenshot:

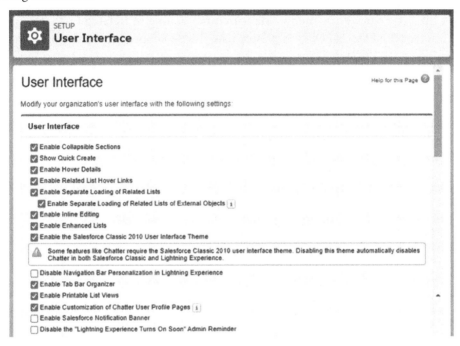

Figure 5.2 – Main User Interface options

From the preceding screenshot, we can observe the following:

- **Enable Collapsible Sections**: This setting enables users to collapse or expand sections on record detail pages in a page layout. This is supported in Salesforce Classic.

- **Show Quick Create**: Setting this option presents the Quick Create section on the sidebar that allows users to create records from within the Quick Create section. This is supported in Salesforce Classic.

- **Enable Hover Details**: This setting enables users to hover the mouse cursor over records in the Recent Items list on the sidebar or in a lookup field on the record detail page to view record details. This is supported in Salesforce Classic.

- **Enable Related List Hover Links**: This option allows users to hover the mouse cursor over records in related lists on the record detail page to view record details. This is supported in Salesforce Classic.

- **Enable Separate Loading of Related Lists**: This setting enables the separate loading of page information in two phases. Firstly, the record detail sections is presented, and secondly, any related list details are loaded. This is supported in Salesforce Classic.

- **Enable Separate Loading of Related Lists of External Objects**: This setting results in the same behavior as the **Enable Separate Loading of Related Lists** setting, but concerns the External Objects-related lists. This is supported in Salesforce Classic.

- **Enable Inline Editing**: This setting enables users to edit field values within the record detail page rather than clicking on the Edit button and displaying the edit page. This is supported in Salesforce Classic.

- **Enable Enhanced Lists**: Setting this option enables users to edit data directly within a list view rather than clicking on the Edit button and displaying the edit page. This is supported in Salesforce Classic.

- **Enable the Salesforce Classic 2010 User Interface Theme**: This setting changes the appearance of the Classic user interface by setting the latest Classic theme, which is Salesforce Classic 2010. This is supported in Salesforce Classic only.

- **Disable Navigation Bar Personalization in Lightning Experience**: This setting prevents users from adding or reordering the items that appear in the navigation bar. This setting is only applicable when used within the Lightning Experience theme.

- **Enable Tab Bar Organizer**: Setting this option results in the tabs in the tab bar being automatically arranged into a drop-down selection whenever the width of the page changes to prevent horizontal scrolling of the page. This is supported in Salesforce Classic.

- **Enable Printable List Views**: This setting enables the printing of list views by presenting a **Printable View** link, shown with a printer logo, to users. Upon clicking the printer logo, located in the top-right corner of list views, a new browser appears to enable the printing of the data.

- **Enable Customization of Chatter User Profile Pages**: Setting this option enables the customization of the tabs that are available for the standard Chatter user profile.

- **Enable Salesforce Notification Banner**: This setting enables the Salesforce notification banner to appear on standard pages, dashboards, and within the Setup menu.

- **Disable the "Lightning Experience Turns On Soon" Admin Reminder**: This setting is a legacy option and was used to allow the suppression of the reminders that were initiated in the Salesforce Classic theme to encourage the transition to Lightning Experience.

Let's now look at the **Sidebar**, **Calendar**, and **Name Settings User Interface** settings, as shown in the following screenshot:

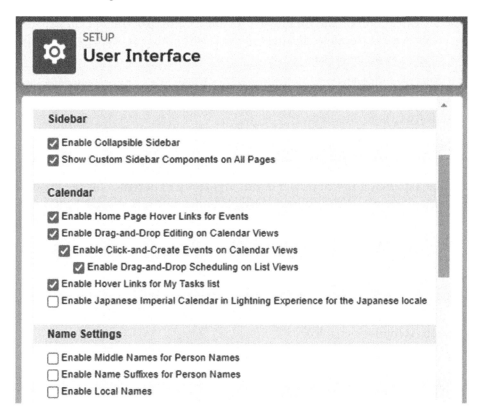

Figure 5.3 – Sidebar and more – User Interface options

These are the **Sidebar** user interface settings:

- **Enable Collapsible Sidebar**: This setting enables users to show or hide the sidebar within the Salesforce Classic user interface.

- **Show Custom Sidebar Components on All Pages**: This option results in any sidebar components being shown on all pages in the Salesforce Classic user interface.

These are the **Calendar** user interface settings:

- **Enable Home Page Hover Links for Events**: This option enables hover links to appear for events on the Salesforce Classic interface.

- **Enable Drag-and-Drop Editing on Calendar Views**: This option enables users to drag and drop existing events between calendar views in the Salesforce Classic interface.

- **Enable Click-and-Create Events on Calendar Views**: This option enables users to create events by double-clicking time slots within the events page within the Salesforce Classic interface.

- **Enable Drag-and-Drop Scheduling on List Views**: This option, when enabled, allows users to create events by dragging items onto the weekly calendar view in the Salesforce Classic interface.

- **Enable Hover Links for My Tasks list**: This option enables hover links in the **My Tasks** section of the **Home** page within the Salesforce Classic interface.

- **Enable Japanese Imperial Calendar in Lightning Experience for the Japanese locale**: This option displays the imperial calendar for users who have their language set to Japanese and their locale set to Japanese (Japan) in the Lightning Experience theme.

These are the **Name Settings** user interface settings:

- **Enable Middle Names for Person Names**: This option, when enabled, adds a **Middle Name** field to the following standard objects: **Contact**, **Lead**, **User**, and **Person Account** (if enabled).

- **Enable Name Suffixes for Person Names**: This option, when enabled, adds a **Suffix** field for the **Name** field within the following standard objects: Contact, Lead, User, and Person Account (if enabled).

- **Enable Local Names**: This option, when enabled, adds a **Local name** field within the following standard objects – **Account**, **Contact**, and **Lead**, and is used to store and display an original or a translated text value.

Let's now look at the **Setup** and **Advanced** user interface settings, as shown in the following screenshot:

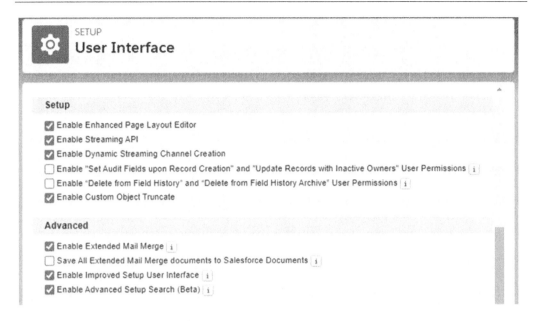

Figure 5.4 – Sidebar and so on – User Interface options

These are the **Setup** user interface settings:

- **Enable Enhanced Page Layout Editor**: This option activates an enhanced version of the editor that is used to edit page layouts.

- **Enable Streaming API**: This option, when enabled, allows the use of the Streaming **API (Application Programming Interface)**, which provides a near real-time stream of data within the Lightning Platform.

- **Enable Dynamic Streaming Channel Creation**: This option is part of the Streaming API and, when enabled, results in the dynamic creation of streaming channels when clients subscribe.

- **Enable "Set Audit Fields upon Record Creation" and "Update Records with Inactive Owners" User Permissions**: This option enables the setting of audit fields that are normally set to be read-only.

- **Enable "Delete from Field History" and "Delete from Field History Archive" User Permissions**: This option, when enabled, activates a user permission that can be set using either a profile or permission set to allow users to delete field history and field history archive data.

- **Enable Custom Object Truncate**: This option enables the truncation of custom objects, resulting in the permanent removal of records from the custom object while retaining the custom object.

These are the **Advanced** user interface settings:

- **Enable Extended Mail Merge**: This option, when enabled, results in the **Mass Mail Merge** link being shown on the Tools area for the following standard objects in the Salesforce Classic interface: Account, Contact, and Lead.

- **Save All Extended Mail Merge documents to Salesforce Documents**: When enabled, this option, which is a Salesforce Classic feature, results in mail merge document no longer being sent as email attachments and instead are stored in the personal documents folder for the user.

- **Enable Improved Setup User Interface**: This option affects the Salesforce Classic interface and how users access their personal settings. When enabled, users access personal settings from the **My Settings** menu via the username menu and, when disabled, the personal settings are accessed from the **Setup** menu.

- **Enable Advanced Setup Search (Beta)**: This option affects the Salesforce Classic interface and, when enabled, allows the searching of the following setup types – setup pages, permission sets, profiles, roles, public group, and users, by using the setup sidebar in **Setup**. When this option is not enabled, only setup pages can be searched.

Let's now look at the mechanisms and options that are available for creating apps and tabs within the Lightning Platform.

Creating apps and tabs in the Lightning Platform

In the Lightning Platform, an app serves as a container for various components, including tabs, objects, and associated processes that are used to provide a business function.

Salesforce provides some out-of-the-box apps, known as **Standard Apps**, which provide core functionality for users and employ general categories of business functions. The standard apps allow the assignment of apps to users who have a particular job function and profile. They include apps such as Marketing, Sales, Call Center, Community, Salesforce Chatter, and Site.com.

In addition to the standard apps, you can create custom apps that allow association with all the elements required for a business function within the app. This is to provide a particular type of function that can be used by users with particular job functions or simply as a way to group a specific set of functions and objects together. One of the main elements within either a standard app or a custom app is a set of tabs.

A **Tab** in the Lightning Platform is a user interface element that, when clicked on, either navigates to a record or set of records to display data or invokes a process.

There are standard and custom tabs. **Standard tabs** are provided out of the box and are used in association with the standard objects where there is a tab for each standard object to gain access to the list of object records. **Custom tabs** enable access to the list of records for a given custom object and also provide options to navigate to custom user interfaces or processes for new custom functionality that has been built.

The features and capabilities that are contained within apps are as follows:

- **Tabs**: Apps contain standard and custom tabs. These are available for the Lightning Experience and Salesforce Classic themes.

- **Objects**: Apps contain standard and custom objects. These are available for the Lightning Experience and Salesforce Classic themes.

- **Visualforce tabs**: Visualforce pages can be associated with a tab to allow easy access to the page by creating a Visualforce tab. This is available for the Lightning Experience and Salesforce Classic themes.

- **Lightning component tabs**: Lightning components can be associated with a tab to allow easy access to the component by creating a Lightning component tab. This is only available for the Lightning Experience and Salesforce mobile app themes.

- **Web tabs**: URLs can be associated with a tab to allow easy access to the URL by creating a Web tab. This is available for the Lightning Experience and Salesforce Classic themes.

Apps and any associated tabs are available as specified for both the Lightning Experience and Salesforce Classic user interface themes. These are accessed by users by either clicking the **App Launcher** or the **App Menu**, depending upon which user interface theme they are using.

In the Lightning Experience user interface, the app launcher is used to access standard and custom apps and this is located at the top-left corner of the Salesforce page, as shown in the following screenshot:

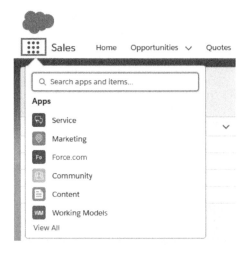

Figure 5.5 – Lightning app options

In the Classic user interface theme, the Apps menu is used to access standard and custom apps and this is located in the top-right corner of the Salesforce page, as shown in the following screenshot:

Figure 5.6 – Classic apps options

To help reinforce the skills and knowledge needed to create an app, there is some practical work to be done in Salesforce. So, if you do not have a Salesforce environment in which to carry this out, create a free developer org as detailed in *Chapter 1, Core Capabilities of the Lightning Platform*.

Let's create our custom app that contains custom tabs for our example lead assignment requirement that we introduced and designed the data model for, in *Chapter 2, Designing and Building a Data Model*, with the following configurations:

- **Lead Assignment custom app**: This is the name of the app for the lead assignment function.

- **Region custom tab**: This is the name of the tab for the **Region** custom object.

- **Location custom tab**: This is the name of the tab for the **Location** custom object.

Using the example scenario, where we have already created the custom tabs for the *Region* and *Location* custom objects during *Chapter 2, Designing and Building a Data Model*, when we created the custom objects, we will now create the custom app to associate the custom tabs.

> **App limits**
>
> Make sure you have not reached the total number of available apps before starting this exercise, otherwise you will encounter an error when attempting to save if the number of apps exceeds the app limit in your org.

At the time of writing, the limits for the number of apps for each edition are as follows: The Developer Edition limit is 10, the Professional Edition limit is 255, the Enterprise Edition limit is 260, and the Unlimited Edition limit is no limit (that is, unlimited).

Refer to the following general limit reference provided by Salesforce: `https://help.salesforce.com/articleView?id=overview_limits_general.htm&type=5`.

To create a custom app using Lightning Experience, first refer to the following screenshot that shows an example app:

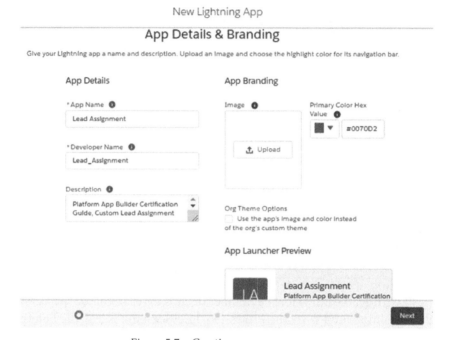

Figure 5.7 – Creating a new app screen

Using the screenshot, perform the following steps:

1. Navigate to **Setup** and then search for App Manager in the **Quick Find** search box located at the top of the **Setup** menu on the left side bar.

2. Click on **App Manager** in the **Setup** menu.

3. Click on **New Lightning App** in the Lightning Experience **App Manager** setup screen.

4. Enter Lead Assignment in the **App Name** textbox.

5. The **Developer Name** textbox defaults to **Lead_Assignment**.

6. Optionally upload an image.

7. Enter Platform App Builder Certification Guide, Custom Lead Assignment Scenario, Custom App in the **Description** textbox.

8. Click on **Next**.

You will be presented with the following app options screen:

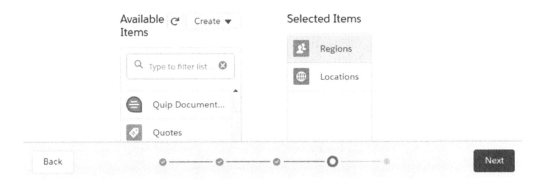

Figure 5.8 – Setting the Navigation Items app screen

Using this, you will you have to do the following:

1. Keep the default options, with **Navigation Style** set to **Standard navigation** and **Supported Form Factors** set to **Desktop and phone**.

2. Click on **Next**.

3. In the **Utility Items (Desktop Only)** setup screen, click on **Next**.

4. In the **Navigation Items** setup screen, select the **Regions** and **Locations** items.

5. Click on **Next**, as shown in the preceding screenshot.

You will be presented with the **User Profiles** screen:

Figure 5.9 – Setting the Profile app screen

From this screen, perform the following steps:

1. Select **Custom Marketing User** and **Custom: Sales Profile** plus the System Administrator profile or custom System Administrator profile that is present in your Salesforce org.

2. Finally, click on **Save & Finish**, as shown in the preceding screenshot:

    After having clicked on **Save & Finish**, you have created a Lightning app that you can select using **App Launcher** to reveal the **Lead Assignment** app, as shown in the following screenshot:

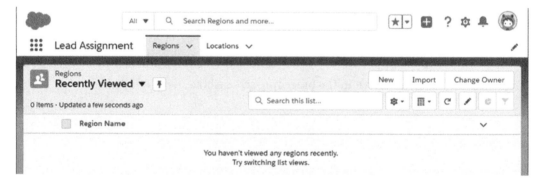

Figure 5.10 – Viewing the Lead Assignment app screen

Let's briefly look at the capabilities and features of record types in the Lightning Platform.

Understanding record types

Record types are a feature of the Lightning Platform that allow you to provide different business processes to different categories of user. An example is where you have a sales department that is split into field sales and internal sales. Here, you can use record types to present a different set of object picklist field values, different page layouts, and an overall different business process. You can assign custom record types within **Profiles** and **Permission Sets**.

From the perspective of the user interface, using different record types allows for the creation and assignment of different page layouts and, since you can use record types to control how the page layouts are assigned to users via their profile, and also by using automation to update the record types based on a business process, you can create a highly customized user interface.

You will learn more about record types and how to implement record types in order to provide different business logic for users in *Chapter 6, Implementing Business Logic*.

Let's now look at the options that are available for creating and assigning page layouts.

Creating and assigning page layouts

Page layouts are comprised of sections that contain various user interface elements, including buttons, links, fields, and related lists. Page layouts can be used to show different views of records and present items of functionality to users. You can create different page layouts for the same object type, but which contain a different set of fields, buttons, and related lists.

You can create a tailored view for specific users that displays the necessary screen objects for when the user is editing or viewing the object record. When used in association with record types, different page layouts can present different information for different business use cases.

In *Chapter 4, Securing Access to Data*, we looked at how field-level security can be used to prevent access to fields for specified users. Within page layouts, field-level security overrides any visibility setting on the page layout. As an example, a hidden field implemented using field-level security permissions will not be displayed regardless of the setting within the page layout.

> **Variations in behavior in terms of page layout and formula fields**
>
> Lightning Experience and Salesforce Classic behave differently in terms of page layouts and formula fields. Formula fields are displayed on the edit screen when using Lightning Experience, but are not displayed when using Salesforce Classic.

Refer to the following knowledge article provided by Salesforce: `https://help.salesforce.com/articleView?id=000335708&type=1&mode=1`.

The fields that are displayed in any related lists are controlled by the settings within page layouts. Here, the name of the related list is determined by the settings of the lookup or master-detail relationship field on any related objects.

There are differences between the page layout elements that are available in Lightning Experience and Salesforce Classic. The features and capabilities of **Page Layouts** are as follows:

- **Blank Space**: Within the **Field** element on the page layout editor, blank spaces allow a space to be added to the page and inserted into the region where a field might exist and are used to help organize the elements within a page.

- **Canvas Apps**: Canvas apps are used to integrate a third-party application within the Lightning Platform. Canvas apps are supported in Lightning Experience.

- **Custom Buttons**: Custom buttons enable custom operations that are used to extend the functionality that appears on standard buttons.

- **Custom Links**: Custom links enable custom operations to extend the standard functions and present a URL link for users to click. Custom links are supported in Lightning Experience and Salesforce Classic and are displayed within the **Details** page.

- **Fields**: **Standard Fields** and **Custom Fields** can be organized on the page using the page layout editor and can be set to **Read-Only** or **Required**.

- **Related Lists**: Related lists allow the viewing of child records for objects with lookup or master-detail relationship fields. Related lists are added to page layouts in the Salesforce Classic theme. An alternative method of adding related lists using Lightning components is carried out in Lightning Experience using the Lightning App Builder.

- **Report Charts**: Report charts are based on reports that have embedded charts and, in the Lightning Experience theme, when included on a page layout, appear within the **Details** tab.

- **Section**: Within the **Field** element on the page layout editor, sections appear along with the fields within the record edit and details pages. The **Section Properties** window contains an option to set a header for the section, and if none is set, the elements within the section appear under the header of the section that is situated above it on the page layout.

- **S-control**: Salesforce no longer supports the creation of new S-controls. S-controls were once a way to create user interface content on a page that uses custom HTML, Excel files, or an Active-X control. Existing S-controls can be edited using Salesforce Classic only.

- **Visualforce Pages**: Visualforce pages can be added to the page layout and appear within the **Details** page. Visualforce pages are only supported in Lightning Experience if the **Available for Lightning Experience** option is set.

> **Page layouts – variations in behavior**
>
> Variations in behavior exist between Lightning Experience and Salesforce Classic in relation to page layouts.
>
> Refer to the following reference provided by Salesforce: `https://help.salesforce.com/articleView?id=layouts_in_lex.htm&type=5`.

To create or customize the page layout for the custom object in `Region__c`, perform the following steps:

1. Navigate to **Setup** and then search for **Object Manager** in the **Quick Find** search box located at the top of the **Setup** menu on the left side bar.

2. Enter `Region` in the **Search** textbox in the **Object Manager** setup page.

3. Click on the presented **Region** object.

4. Click on **Page Layouts** in the **Object Manager** setup menu on the left side bar.

5. Click on **Region Layout** in the **Page Layouts** set screen to present the **Page Layouts** edit screen as shown in the following screenshot:

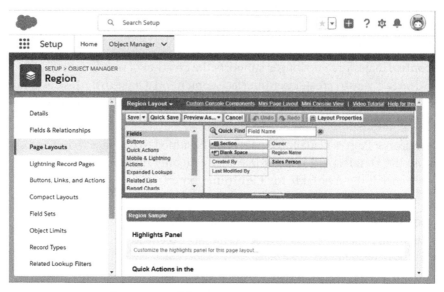

Figure 5.11 – Editing the Page Layouts screen

6. Now, locate the **Sales Person** field.

7. Drag and drop the Sales Person field onto the page layout section.

8. Finally, click on the **Save** button, as shown in the following screenshot:

Figure 5.12 – Saving the Page Layouts screen

To assign the Region page layout to users, perform the following steps:

1. Click on **Page Layouts** in **Object Manager** for the Region object within the **Setup** menu on the left side bar.

2. Click on **Page Layout Assignment** in the **Page Layouts** list, as shown in the following screenshot:

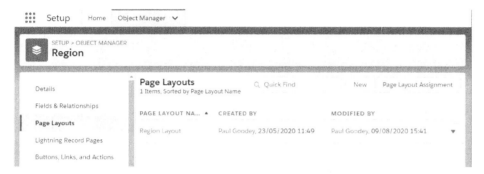

Figure 5.13 – Page Layouts assignment screen

3. Click on **Edit Assignments** in the **Page Assignment** page.

4. Select which profiles are to use the page layouts and click **Save**, as shown in the following screenshot:

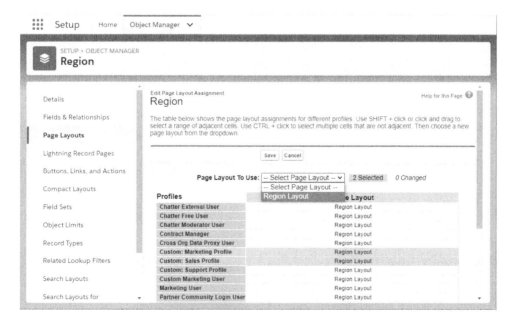

Figure 5.14 – Page Layouts profile selection screen

Having created and assigned a page layout, let's look at the mechanisms and options that are available for you to customize buttons, links, and actions within the Lightning Platform.

Customizing buttons, links, and actions

In the Lightning Platform, buttons, links, and actions can generally be found on page layouts, related lists, and search layouts, and there are standard buttons, links, and actions that are provided out of the box. These standard buttons, links, and actions provide out-of-the-box functionality, such as the creating, viewing, and deleting of standard object records and default record operation buttons for custom objects.

You can customize some of the standard buttons to change their behavior, and this is known as a **button override**. Depending upon whether you are using Lightning Experience or Salesforce Classic, standard buttons can be overridden with Visualforce Pages and/or Lightning Components.

Let's look at the options that are available for creating custom buttons and links.

Creating custom buttons and links

In addition to the standard buttons and links, you can create custom buttons and links that enable custom operations that extend the operations and actions found in standard features. Examples of these custom operations include populating field values when creating records, navigating to external web resources, invoking custom pages with Visualforce pages, or calling functions in Salesforce, such as reports.

When creating custom buttons and links, there are various properties you can select that determine how the button or link is displayed and the type of operation that is invoked when the button or link is clicked on by a user. These properties are controlled by setting the **Display Type**, **Behavior**, and **Content Source** fields, where the following options are available to select:

- **Display Type**: The options for the display type are **Detail Page Link**, **Detail Page Button**, and **List Button**.

- **Behavior**: The options for behavior are **Display in new window, Display in existing window with sidebar, Display in existing window without sidebar, Display in existing window without sidebar or header**, and **Execute JavaScript**.

- **Content Source**: The options for content source are **URL, Custom S-Control, OnClick JavaScript**, and **Visualforce Page**.

> **Options not supported in Lightning Experience**
>
> Behavior options and the use of JavaScript are not supported in Lightning Experience. In Lightning Experience, the behavior of custom buttons and links is to display in a new window. JavaScript is not supported and so cannot be used within a URL or as an **OnClick JavaScript** content source.

To create or customize a button or link, perform the following steps:

1. Navigate to **Setup** and then search for **Object Manager** in the **Quick Find** search box located at the top of the **Setup** menu on the left side bar.

2. Select the object (in this example, we've selected the **Account** object).

3. Click on **Buttons, Links, and Actions** in the **Account Object** setup menu.

4. Click on **New Button** or **Link** in the **Buttons, Links, and Actions** setup screen, as shown in the following screenshot:

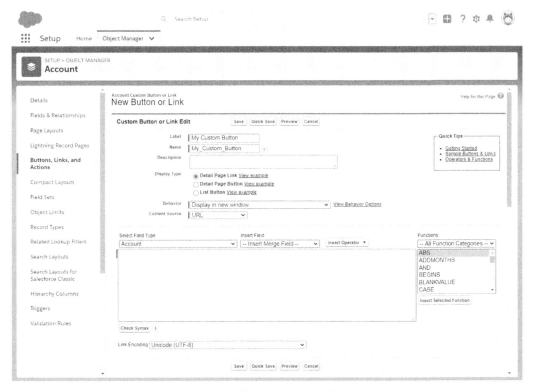

Figure 5.15 – Creating a custom button

Let's look at the options that are available for building actions.

Building actions

Actions can be used to save users' time by presenting convenient record creation buttons, and buttons that allow pre-populated record creation screens, and so on. There are several types of actions within the Lightning Platform and these allow you to present navigation to custom functionality using graphical elements that also appear as buttons within the user interface.

When creating new actions, there are several types and options available for creating the action that allows functionality, such as sending emails, creating or updating records, and posting to Chatter.

The mechanisms and choices for creating actions that are available to you in your Salesforce org depend on which options have been selected beforehand in your org, when your environment was first initiated, and whether the action is being used in Lightning Experience or Salesforce Classic.

In general, the main types of action that we consider in this section are known as **quick actions** or **productivity actions**, the features and capabilities of which are as follows:

- **Create a Record**
- **Update a Record**
- **Send Email**
- **Log a Call**
- **Invoke a custom Visualforce page**
- **Invoke a Lightning component**
- **Launch a Lightning Flow**

When building quick actions, the action and resulting button can be applied to two types of action within the Lightning Platform, either as an object-specific action or as a global action.

Object-specific actions are applied within the page layout for a given object and are applied by dragging and dropping the action button onto the page layout actions area. Global actions are applied within the global publisher layout, which is not related to any given object. You can create a record, but cannot update a record by using a global action.

To access the object-specific actions, users navigate to the record and click the action button on the detail page in the same way as users access standard and custom buttons.

To access the global actions, users navigate to the global actions menu by clicking the **GLOBAL ACTIONS** menu icon located within the Salesforce header. They can then choose the global action. By way of an example, a global action has been created called **New Account (Global Action)**, as shown in the following screenshot:

Figure 5.16 – Accessing global actions

Let's look at an example of building an object-specific action with the use of a **Create a Record** action to create an **Account** record with the help of the following steps:

1. Navigate to **Setup** and then search for **Object Manager** in the **Quick Find** search box located at the top of the **Setup** menu on the left side bar.

2. Click on the **Account** object.

3. Click on **Buttons, Links, and Actions** in the **Setup** menu.

4. Click on the **New Action** button in the **New Actions** setup screen.

5. Enter the details for the action by entering or selecting the following: **Action Type (Create a Record)**, **Target Object**, **Standard Label Type**, **Label**, **Name**, **Description**, **Create Feed Item**, **Success Message**, and **Icon**.

6.   Click on **Save**, as shown in the following screenshot:

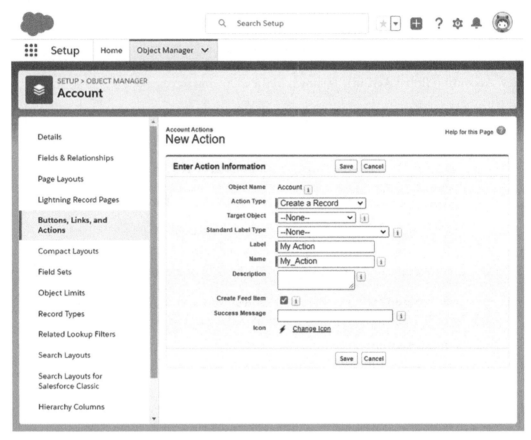

Figure 5.17 – Creating actions

Having built an object-specific action, let's now look at the declarative options for using Lightning Components and building apps with the Lightning App Builder within the Lightning Platform.

Using declarative options with Lightning components

Lighting components, from a declarative perspective, are reusable visual elements that can be used to provide standard and customized features and functionality on a Lightning Page within the Lightning Platform.

There are several types and flavors of Lightning Components and these allow you to present a combination of standard and custom functionality that is presented within the Lightning Experience user interface.

The mechanism that enables you to customize the user interface and apply Lightning Components is known as the **Lightning App Builder**. Let's look at the options that are available for using declarative options with Lightning Components and for configuring and building Lightning pages.

Building apps with the Lightning App Builder

The Lightning App Builder provides features and functionality that allow the configuration of apps. You can customize the styling or branding for the app, the paths or navigation options presented to users, and control how Lightning pages are associated with the app by building apps with the Lightning App Builder.

You can use the app builder to build the following types of pages in the Lightning Platform:

- **App Page**: This option allows you to build various types of customized functional apps. For example, you can build apps that present activities, apps that provide a particular function such as a vacation booking system, or apps that simply navigate to a standard Lightning Platform page.

- **Home Page**: This option allows you to build pages that replace the standard Lightning home page and you can build different home pages for different types of users so that they have access to the components and functionality that is relevant to them.

- **Record Page**: This option allows you to build pages for both standard and custom objects that can be tailored to present the components and functionality for users.

The Lightning App Builder allows the dragging and dropping of standard and custom components from the **Components Navigation** toolbar onto the main area known as the **canvas** as shown for the **Home Page**, as indicated in the following screenshot:

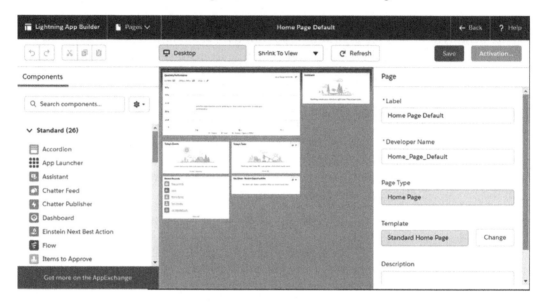

Figure 5.18 – Building apps with the Lightning App Builder

Let's look in more detail at the building blocks associated with the configuration of Lighting Pages and see what Lightning Components can be added.

Adding Lightning Components to Lightning Pages

You can add various types of components to Lightning pages in the Lightning Platform and each Lightning page can have a maximum of 100 components. Lightning Components can be added from the following types of components:

- **Standard components**: Standard components are Lightning components built by Salesforce.

- **Custom components**: Custom components are Lightning components that you or someone else has created. You can configure custom Lightning components to work in Lightning App Builder.

- **Third-party components on AppExchange**: The AppExchange provides a marketplace for Lightning components. You can find packages containing components already configured and ready to use in the Lightning App Builder.

Let's now look at the standard components that can be included in Lightning Pages in the Lightning Platform.

Inclusion of standard components

There are a number of standard components that are available to be added to a Lightning page. Some Lightning Components are only available for certain types of page, and some components only become visible for selection under certain conditions.

New and updated standard components

Salesforce is continually adding to the list of standard components that are available and new components are released during each major update.

For the latest list of available standard components, refer to the following help page provided by Salesforce: `https://help.salesforce.com/articleView?id=lightning_page_components.htm&type=5`.

The following list of components is not a comprehensive list of all available standard components and others are available depending upon the type of Lightning page, the type of object, and the form factor. Let's look at some of the key **standard Lightning components** on Lightning Pages that are available for the **Home** and **Record** page types under the following conditions:

- **Accordion**: The **Accordion** component enables other Lightning Components to be grouped together within a collapsible page section. Configuring the **Accordion** component is a two-step process. First, you drag and drop the component onto the canvas and then you drag and drop one or more components to be grouped into a section and set the section name within the **Accordion** component. A maximum of 25 sections can be added for each **Accordion** component.

- **App Launcher**: The **App Launcher** component is used to present the apps that are available to allow the user to navigate from one app to another.

- **Assistant**: The **Assistant** component enables the automatic presentation of key updates on the **Home** page. By way of an example, the following types of updates can automatically appear in the **Assistant** section of the Lightning home page: Lead records that have been assigned to you, or Opportunity records that are overdue. A maximum of 10 updates are displayed in the **Assistant** section.

- **Activities**: The **Activities** component enables the activities timeline to be displayed in a section on a Lightning record page. The **Activities** component is only presented if the **Default Activities View** is set to **Activity Timeline**, which is accessed from **Setup | Record Page Settings**.

- **Chatter Feed**: The **Chatter Feed** component allows the feeds from Chatter to be presented in a section on a Lightning record page.

- **Dashboard**: This allows a dashboard to be presented in a section on a Lightning home page.

- **Highlights Panel**: This enables the presentation of fields that are specified in compact layouts along with actions that are specified in page layouts.

- **List View**: This enables the inclusion of a list view within the Lightning page and presents an initial set of records based on the view. A maximum of 30 records can be configured to be displayed.

- **Recent Items**: This enables the presentation of a list of recently accessed records for specified objects. A maximum of 30 items can be configured to be displayed.

- **Related List - Single component**: This enables the inclusion of a single related list of a specified object type. In addition to displaying the child records, such as via lookup or master-detail fields, this component can also be used to show details of a parent record.

- **Related List Quick Links component**: This enables links to any related lists for an object to be displayed and allows users to hover over the links and dynamically view the columns within the related list.

- **Related List**: This enables the inclusion of one or more related lists of a specified object type. In addition to displaying the child records, such as via lookup or master-detail fields, this component can also be used to show details of a parent record.

- **Related Record**: This allows related records for an object to be shown within a record Lightning page. In addition to displaying the child records, such as via lookup or master-detail fields, this component can also be used to show details of a parent record.

- **Report Chart**: This enables the inclusion of a chart that is contained within a report to be displayed in the Lightning page. Within the **Chart** component is a link to allow navigation to the report.

- **Rich Text**: This allows the addition of text within the section of the Lightning page.

- **Tabs**: This enables other Lightning Components to be grouped together within a set of tabs. Configuring the **Tabs** component is a two-step process. First, you drag and drop the component onto the canvas, and then you can either create a custom tab with a label or select one of the standard tabs and then drag and drop a component into the **Tab** section. A maximum of 100 tabs can be configured within the **Tabs** component.

- **Visualforce**: The Visualforce page component enables the inclusion of a Visualforce page within the Lightning page. The Visualforce page needs to have the **Available for Salesforce mobile apps and Lightning pages** setting enabled.

Let's now look at the features and capabilities that exist in the Lightning Platform for configuring Lightning Pages.

Configuring Lightning Pages

Three types of Lightning pages, **App Page**, **Home Page**, and **Record Page**, are available for different devices and render differently depending on which device is being viewed.

When creating Lightning pages, you specify a particular template that determines how the areas of the page appear when viewed on a given device. These Lightning page templates allow various options to be selected that separates the page into sections or regions. The templates are used to support the style of user interface that is termed the *form factor*, which can be either desktop or phone.

Templates that are used for **App Page** and **Record Page** support both the desktop and phone form factors. Templates that are used for **Home Page Lightning** pages only support the desktop form factor. The Lightning App Builder has a function called the **form factor switcher**, which allows you to preview how the page appears in each of the form factors when more than one form factor is supported.

With the use of an appropriate template that is supported for the form factor of the device you plan to use, you can then configure the areas of the page where the content is to be shown. The options that are available for configuring the Lightning app page content depend on the template and the form factor that has been selected.

Lightning App Builder Editor enables the dragging and dropping of components onto the area of the template that you have selected. This area is called the **Lightning Page Canvas** and, along with other sections in the editor screen, it allows you to build your page within the Lightning App Builder Editor. The sections when building a Lightning page can be seen in the following screenshot:

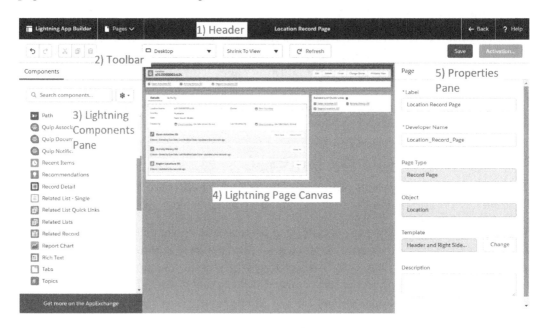

Figure 5.19 – The Lightning app page

The features and capabilities that exist in the Lightning Platform for configuring Lightning Pages are as follows:

- **Header**: The header section, at the top of the page, contains the **Pages** drop-down list, which displays the latest ten modified Lightning Pages and the label for the Lightning app page.

- **Toolbar**: The toolbar section allows you to save and activate the Lightning page. Other actions that can performed are undo and redo, as well as cut, copy, and paste Lightning page content. In addition, you can select options to view the page in different device formats.

- **Lightning components pane**: The **Lightning components** pane contains standard and custom Lightning components that you can drag and drop onto the Lightning page canvas. In general, only the components that are supported for the type of Lightning page and form factor are available for selection in the pane.

- **Lightning Page Canvas**: The Lightning page canvas is the section that Lightning components are added to and arranged for viewing in the Lightning app page.

- **Properties Pane**: The **Properties** pane renders whenever you click either the main page section or on a component to display either of the properties for the selected component.

Having configured Lightning Pages, let's now look at the options that enable appropriate user interface designs to be produced when building apps within the Lightning App Builder.

Determining appropriate user interface designs

When building Lightning app pages and configuring Lighting Components, you have various options available to you to produce a suitable design. Every use case will be different, but there are some fundamental approaches and recommendations by Salesforce that will result in an appropriate design.

When considering the user experience within the Lightning Platform, you should try to achieve the most optimum way for information to be accessed as this affects user efficiency and page performance. Some very basic consistency measures include setting all Lightning pages to show the **Details** section by default and making the order of tabs consistent across all page layouts.

By determining an appropriate user interface design, you can provide an experience that avoids too much scrolling and reduces the number of clicks, which can drive increased user adoption and engagement. Let's consider some of the key standard components that we detailed earlier in this chapter.

Considering Lightning components and performance

Be mindful of the limits that a standard Lightning component has, but also of the recommendations in terms of numbers that Salesforce recommends. In the case of the **Accordion** component, for example, which enables other Lightning Components to be grouped together within a collapsible page section, you can configure a maximum of 25 sections. However, Salesforce recommends a maximum of 10.

Generally, if there are a large number of Lightning components on a page, the Lightning page will take a long time to load. To improve loading and response times, Salesforce recommends repositioning some components, whenever performance is of concern, into an **Accordion** component or a **Tab** (non-default) section.

Here are two specific recommendations for using standard Lightning Components:

- **Highlights Panel**: The **Highlights Panel** component allows users to easily access key information at the top of a record page.

- **Related List Quick Links**: The **Related List Quick Links** component reduces the amount of space taken up by the other components used to render related lists. So it provides a more responsive and interactive way for users to access the relevant related list information.

> **Lightning App Builder considerations**
>
> Guidance and recommendations for the building of Lightning pages and Lightning apps in the Lightning App Builder are available within the following help page provided by Salesforce:
>
> ```
> https://help.salesforce.com/
> articleView?id=lightning_app_builder_
> considerations.htm&type=5
> ```

We will now present eight questions to help assess your knowledge of the features and capabilities that exist in the Lightning platform to customize the user interface. The answers can be found at the end of the chapter.

Questions to test your knowledge

The following questions serve to assess your readiness in completing the user interface part of the Salesforce Certified Platform App Builder exam. Here, you will be presented with four questions to test your understanding of the user interface customization options and the building of custom buttons, links, and actions. You will also be asked another four questions to help determine the declarative options available for incorporating Lightning Components and when, given a certain scenario, how to determine an appropriate user interface design.

Question 1 – Navigating between apps

Which of the following statements is true about navigating between apps in the Lightning Platform? (Select one)

a) Navigation between apps can only be done by clicking the **App** menu within the Lightning Experience theme.

b) Navigation between apps can be done by clicking **App Launcher** within the Lightning Experience theme and the Salesforce Classic theme.

c) Navigation between apps can be done by clicking **App Launcher** within the Lightning Experience theme and by clicking the **App** menu within the Salesforce Classic theme.

d) Navigation between apps can be done by clicking the **App** menu within the Lightning Experience theme and the Salesforce Classic theme.

Question 2 – Custom buttons and links

Which of the following is not a type of custom button or link in the Lightning Platform? (Select one)

a) The **Detail Page** link

b) The **List** button

c) The **JavaScript** button

d) The **Detail Page** button

Question 3 – Actions

What functionalities can be carried out using an action? (Select three)

a) Launch a Lightning flow.

b) Send email and log a call.

c) Create, update, and delete a record.

d) Invoke a custom Visualforce page.

Question 4 – Global actions

Which action type is not available for global actions? (Select one)

a) Invoke a custom Visualforce page.

b) Send an email.

c) Update a record.

d) Log a call.

Question 5 – Lightning App Builder

When using the Lightning App Builder, where can you see standard Lightning Components? (Select two)

a) The header

b) Compact layouts

c) The Lightning Page canvas

d) The Lightning components pane

Question 6 – Lightning home page

The marketing team in your company has asked you to add marketing users to the Lightning Platform org. The marketing team does not only want to see the sales performance charts and top deals when they log in to the system, but also a list of campaigns. However, the sales team does not want to see their view *cluttered up with campaign information*. What could you, as the app builder, do to fulfil this requirement? (Select one)

a) Explain to the sales team that there must be a common home page and ask them to just ignore the campaign information once you've added the campaign information.

b) Explain to the marketing team that they can just go ahead and customize their own home page.

c) Use the Lightning App Builder to create and customize the home page for each team's profile.

d) Develop a Visualforce page to show information based on the users' profiles.

e) Explain to the marketing team that they cannot view campaigns as it is not possible to change the standard sales information on the home page.

Question 7 – Standard Lightning Components options

Which of the following are standard Lightning Components available for Lightning record pages? (Select three)

a) Visualforce

b) Reports

c) Rich text

d) Dashboards

e) List view

Question 8 – Standard Lightning Components – key information

The marketing team in your company has asked you to ensure that certain key values can be presented within the campaign record. Which of the following standard Lightning Components would allow these key fields to be prominent in a Lightning app page? (Select one)

a) Accordion

b) Harmonica

c) Highlights panel

d) Rich text

Here are the answers to the eight questions that were presented to help verify your knowledge of building and configuring the user interface elements for the Salesforce Certified Platform App Builder exam.

Answer 1 – Navigating between apps

The answer is: c) Navigation between apps can be done by clicking **App Launcher** within the Lightning Experience theme and by clicking the **App** menu within the Salesforce Classic theme.

The following are incorrect:

a) Navigation between apps can only be done by clicking the **App** menu within the Lightning Experience theme.

b) Navigation between apps can be done by clicking **App Launcher** within the Lightning Experience theme and the Salesforce Classic theme.

d) Navigation between apps can be done by clicking the **App** menu within the Lightning Experience theme and the Salesforce Classic theme.

Answer 2 – Custom buttons and links

The answer is: c) The JavaScript button.

The following are incorrect as they are all types of custom buttons or links in the Lightning Platform:

a) The **Detail Page** link, b) The **List** button, and d) The **Detail Page** button

Answer 3 – Actions

The answers are: a) Launch a Lightning flow, b) Send email and log a call, and d) Invoke a custom Visualforce page.

The following is incorrect as it is not possible to delete a record using a standard action:

c) Create, update, and delete a record.

Answer 4 – Global actions

The answer is: c) Update a record – it is not possible to update a record as **Global Actions** are not associated with an object.

The following are incorrect:

a) Invoke a custom Visualforce page, b) Send email, and d) Log a call.

Answer 5 – Lightning App Builder

The answers are: c) Lightning Page canvas and d) Lightning Components pane – You drag a standard Lightning component from the Lightning Components pane to the Lightning Page canvas.

The following are incorrect: a) Header and b) Compact layouts.

Answer 6 – Lightning home page

The answer is: c) Use the Lightning App Builder to create and customize the home page for each team's profile.

The following are incorrect:

a) Explain to the sales team that there must be a common home page and ask them to just ignore the campaign information once you've added the campaign information.

b) Explain to the marketing team that they can just go ahead and customize their own home page.

d) Develop a Visualforce page to show information based on the users' profiles.

e) Explain to the marketing team that they cannot view campaigns as it is not possible to change the standard sales information on the home page.

Answer 7 – Standard Lightning Components options

The answers are: a) Visualforce, c) Rich text, and e) List view.

The following are incorrect: b) Reports, and d) Dashboards.

Answer 8 – Standard Lightning Components – key information

The answer is: c) Highlights panel.

The following are incorrect:

a) Accordion, b) Harmonica, and d) Rich text

Summary

In this chapter, you have gained knowledge of the options and settings that are available for controlling the user interface in the Lightning platform.

You have learned how to configure custom buttons, links, and actions and have acquired skills and knowledge in terms of the declarative building of Lightning Pages and using Lightning Components.

You discovered how to design an appropriate user interface when presented with various scenarios and how different configuration options exist for various use cases.

In the next chapter, you will learn how to implement record types that enable different business logic for users and shared functions. You will discover how formula fields and roll-up summary fields allow the building of values for certain business logic and learn how validation rules can be used to further enforce business logic.

6
Implementing Business Logic

In this chapter, you will gain the knowledge to be able to implement business logic in the Lightning Platform.

You will learn about the record types feature, which enables various types of business logic to be applied, and how to build custom field types for formula and roll-up summary calculations, which serve to apply field calculations.

With this chapter, you will also understand how data quality can be improved and how record values can be enforced in line with business data quality criteria with the use of validation rules.

At the end of it, you will be presented with a number of questions about the capabilities of and use cases for record types, formula fields, roll-up summary fields, and validation rules in the Lightning Platform.

In this chapter, we will cover the following:

- Exam objectives – Business Logic and Process Automation
- Using record types to control business logic
- Building custom field types for formula and roll-up summary calculations
- Enforcing data quality with the use of validation rules
- Questions to test your knowledge

Exam objectives – Business Logic and Process Automation

To complete the Business Logic and Process Automation section of the Certified Platform App Builder exam, app builders are expected to be able to carry out the following:

1. Describe the capabilities of and use cases for record types.
2. Describe the capabilities of and use cases for formula fields.
3. Describe the capabilities of, use cases for, and implications of roll-up summary fields.
4. Describe the capabilities of and use cases for validation rules.
5. Describe the capabilities of and use cases for approval processes.
6. Describe the capabilities of and use cases for workflows, Flow, and Process Builder.
7. Given a set of business requirements, recommend a solution to automate business processes.
8. Describe the ramifications of field updates and the potential for recursion.

Reference: Salesforce Certified Platform App Builder Exam Guide

This guide is published by Salesforce and can be referenced at: `https://trailhead.salesforce.com/help?article=Salesforce-Certified-Platform-App-Builder-Exam-Guide`.

In the Salesforce Certified Platform App Builder Exam Guide, the total number of questions is given, a percentage breakdown for each of the objectives, and an indication of the number of features/functions that can be expected in each of the objectives.

By analyzing these objectives, percentages, and question counts, we can determine the likely number of questions that will appear in the exam, and for the Business Logic and Process Automation objective this is as follows:

> **Business Logic and Process Automation: Total number of exam questions**
>
> There are likely to be 16 questions in total. This is calculated as 27% of 60 total exam questions (which equals 16.2).
>
> The process automation objectives are covered in *Chapter 7, Building Business Process Automation*.

The business logic section of the Certified Platform App Builder exam requires knowledge of the following, which also are the objectives and mechanisms for implementing business logic within the Salesforce Lightning Platform:

1. Describe the capabilities of and use cases for record types.

2. Describe the capabilities of and use cases for formula fields.

3. Describe the capabilities of, use cases for, and implications of roll-up summary fields.

4. Describe the capabilities of and use cases for validation rules.

The number of items that are likely to be assessed and the approximate number of business logic questions can be estimated as follows:

- Using record types to control business logic: two questions

- Building custom field types for formula and roll-up summary calculations: three or four questions

- Applying data quality with the use of validation rules: two questions

To help reinforce the skills and knowledge to configure business logic, there is some practical work for you to do in Salesforce, so if you do not have a Salesforce environment to carry this out in, create a free developer org as detailed in *Chapter 1, Core Capabilities of the Lightning Platform*.

We will use an example business scenario that we covered in *Chapter 2, Designing and Building a Data Model*, to demonstrate how the features in the Lightning Platform can be used to carry out the required business logic.

Now, let's look at how record types can be used to control business logic.

Using record types to control business logic

Record types allow you to create different business processes and views of information for users and records in the Lightning Platform. In *Chapter 5, Setting Up the User Interface,* we outlined how record types can be used to provide users that have access to a particular object with a different set of object picklist field values and different page layouts for the object.

An example is where you have a sales department that is split into field sales and internal sales whereby all sales users have access to an opportunity record, say, and the records are to be segmented into internal sales and field sales. With the use of record types, a different set of object picklist field values and page layouts, and a different business process can be presented to the different categories of sales users.

Record types can be created on both standard and custom objects to enable the records of that object type to be segmented. By segmenting records in this way, users that have been assigned to the different record types can carry out different actions and access different fields within the object records.

The use of record types allows the control of business logic by segmenting records through the use of page layouts and through the use of different picklist values. Page layouts can be associated with different page layouts and there are the two main use cases where record types should be considered. One is where there are different varieties of records and the other is for different processes for users.

Let's now consider how record types allow different varieties of records to be structured.

Implementing different varieties of records

This use case is when there is a business requirement for the same core functionality but there are flavors of record that do not require the inclusion of a given field or the record choice requires a different set of picklist value fields being entered on the associated page layouts.

As an example, say you have lead records that are entered using a public-facing web-to-lead form with a small number of fields to encourage people to sign up. You could create a record type for the web-to-leads that differs from leads that are entered by Salesforce users. Here, you can not only present more detail and mandatory fields for the manually entered leads but can also process and generate reports for the different lead record types accordingly.

Presenting different processes for users

This use case is when a given user or set of users have different business requirements for accessing particular fields on the associated page layouts or are allowed to only view or edit certain fields.

This can be controlled by the assignment of record types within profiles or permission sets and an example use case is when displaying fields that are used to process automation but are not required to be manually updated. In this situation, you would want to display the given fields on a page layout that is used by a system administrator for debugging purposes but not show the fields to standard users.

Before creating record types, you should carefully consider whether the business requirement warrants the use of record types as there are several overheads and maintenance concerns after record types have been created. In some situations, simply adding a picklist or checkbox can meet the requirement for capturing the information, and therefore, a record type may not always be absolutely necessary.

When creating record types, you create an additional layer of customization for the business process.

Let's now look at the impact of using record types, which create additional administration and configuration of picklist values and page layout assignments.

Considering the impact of creating record types

All objects have a hidden master record type by default, whether they are in use or not, and when you create a new record type, you can use this as the value setting for all picklist values for the object.

You can optionally clone any existing record type for the object that you are working with and if record types are created without having first cloned an existing one, the newly created record type automatically includes all the master picklist values for any given picklists for the object.

The master picklist values include both standard and custom picklists and you can then customize the picklist values for the new record type.

The features and capabilities and other areas to consider when creating record types are as follows:

- **Create a page layout in advance**: When creating record types, you must have already created the page layout to assign to the new record type.

- **Assignment of record types to users**: Users are provided with access to record types with the use of profiles and permission sets.

- **Multiple record types assigned to users**: When users have multiple record types assigned to them via their profile or permission set, they are presented with a choice of record type to select when they create new records for that particular object.

- **Use of record types with objects**: Objects are configured with one or more record types and these can be created for both standard and custom objects.

The standard objects Opportunity, Lead, Case, and Solution present some differences when using record types as we will now consider.

Using record types with standard objects

The standard objects Opportunity, Lead, Case, and Solution use a feature termed as a **Business Process** and these change the way that some of the standard picklist values for these standard objects are modified when configuring record types.

Business processes result in certain picklist fields for these standard objects not being available for record types as they are instead used via the business processes, which have the following features and capabilities:

- **Sales process**: The sales process is used to manage the business process for the standard Opportunity object and configure different business processes using the picklist values within the standard **Stage** field. The **Stage** field is therefore not available to be set by record types but other standard Opportunity fields, such as **Lead Source** or **Type**, can be set.

- **Lead process**: The lead process is used to manage the business process for the standard Lead object and to configure different business processes using the picklist values within the standard **Lead Status** field. The **Lead Status** field is therefore not available to be set by record types but other standard Lead fields such as **Industry** and **Rating** can be set.

- **Lead conversion**: When a lead record is converted to an account, contact, and optionally, an opportunity record, the new records are set with the default record types that have been set on the lead record owner. In the situation where the lead record owner has more than one record type, for each object assigned to them, they are presented with a choice of which record type to set on the lead conversion screen.

- **Support process**: The support process is used to manage the business process for the standard Case object and to configure different business processes using the picklist values within the standard **Case Status** field. The **Case Status** field is therefore not available to be set by record types but other standard support fields, such as **Priority** and **Type** can be set.

Using record types and picklists in the Lightning Platform

For a full list of considerations when using record types in the Lightning Platform, see the following guide from Salesforce:

```
https://help.salesforce.com/
articleView?err=1&id=customize_recordtype_
considerations.htm&type=5
```

Let's now look at the features and functionality that allow you to build formula and roll-up summary fields.

Building custom field types for formula and roll-up summary calculations

In *Chapter 2*, *Designing and Building a Data Model*, we looked at custom fields in the Lightning Platform and at the selection of a data type when creating custom fields. In this section, we will look at two such data types in particular, namely, formula fields and roll-up summary fields.

Understanding formula calculations

Formulas can be created in a number of areas within the Lightning Platform and are used to generate a new value that is calculated or derived from values in other expressions or fields within the platform.

In this section, we will describe the features and functionality when creating formulas for custom fields, however, formulas can also be built within areas such as approval processes, assignment and auto-response rules, custom buttons and links, validation rules, and workflow rules.

We have already learned about assignment rules, auto-response rules, and custom buttons and links in previous chapters and we will cover validation rules later in this chapter. Approval processes and workflow rules will be covered in *Chapter 7, Building Business Process Automation*.

> **Areas of use and differences between formulas in the Lightning Platform**
>
> For a full list of where formulas can be used in the Lightning Platform and to understand how they differ in capability and how they are used, see the following guide from Salesforce:
>
> ```
> https://help.salesforce.com/
> articleView?id=customize_formula_where.htm&type=5
> ```

Let's look at the features and functionality when building custom formula fields:

- **Formula Data Types**: Formula fields are configured to return particular types of data, which include the following data types: **Checkbox, Currency, Date, Date/Time, Number, Percent**, and **Text**.

- **Formula Limits for Text**: There is a limit of 3,900 characters that can be entered for **Text** formula fields.

- **Formula Limits for Currency, Number, and Percent**: There is a limit of 18 digits for **Currency, Number**, and **Percent** formula fields.

- **Formula restrictions**: The restriction that **Text Area, Encrypted**, and **Description** data types cannot be referenced in a formula field exist for formula fields.

- **Deleting fields that are referenced in formula fields**: Fields that are referenced in formula fields cannot be deleted. You must first modify or delete the formula fields so that the fields are no longer referenced before the fields can be deleted.

- **Formula elements**: Formula fields are configured to calculate or determine values using the following types of elements: **Literal Value**, **Field Reference**, **Function**, or **Operator**. In addition, you can optionally add **Comment** elements, which allow you to describe the details within the formula and help to make the formula easier to understand and maintain.

Let's look at the elements of a formula in more detail and at the types of functions and operators, which are as follows:

- **Literal value**: A literal value is a hardcoded keyed value that is either numeric or a string of text.

- **Field reference**: A field reference is a value that is derived from either the object record or via a relationship with the record to retrieve the value of another field. The referenced field can be either a standard or a custom field and is known as a *merge* field.

- **Date and time functions**: Date and time functions generate data types: **Date**, **Date/Time**, and **Time**, and allow you to convert text values to date and time values, and to calculate the difference between two date or time values.

- **Logical functions**: Logical functions are used to return a value after checking logical comparisons such as whether an expression contains a specified value, is true or false, or whether a record has a specified property such as new or cloned, and so on.

- **Math functions**: Math functions generate **Number** and **Geolocation** data types and are used to determine various types of numerical calculations such as an absolute value of a given number, the **Geolocation** value for the given latitude and longitude values, and the square root of a number, and so on.

- **Text functions**: Text functions generate the **Text** data type and allow you to apply various types of conversions and comparisons between different data types and are used to determine whether specific characters appear at the start of a string, generate a URL link, convert a string of text to a numeric value, and so on.

- **Advanced functions**: Advanced functions generate the data types **Currency**, **Text**, and **URL** and apply various types of calculations, conversions, and comparisons between different data types. Advanced functions enable comparison between a field value and its previous value, comparisons using regular expressions to find matched values, the calculation of a value having looked up a related value contained on a custom object field, and so on.

- **Math operators**: Math operators provide the functionality for mathematical operations that enable various calculations, such as the summing of two values, the multiplication of two values, calculating the exponential number of a given number value, and so on.

- **Logical operators**: Logical operators provide the functionality for logical operations that enable various evaluations such as whether two values are equal, whether one value is greater than another value, whether one or more expressions or calculated values are true, and so on.

- **Text operators**: The text operator uses the expression &, which is used to concatenate values and enables two or more text strings to be connected.

Let's build a custom formula field that is used to show whether a salesperson is an active user. The use case for this formula is that we would not want users to choose an inactive salesperson, which would result in incoming leads being assigned to an inactive user record.

Building a custom formula field

In *Chapter 2*, *Designing and Building a Data Model*, we created a custom object called **Region** to meet the requirements for a custom lead assignment app. We will now create a formula field that will be added to the **Region** page layout and show whether the selected salesperson is active or inactive.

Let's go ahead and create the **Sales Person Active** formula field on the **Region** custom object by following these steps:

1. Navigate to **Setup** and then search for Object Manager in the **Quick Find** search box located at the top of the **Setup** menu on the left sidebar.

2. On the **Object Manager** screen, search for **Region** in the **Quick Find** search box located at the top right of the page.

3. Select the **Region** object and click on **Fields & Relationships**.

Now click on **New** and complete the following details in the sections of the **New Custom Field** setup page:

1. Choose the field type **Formula** on the **Step 1. Data Type** page.

2. Click on **Next** to continue.

3. On the **Step 2. Choose output type** page, enter the following:

    Field Label: **Sales Person Active**

    Field Name: **Sales_Person_Active** (automatically set)

    Formula Return Type: **Checkbox**

4. Click on **Next** to continue.

5. On the **Step 3. Enter formula** page, enter the following in the formula textbox:

    `Sales_Person__r.IsActive:`

6. In the lower section of the **Step 3. Enter formula** page, enter the following:

    Description: `Platform App Builder Certification Guide, Custom Lead Assignment Scenario, Sales Person Active Formula Field`

    Help Text: (do not set)

    On the **Step 3. Enter formula** page, the formula editor and the **Description** fields will appear as shown in the following screenshot:

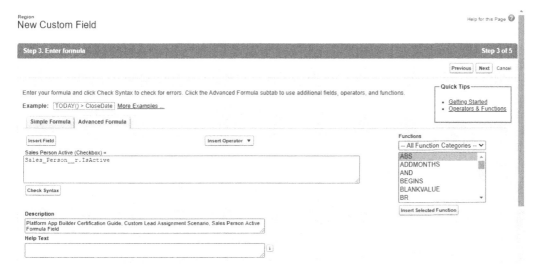

Figure 6.1 – Scenario Salesforce region Sales Person Active Formula

Blank Field Handling: (do not set)

7. Click on **Next** to continue.

8. On the **Step 4. Establish field-level security** page:

    No option to set (accept default visible for all profiles)

9. Click on **Next** to continue.

10. On the **Step 5. Add to Page Layouts** page:

    No option to set (accept default **Region** Layout)

11. Finally, click on **Save** to complete the creation of the formula field.

Having entered these details and saved the formula field, you will have created the custom field as shown in the following screenshot:

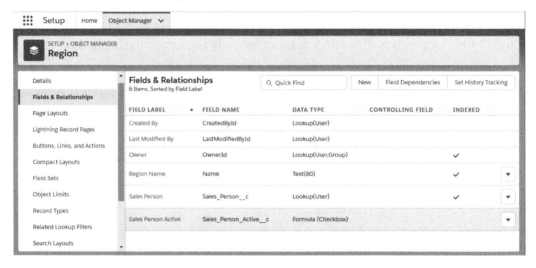

Figure 6.2 – Scenario Salesforce Region Sales Person active

When the field appears on the page layout and **Sales Person** has been selected, the page appears as shown in the following screenshot:

Figure 6.3 – Scenario Salesforce Region Sales Person Active view

In this formula, we referenced a field on the **User** object to show on the custom **Region__c** page layout. There are other mechanisms to show fields that are on objects that are related to the primary object and this includes cross-object formulas and using functions and operators in the formula fields.

Functions and operators in the Lightning Platform

For a full list of the functions and operators that can be used within formulas in the Lightning Platform, see the following guide from Salesforce:

```
https://help.salesforce.com/
articleView?id=customize_functions.htm&type=5
```

There is also the following formula cheat sheet provided by Salesforce:

```
http://resources.docs.salesforce.com/rel1/doc/en-
us/static/pdf/SF_Formulas_Developer_cheatsheet_
web.pdf
```

Let's now look at how best practices can be applied when building formula fields in the Lightning Platform.

Applying best practices when building formula fields

When formulas are created and edited within the formula editor, there is no automatic formatting of the completed formula expression. The lack of formatting poses no issues when building simple formulas as they are relatively easy to understand. However, for formulas that are more complex, there are some techniques and best practices that you can apply to help improve the readability and ease the maintenance of the formula.

The following best practices and techniques can be considered when creating and maintaining formula fields to help with the readability and understanding the formula:

- **Formatting with carriage returns and indenting spaces**: Consider including carriage returns and indenting spaces in formula text rather than writing the formula in one string of text on a single line. The readability of the formula is vastly improved by placing the text, such as function names, on separate lines and indenting. For example, instead of writing the following:

```
IF(AND(ISBLANK(My_Custom_Field__c)...
```

  Consider using carriage returns and indenting spaces, as in the following:

```
IF(
  AND(
    ISBLANK(My_Custom_Field__c)
    ...
```

- **Writing functions and keywords in uppercase**: Write formula functions or keyword names using uppercase text such as AND, OR, IF, instead of using lowercase text such as and, or, and if to make it clearer and more obvious where these keywords appear. For example, IF(TEXT(Country__c) = "Australia", "Kilometer"... rather than if(text(Country__c) = "Australia", "Kilometer".

- **Including the use of comments**: Comments are snippets of text that are simply ignored when the formula field is run. Here, the commenting text starts with a forward slash and an asterisk (/*), and the commenting text finishes with an asterisk and a forward slash (*/); for example, /* This is a comment */.

There are limits to the amount of text that can be included when building formula fields. There is also a limit on the resulting formula after the formula text has been compiled within the Lightning Platform. Let's look at how to troubleshoot formula text and compilation limits.

Troubleshooting formula text and compilation limits

Formula fields have a text size limit of 3,900 characters and a compilation limit of 5,000 characters and when these limits are reached, you cannot save the formula field. Here, you will receive an error message during the attempt to save the formula, which appears similar to the following error:

```
Compiled formula is too big to execute (7,085 characters).
Maximum size is 5,000 characters.
```

It is common to encounter these limits when building complicated formula field calculations. These limits often appear, and particularly so when building formulas that reference other formula fields. While there is no way to increase this limit, there are the following methods to help avoid and work around these limitations:

- **Use the CASE function instead of IF**: For formulas that use multiple branch conditions to derive the values, as in the preceding example formula, which is used to check whether the market is US and the state is California, Nevada, or Utah, you can replace the nested `IF` statements and instead use the `CASE` statement. The reason for the replacement is due to nested `IF` statements often resulting in larger compiled sizes since the `IF` function is used multiple times.

- **Use algebra**: The compiled size of formula fields increases as you increase the number of fields that are referenced. This is compounded when you are referencing fields that are themselves formula fields. A way to reduce the overall size is to use algebra to avoid the need to reference fields, wherever possible. The following example shows how the `Item_Price__c` and `Support_Price__c` fields are used multiple times:

  ```
  Total Price = (Item_Price__c + (Item_Price__c * Sales_
  Tax__c)) + (Support_Price__c + (Support_Price__c * Sales_
  Tax__c))
  ```

  To reduce the compiled size, use simple algebra to avoid multiple uses of the `Item_Price__c` and `Support_Price__c` fields, as in the following example:

  ```
  Total Price = (Item_Price__c * (1 + Sales_Tax__c)) +
  (Support_Price__c * (1 + Sales_Tax__c))
  ```

Let's now look at the features and functionality for creating roll-up summary fields.

Understanding roll-up summary calculations

Roll-up summary fields are created on master object records and are used to summarize the values within the child records that are associated with the master record. The association between the master record and the child record, known as the *detail*, is created by the use of a master-detail relationship field.

You can create roll-up summary fields on standard and custom objects provided that the object serves as the master object as part of a master-detail relationship with an associated detail object.

The use cases for roll-up summary fields include calculating the sum of all won opportunity amounts for a given account, calculating the total number of contact records associated with a given account, or calculating the oldest case record that has not been closed for a given account, and so on.

The following roll-up types used for calculations can be performed by using a roll-up summary field:

- COUNT: The COUNT roll-up type is used to count the number of detail records that meet the optional criteria in the summary filter.

- MIN: The MIN roll-up type is used to derive the minimum value of the detail records that meet the optional criteria in the summary filter. The data type of the MIN roll-up summary field can be either Number, Currency, Percent, Date, or Date/time.

- MAX: The MAX roll-up type is used to derive the maximum value of the detail records that meet the optional criteria in the summary filter. The data type of the MAX roll-up summary field can be either Number, Currency, Percent, Date, or Date/time.

- SUM: The SUM roll-up type is used to add the sum of field values within the detail records that meet the optional criteria in the summary filter. The data type of the SUM roll-up summary field can be either Number, Currency, or Percent.

When implementing roll-up summary fields, consider the following features and capabilities:

- **Field-level security**: You need to ensure the field-level security is appropriate when creating a roll-up summary field. If there are data concerns about the visibility of the values that are to be calculated, you must set them using field-level security as the values will be shown irrespective of the field-level security of the detail records. In other words, the field-level security of the detail record is not passed up to the parent record roll-up summary.

- **Deleting detail records**: When detail records used within a roll-up summary field are deleted, the value of the roll-up field is not automatically recalculated. To calculate the correct value, you have to manually click the **Force a mass recalculation of this field** option, which is available on the setup page for the roll-up summary field.

- **Assignment rules**: If there is an assignment rule with criteria that includes the roll-up summary field, then whenever the roll-up summary field value is recalculated and the new value meets the criteria specified in the assignment rule, then the assignment rule is triggered and the record is reassigned accordingly.

- **Non-supported field types in summary filters**: There are a number of field types that are not supported for use within the summary filter. These include **Auto number** fields, **Long Text Area** and **Picklist (Multi-select)** fields, plus **Lookup Relationship** fields, **System** fields, some **Formula** fields, and so on.

When a roll-up summary field has been created on an object, it becomes no longer possible to modify the relationship field type from master-detail to lookup.

Implementation tips and best practices

For a full list of implementation tips and best practices for **Roll-Up Summary** fields in the Lightning Platform, see the following guide from Salesforce:

```
https://help.salesforce.com/articleView?id=fields_
about_roll_up_summary_fields.htm&type=5
```

Let's go ahead and create the **Region Location Count Roll-Up Summary** field on the **Region** custom object by following these steps:

1. Navigate to **Setup** and then search for `Object Manager` in the **Quick Find** search box located at the top of the **Setup** menu on the left sidebar.

2. On the **Object Manager** screen, search for `Region` in the **Quick Find** search box located at the top right of the page.

3. Select the **Region** object and click on **Fields & Relationships**.

Now click on **New** and complete the following details in the sections of the **New Custom Field** setup page:

1. Choose the field type **Roll-Up Summary** on the **Step 1. Data Type** page.

2. Click on **Next** to continue.

3. On the **Step 2. Choose output type** page, enter the following:

Field Label: Region Location Count

Field Name: Region_Location_Count (automatically set)

Description: Platform App Builder Certification Guide, Custom Lead Assignment Scenario, Region Location Count Rollup Summary Field

Help Text: Platform App Builder Certification Guide, Custom Lead Assignment Scenario, Region Location Count Rollup Summary Field

4. Click on **Next** to continue.

On the **Step 3. Define the summary calculation** page, enter the following:

Summarized Object: Region Locations

Select Roll-Up Type: COUNT

Filter Criteria: All records should be included in the calculation

The page and field settings should be set as shown in the following screenshot:

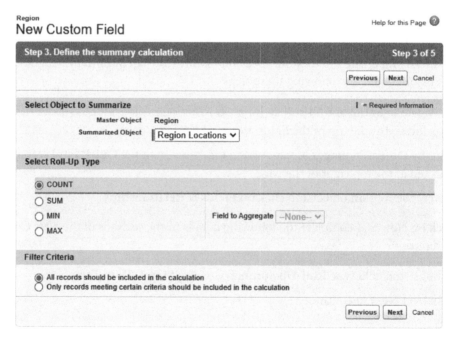

Figure 6.4 – Scenario of Salesforce Region, Region Locations COUNT Roll-Up Summary

5. Click on **Next** to continue.

6. On the **Step 4. Establish field-level security** page:

    No option to set (accept default visible for all profiles)

7. Click on **Next** to continue.

8. On the **Step 5. Add to Page Layouts** page:

    No option to set (accept default **Region** layout)

9. Finally, click on **Save** to complete the creation of the **Roll-Up Summary** field.

Having entered these details and saved the **Roll-Up Summary** field, you will have created the custom field as shown in the following screenshot:

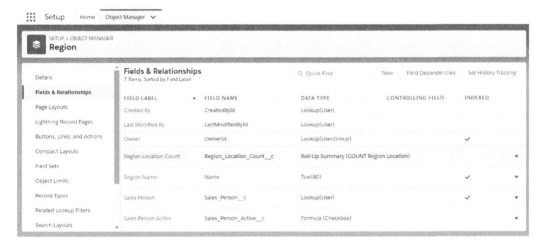

Figure 6.5 – Scenario Salesforce Region, Region Location Count Roll-Up Summary field

Let's now look at the features and functionality that allow you to enforce data quality by using a validation rule.

Enforcing data quality with the use of validation rules

Validation rules are used to prevent records from being created or updated with inconsistent or missing values that do not conform to your data quality rules. Validation rules make use of error formulas or expressions that specify the criteria for the inconsistent or missing values.

When there is a match for the formula or expression and the criteria return true, then the validation rule is activated and the error message is displayed. Here, you can choose to present the error message in one of two places: either at the top of the record page or under a specified field on the page.

We will now create a validation rule that enforces the setting of an active salesperson when creating or editing records within the **Region** object.

Let's go ahead and create the validation rule on the **Region** custom object by following these steps:

1. Navigate to **Setup** and then search for `Object Manager` in the **Quick Find** search box located at the top of the **Setup** menu on the left sidebar.

2. On the **Object Manager** screen, search for `Region` in the **Quick Find** search box located at the top right of the page.

3. Select the **Region** object and click on **Validation Rules**.

   Now click on **New** and complete the following details in the sections of the **New Validation Rule** setup page:

   Rule Name: `Region Check Active Sales Person` (when you navigate from the **Rule Name** textbox, the name changes to **Region_Check_Active_Sales_ Person**)

   Active: Checked (checked by default)

   Description: `This validation rule checks that an active user is set in the Sales Person lookup field before creating or updating a region record`

   In the **Error Condition Formula** section, enter the following:

   ```
   OR (
     ISBLANK(Sales_Person__c),
     NOT(Sales_Person__r.IsActive)
   )
   ```

In the **Error Message** box, enter the following:

```
Please select an active user
```

4. Set the **Error Location** option to **Field**: **Sales Person** as shown in the following
    screenshot:

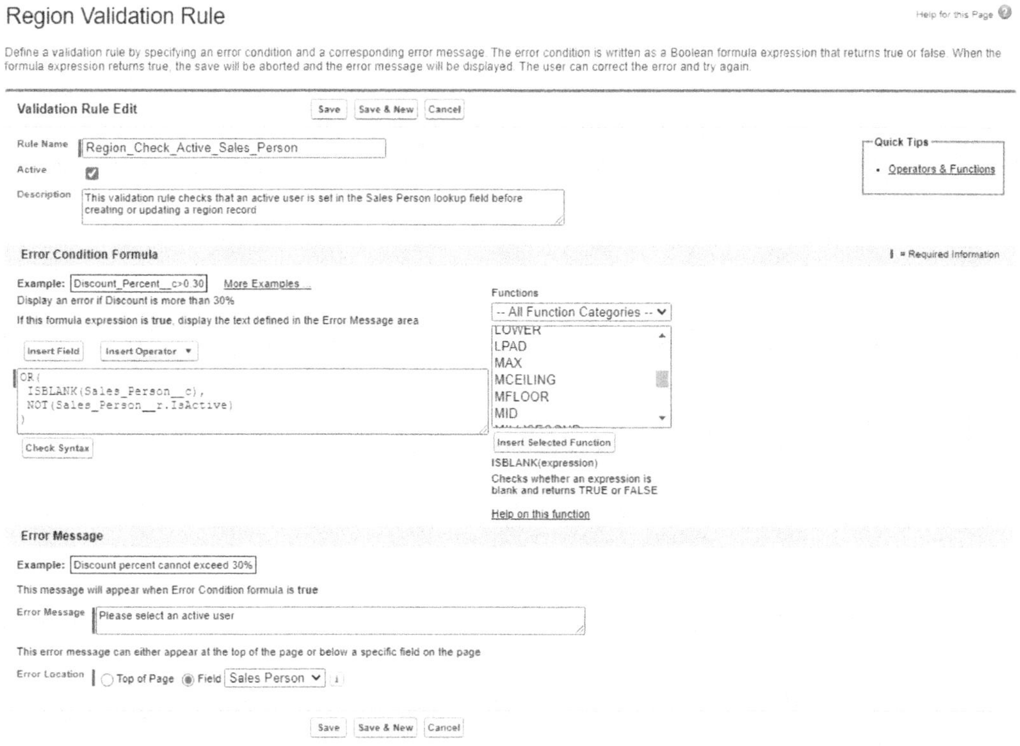

Region Validation Rule   Help for this Page ❓

Define a validation rule by specifying an error condition and a corresponding error message. The error condition is written as a Boolean formula expression that returns true or false. When the
formula expression returns true, the save will be aborted and the error message will be displayed. The user can correct the error and try again.

Validation Rule Edit	Save Save & New Cancel	

Rule Name | Region_Check_Active_Sales_Person |

Active   ☑

Description This validation rule checks that an active user is set in the Sales Person lookup field before
             creating or updating a region record

┌─ Quick Tips ──────────
│ • Operators & Functions

Error Condition Formula   ‖ = Required Information

Example: Discount_Percent__c>0.30   More Examples...
Display an error if Discount is more than 30%

If this formula expression is **true**, display the text defined in the Error Message area.

[Insert Field] [Insert Operator ▼]

```
OR(
  ISBLANK(Sales_Person__c),
  NOT(Sales_Person__r.IsActive)
)
```

[Check Syntax]

Functions
[-- All Function Categories -- ▼]

LOWER
LPAD
MAX
MCEILING
MFLOOR
MID

[Insert Selected Function]

ISBLANK(expression)
Checks whether an expression is
blank and returns TRUE or FALSE

Help on this function

Error Message

Example: Discount percent cannot exceed 30%

This message will appear when Error Condition formula is true

Error Message   Please select an active user

This error message can either appear at the top of the page or below a specific field on the page.

Error Location ◯ Top of Page ⦿ Field [Sales Person ▼] ⅈ

[Save] [Save & New] [Cancel]

Figure 6.6 – Scenario Salesforce Region Sales Person Validation Rule

5.   Finally, click on **Save** to complete the creation of the validation rule.

Having entered these details and saved the validation rule, you will have created the custom field as shown in the following screenshot:

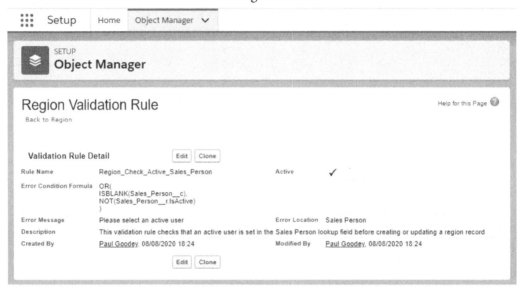

Figure 6.7 – Scenario Salesforce Region Sales Person validation rule

Whenever a user attempts to save the **Region** records, either when creating or updating, and there is either no **Sales Person** selected or the **Salesperson** is not active, an error message appears as shown in the following screenshot:

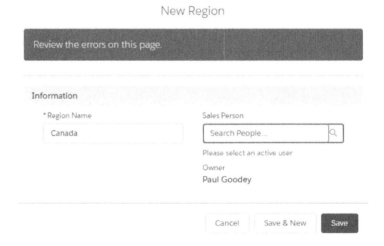

Figure 6.8 – Scenario Salesforce Region Sales Person error

The user is thus presented with an error message and they are unable to save the record unless they select a value within the **Sales Person** field.

Let's now look at some questions to test your knowledge.

Questions to test your knowledge

We'll now present six questions to help assess your knowledge of implementing business logic on the Lightning Platform. There are questions about the capabilities of record types, formula fields, roll-up summary fields, and validation rules.

Question 1 – Record type capabilities

Which of the following statements are true about the capabilities of record types on the Lightning Platform? (Select three)

a) Record types allow users that have access to a particular object to have a different view of records through the use of different page layouts.

b) Record types can be created on standard objects and custom objects.

c) Record types allow users that have access to a particular object to have a different set of object picklist field values.

d) Record types allow users that have access to a particular object to have a different view of records through the use of checkbox fields.

Question 2 – Record types and standard fields

Which of the following set of standard picklist fields can be used with record types on the Lightning Platform? (Select one)

a) The **Lead Source** field within the **Opportunity** object, the **Status** field within the **Lead** object, and the **Status** field within the **Case** object.

b) The **Lead Source** field within the **Opportunity** object, the **Industry** field within the **Lead** object, and the **Priority** field within the **Case** object.

c) The **Stage** field within the **Opportunity** object, the **Industry** field within the **Lead** object, and the **Priority** field within the **Case** object.

d) The **Stage** field within the **Opportunity** object, the **Industry** field within the **Lead** object, and the **Status** field within the **Case** object.

Question 3 – Formula field data types

Which of the following data types can be returned using formula fields on the Lightning Platform? (Select two)

a) Date/Time

b) Time

c) Checkbox

d) Email

e) Text (Encrypted)

Question 4 – Roll-Up Summary field functions

Which of the following functions are available within the **Roll-up Summary** field on the Lightning Platform? (Select two)

a) AVG

b) COALESCE

c) SUM

d) MAX

Question 5 – Roll-Up Summary field capabilities

Which of the following statements are true about the capabilities of the roll-up summary field on the Lightning Platform? (Select two)

a) Roll-up summary fields can only be created on objects that are the master as part of a master-detail or lookup relationship.

b) The roll-up summary field shows data to users even if the user cannot see the **Detail** object field data due to field-level security.

c) Changes to the value of a roll-up summary field can automatically trigger any assignment rule that contains criteria that includes the roll-up summary field.

d) All types of field data types can be used in the **Field** column of roll-up summary filters.

Question 6 – Validation rule capabilities

Which of the following statements is true about the capabilities of validation rules on the Lightning Platform? (Select one)

a) The error message for a validation rule can be set to either appear at the top of the page or above a specific field on the page when the validation rule evaluates to true only when creating a record.

b) The error message for a validation rule can only appear at the top of the page when the validation rule evaluates to true when either creating or updating a record.

c) The error message for a validation rule can be set to appear above a specific field on the page when the validation rule evaluates to true when either creating or updating a record.

d) The error message for a validation rule can be set to either appear at the top of the page or below a specific field on the page when the validation rule evaluates to true when either creating or updating a record.

Here are the answers to the six questions.

Answer 1 – Record type capabilities

The answers are a), b), and c):

a) Record types allow users that have access to a particular object to have a different view of records through the use of different page layouts.

b) Record types can be created on standard objects and custom objects.

c) Record types allow users that have access to a particular object to have a different set of object picklist field values.

The following choice is not correct:

d) Record types allow users that have access to a particular object to have a different view of records through the use of checkbox fields.

Answer 2 – Record types and standard fields

The answer is b) The **Lead Source** field within the **Opportunity** object, the **Industry** field within the **Lead** object, and the **Priority** field within the **Case** object.

The following choices are not correct:

a) The **Lead Source** field within the **Opportunity** object, the **Status** field within the **Lead** object, and the **Status** field within the **Case** object.

c) The **Stage** field within the **Opportunity** object, the **Industry** field within the **Lead** object, and the **Priority** field within the **Case** object.

d) The **Stage** field within the **Opportunity** object, the **Industry** field within the **Lead** object, and the **Status** field within the **Case** object.

Answer 3 – Formula field data types

The answers are a) and c):

a) Date/Time

c) Checkbox

The following choices are not correct as these data types cannot be returned using formula fields:

b) Time

d) Email

e) Text (Encrypted)

Answer 4 – Roll-Up Summary field functions

The answers are c) and d):

c) SUM

d) MAX

The following choices are not correct:

a) AVG

b) COALESCE

Answer 5 – Roll-Up Summary field capabilities

The answers are b) and c):

b) The **Roll-Up Summary** field shows data to users even if the user cannot see the **Detail** object field data due to field-level security.

c) Changes to the value of a roll-up summary field can automatically trigger any assignment rule that contains criteria that includes the roll-up summary field.

The following choices are not correct:

a) Roll-up summary fields can only be created on objects that are the master as part of a master-detail or lookup relationship.

d) All types of field data types can be used in the **Field** column of roll-up summary filters.

Answer 6 – Validation rule capabilities

The answer is d):

d) The error message for a validation rule can be set to either appear at the top of the page or *below* a specific field on the page when the validation rule evaluates to true when either *creating* or *updating* a record.

The following choices are not correct:

a) The error message for a validation rule can be set to either appear at the top of the page or above a specific field on the page when the validation rule evaluates to true only when creating a record.

b) The error message for a validation rule can only appear at the top of the page when the validation rule evaluates to true when either creating or updating a record.

c) The error message for a validation rule can be set to appear above a specific field on the page when the validation rule evaluates to true when either creating or updating a record.

Summary

In this chapter, you have gained an understanding of how to use record types to control business logic by segmenting records through the use of page layouts and through the use of different picklist values.

You have learned about the features and capabilities of formula fields and how to build custom field types for formula and roll-up summary calculations. Knowing about roll-up summary fields and master-detail relationships, in general, is particularly important for an app builder. It is vital to understand where roll-up summary fields can be used and the calculations that can be performed.

You have discovered and learned how to build validation rules to prevent records that do not match formulae and expressions from being saved, and the options that are available will equip you with the necessary skills and confidence to configure and build rules that enforce data quality on the Lightning Platform.

In the next chapter, we will continue to look at the exam objectives: Business Logic and Process Automation. Here, you will be presented with the features that are available on the Lightning Platform to automate your business processes with approvals, workflows, Process Builder, and Flow.

7
Building Business Process Automation

In this chapter, we'll look at the features and capabilities available to automate business processes in Salesforce Lightning.

From this chapter, you will learn how workflow rules, Flow, and Process Builder can be configured to automate processes for given business requirements and the features, use cases, and considerations to be applied when building automation to create and update records.

You will discover how, with the use of approval processes, the mechanisms of approving or rejecting records can be automated from within the Lightning Platform and by responding to email requests.

At the end of the chapter, you will be presented with a number of questions about the capabilities of and use cases for Workflow, Flow, Process Builder, and approval processes in the Lightning Platform.

In this chapter, we will cover the following:

- Exam objectives: Business Logic and Process Automation
- Assessing the capabilities of process automation in the Lightning Platform
- Understanding the use cases for Workflow, Flow, Process Builder, and approvals
- Translating business requirements into process automation solutions
- Understanding the implications of auto-updating fields and recursion issues within process automation
- Questions to test your knowledge

Exam objectives: Business Logic and Process Automation

To complete the Business Logic and Process Automation section of the Certified Platform App Builder exam, app builders are expected to be able to carry out the following:

1. Describe the capabilities of and use cases for record types.
2. Describe the capabilities of and use cases for formula fields.
3. Describe the capabilities of, use cases for, and implications of roll-up summary fields.
4. Describe the capabilities of and use cases for validation rules.
5. Describe the capabilities of and use cases for approval processes.
6. Describe the capabilities of and use cases for Workflow, Flow, and Process Builder.
7. Given a set of business requirements, recommend a solution to automate business processes.
8. Describe the ramifications of field updates and the potential for recursion.

> **Reference: Salesforce Certified Platform App Builder Exam Guide**
>
> This guide is published by Salesforce and can be referenced at `https://trailhead.salesforce.com/help?article=Salesforce-Certified-Platform-App-Builder-Exam-Guide`

In the *Salesforce Certified Platform App Builder Exam Guide*, the total number of questions, a percentage breakdown for each of the objectives, and an indication of the number of features/functions that can be expected in each of the objectives is given.

By analyzing these objectives, percentages, and question counts, we can determine the possible number of questions that will appear in the exam, and for the Business Logic and Process Automation objective, this is as follows:

> **Business Logic and Process Automation: Total number of exam questions**
>
> There are likely to be 16 questions in total. This is calculated as 27% of 60 total exam questions (which calculates the score to as 16.2).
>
> The Business Logic objectives are covered in *Chapter 6, Implementing Business Logic*.

The process automation objectives within the Certified Platform App Builder exam require knowledge of the following:

- Describe the capabilities of and use cases for approval processes.
- Describe the capabilities of and use cases for Workflow, Flow, and Process Builder.
- Given a set of business requirements, recommend a solution to automate business processes.
- Describe the ramifications of field updates and the potential for recursion.

The number of items that are likely to be assessed and the approximate number of questions on process automation can be estimated as follows:

- Using approvals: 2 questions
- Workflow, Flow, and Process Builder: 5 questions
- Auto-updating fields and recursion issues: 1 or 2 questions

To help reinforce the skills and knowledge needed for configuring process automation, there is practical work for you to do in Salesforce. So, if you do not have a Salesforce environment to carry this out, create a free developer org as detailed in *Chapter 1, Core Capabilities of the Lightning Platform*.

We will continue to use an example business scenario, which we covered in *Chapter 2, Designing and Building a Data Model*, to demonstrate how the features in the Lightning Platform support the building of business logic and process automation.

Now, let's look at the capabilities of the process automation features in the Lightning Platform.

Assessing the capabilities of process automation in the Lightning Platform

As an app builder, you will often be presented with scenarios or requests by users within your organization where manual and time-consuming processes can be replaced using process automation in the Lightning Platform. Furthermore, in the same way that people have become accustomed to notifications when using non-Salesforce systems, such as receiving an acknowledgment that an online shopping order has been placed, customers will expect to receive some form of automation whenever they interact with your organization.

Not only do automation processes allow notifications – both internally and externally, but they can also be used to improve data quality, reduce inefficiencies, and increase productivity. Ultimately, with the use of process automation, data integrity increases and operational costs are lowered.

In the Lightning Platform, we can build these types of automation using Workflow, Flow, Process Builder, and approvals and we will now look at these features.

Understanding the types of process automation

The mechanisms for building automation processes that are available in the Lightning Platform have evolved over the years since the platform was first launched. These mechanisms continue to be developed and refined as more functionality is made available and changes are made to the way the underlying architectures for process automation are carried out by Salesforce. For example, there are recent point-and-click tools that are used for building processes in Flow and Process Builder that differ to the wizard-type screens that are used to build workflows and approval processes.

Within the various declarative tools for creating automation processes, there are some common areas of understanding, such as the need to have previously created email alerts whether building the email automation actions with Workflow, approvals, or Lightning Flow.

There are significant differences and capabilities between the automation tools, which you, as an app builder, must be aware of before deciding which tool to use. In addition, there are names and terminologies that are used when describing the building of the automation processes and the tools used that are available in the Lightning Platform.

It is important for you to understand the following high-level terms for process automation in the Lightning Platform:

- **Workflow rule**: This is the mechanism that allows you to build workflow processes using if/then types of statements and function logic to build a single step and a single set of automation actions.

- **Workflow**: This is the product name for workflow rules.

- **Lightning Flow**: This is the name of the mechanism that is used for Process Builder and Flow.

- **Process Builder**: This is the visual interface that allows you to build Process Builder processes using point-and-click features to build multiple steps and different sets of automation actions.

- **Flow Builder**: This is the visual interface that allows you to build Flow Builder processes using point-and-click features to build multiple steps and different sets of automation actions.

- **Approvals**: This is the name of the feature to control the logic for how records are approved in the Lightning Platform. By using approval processes, you can use if/then types of statements and logic to specify various approval steps, which include the approver and the action or actions that are to be performed during each step of the approval process.

- **Action**: This is the item or set of items within the process automation container, such as sending an email, creating a task, and so on. Depending on the type of initiating process, actions can either be carried out immediately or scheduled as a time-based action.

Let's now compare and contrast the options that exist for building process automation in the Lightning Platform using Workflow, Flow, Process Builder, and approvals.

Using Workflow to build process automation

Workflow provides business processes using workflow rules that enable you to build process automation with limited flexibility. Workflow rules are built using a declarative wizard-like interface using if/then types of statements.

The actions that workflow rules can perform are as follows:

- Sending email alerts

- Updating records

- Creating task records

- Sending a message to an external system with an **Outbound Message**, which provides a simple form of system integration

The resulting actions associated with workflow rules run in the background. The declarative wizard-like interface that enables the building of processes results in a **Workflow Rules** screen that includes the associated actions as shown in the following screenshot:

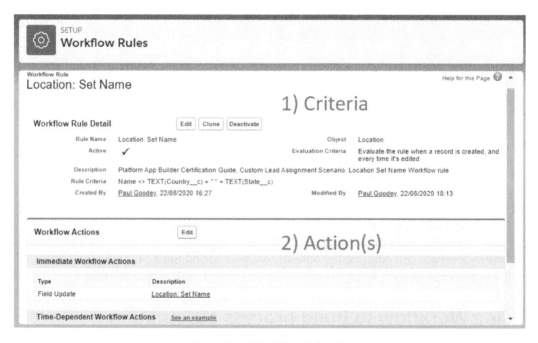

Figure 7.1 – Workflow Rules UI

The user interface for Workflow comprises the **Criteria** and **Actions** sections, which are used within workflow rules for the following:

- **Criteria**: The criteria section is the record detail that has to be met in order for the workflow rule to invoke the actions. The criteria can be thought of as the `if` element within our notional `if...then` statement.

- **Actions**: The action or set of actions is what is executed when the criteria are met within a given record. Actions can be thought of as the "then" element within our notional if...then statement.

Let's now look at the mechanism for building automation processes with Flow.

Building process automation with Flow

Flow allows you to build process automation with greater complexity and flexibility than Workflow. Flow Builder enables automation processes with multiple steps and associated actions. The actions that Flow Builder can perform include all the actions that can be done with Workflow (with the exception of **Outbound Messages**) and also allow the creation, updating, editing, and deleting of various types of records.

In addition, processes can be created that run in the background, known as an autolaunched flow, or via a user interface, known as a screen flow. Flow Builder is part of the Lightning Flow product and provides a visual interface for building processes using point-and-click features as shown in the following screenshot:

Figure 7.2 – Flow Builder UI

The user interface for Flow Builder comprises the sections **Button Bar**, **Toolbox**, and **Canvas**:

- **Button Bar**: The **Button Bar** section contains features and options to manage the process, such as activating or de-activating the flow version, debugging the flow, duplicating elements, editing version properties, and so on.

- **Toolbox**: The **Toolbox** section contains two tabs: the **Elements** tab and the **Manager** tab. The **Elements** tab allows you to add new elements to the flow, such as **Screen**, **Create Records**, **Get Records**, **Update Records**, **Assignments**, and so on. The **Manager** tab allows you to view a listing of all the elements and other resources that have been created within the flow. Within the **Manager** tab, you can also create variables, stages, choices, and so on, which are used within the flow.

- **Canvas**: The **Canvas** section is the location where the elements are dragged and dropped and connected to build the ordering and logic that is used to perform the functionality for the Flow. The Flow canvas allows elements to be moved and positioned to create a visual representation of the logical paths of a flow.

Let's look at the mechanism for building automation processes with Process Builder.

Implementing process automation with Process Builder

Process Builder provides moderate flexibility and allows you to build more complex process automation than Workflow but offers less functionality when compared to Flow. The actions that Process Builder can perform are the same as Workflow (again, with the exception of Outbound Messages), and also allow the creation, updating, editing, and deleting of various types of records.

As with Workflow, the resulting actions associated with Process Builder run in the background only. Process Builder is also part of the Lightning Flow product and provides a visual interface for building processes using point-and-click features and enables automation processes with multiple steps and associated actions as shown in the following screenshot:

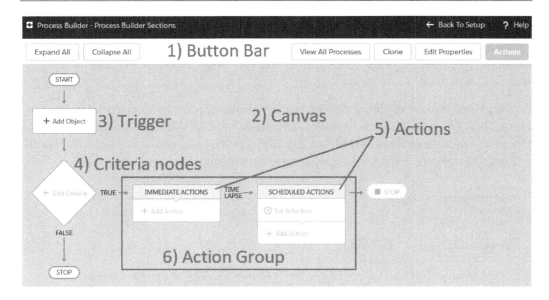

Figure 7.3 – Process Builder UI

- **Button Bar**: The **Button Bar** section contains features and options to manage the process, such as the editing of properties, or to view a list of all processes, and so on.

- **Canvas**: The **Canvas** section is the location where the criteria and actions exist to build the logic that is used to perform the functionality of the Process Builder.

- **Trigger**: This is the object interaction trigger location.

- **Criteria nodes**: The criteria nodes are the elements that define the condition that has to be met in order for Process Builder to execute the actions.

- **Actions**: The actions are what is invoked when the required criteria are met within a given criteria.

- **Action Group**: This group is the set of actions that are invoked within Process Builder.

Let's now look at the mechanism for building automation processes with approvals.

Creating approval processes with approvals

Approvals are automation processes that comprise a logical set of steps that are used to request and receive formal approval for records within the Lightning Platform. Approval processes can range in scale from a simple, single step to multiple logic with associated routing that provides highly complex approval mechanisms.

When creating approvals, you must specify who the initial submitters are, which approval steps are to be taken, and the criteria that the record must meet before the record can be submitted for approval. Within the approval steps are actions that are triggered as the steps are carried out.

As with Workflow, the resulting actions associated with approval processes run in the background only and the declarative wizard interface that enables the building of approval processes results in an **Approval** screen that includes the process definition detail, various actions, and associated approval steps as shown in the following screenshot:

Figure 7.4 – Approval Processes user interface

The user interface for the approval process comprises the **Process Definition Detail**, **Initial Submission Actions**, **Approval Steps**, **Final Approval Actions**, **Final Rejection Actions**, and **Recall Actions** sections, which are used within the approval process as described in the following:

- **Process Definition Detail**: This section contains the entry criteria that contains the `if/then` statement for the record that has to be met in order for the approval process to be invoked along with the approval assignment email template, record editability, and initial submitters.

- **Initial Submission Actions**: The action or set of actions that are executed when the criteria are met after a user submits a record for approval.

- **Approval Steps**: The specific steps that the record can transition through the approval with each step as a chain in the overall path. This is covered in more detail later in this section.

- **Final Approval Actions**: The action or set of actions that is executed when every approval step has been completed.

- **Final Rejection Actions**: The action or set of actions that is executed when any approver has rejected the approval request.

- **Recall Actions**: The action or set of actions that is executed when a submitter or system administrator has set the approval request to be recalled.

Within **Approval Steps**, you set the specific steps that the record will transition through to the approval, with each step a chain in the overall path. Here, you can specify further criteria to determine which records may reach a given step, who to assign the step to in the approval request, and whether each approver's delegated approver can also approve.

The steps include the specific actions that provide for the sending of email alerts, creating task records, sending calls to external systems known as **Outbound Messages**, and field updates as shown in the following screenshot:

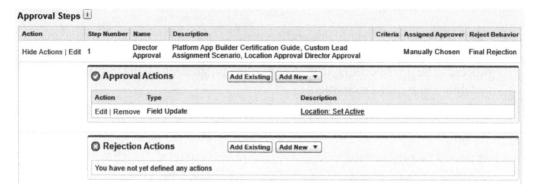

Figure 7.5 – Approval process steps and actions

Let's now look at the specific features and capabilities of the Workflow, Flow, and Process Builder process automation mechanisms.

Considering limits for approvals, Workflow, Flow, and Process Builder

There are a number of limits applied by Salesforce to restrict the number of process automations that can either be active or can be created in total. There are also limits for the number of actions that can be created and performed for approvals, Workflow, Flow, and Process Builder.

There is a limit at the org level for the number of email alerts sent using process automation. This limit is set at 1,000 emails per day for each Salesforce license and there is a total limit per org of 2,000,000 email alerts. This limit applies to email alerts sent using workflow rules, approval processes, flows, and processes, plus the REST API. There is a separate limit within the Developer Edition org, which is 15 emails per day for each Salesforce license.

The following limits apply for approvals in the Lightning Platform:

- Total number of approval processes per org: 2,000
- Total number of active approval processes per org: 1,000
- Total number of approval processes per object: 500

- Total number of active approval processes per object: 300

- Total number of steps per approval process: 30

- Total number of approvers per step: 25

> **Approvals limits in the Lightning Platform**
>
> For more details about the limits for approvals, refer to the following article:
>
> ```
> https://help.salesforce.com/
> articleView?id=approvals_limits.htm&type=5
> ```

The following core limits apply to Workflow in the Lightning Platform:

- Total number of active or inactive workflow rules per org: 2,000 (this limit includes automation via Workflow plus assignment rules, auto-response rules, and escalation rules)

- Total number of active or inactive workflow rules per object: 500 (this limit includes automation via Workflow plus assignment rules, auto-response rules, and escalation rules)

- Total number of active workflow rules per object: 50 (this limit includes automation via Workflow plus assignment rules, auto-response rules, and escalation rules)

- Total number of immediate actions per workflow rule: 40

- Total number of time triggers per workflow rule: 10

> **Workflow limits in the Lightning Platform**
>
> For more details about the limits for workflow rules, refer to the following article:
>
> ```
> https://help.salesforce.com/
> articleView?id=workflow_limits.htm&type=5
> ```

The following core general limits apply for Flow in the Lightning Platform:

- Total number of flows per flow type per org: 4,000

- Total number of active flows per flow type per org: 2,000

- Total number of executed elements at runtime per flow: 2,000

- Total number of versions per flow: 50

- Total number of schedule-triggered flow interviews per 24 hours: 250,000 (this limit is set as 250,000 or the number of user licenses in your org x 200, whichever number is greater)

Flow limits in the Lightning Platform

For more details about the limits for flows, refer to the following article:

```
https://help.salesforce.com/articleView?id=flow_
considerations.htm&type=5
```

The following limits apply for Process Builder in the Lightning Platform:

- Total number of processes per type per org: 4,000

- Total number of active processes per type per org: 2,000

- Total number of active processes per type per org per object: 50 (record change processes and rules)

- Total number of criteria nodes that are evaluated and actions that are executed at runtime per process: 2,000

- Total number of groups of scheduled actions that are executed or flow interviews that are resumed per hour: 1,000

Let's look at the use cases for building automation processes with approvals, Workflow, Flow, and Process Builder.

Understanding the use cases for approvals, Workflow, Flow, and Process Builder

Understanding the use cases for process automation tools in the Lightning Platform is considered an important skill for an app builder and this competency is tested in the Salesforce Certified Platform App Builder Exam as part of the test criteria:

- Describe the capabilities of and use cases for approval processes.

- Describe the capabilities of and use cases for Workflow, Flow, and Process Builder.

Let's look at the use cases for approvals, Workflow, Flow, and Process Builder and begin by considering the use cases for approvals.

Use cases for approvals

Approval processes are manually triggered by users and also automatically when the approval is specified for auto launching by other process automation tools (provided that the entry criteria matches the specified record field values). Approval processes consist of multiple steps, whereby actions are executed depending upon whether the record is approved or rejected. Approval processes result in the approval history being automatically tracked and when an approval is initiated, the record is *locked down* and can only be amended by the approver or system administrator.

Approval processes contain steps with actions that are executed to perform the following action types:

- Sending email alerts

- Updating records

- Creating task records

- Sending a message to an external system with an Outbound Message, which provides a simple form of system integration

Use cases for Workflow

Workflow is the most established process automation tool within the Lightning Platform and allows you to build workflow rules that offer limited flexibility using if/then types of statements.

The following examples of process automation can be accomplished using Workflow:

- Automatically send an email to an external individual, such as a prospect or customer after a period of time has elapsed since a record was created, such as an incoming web-to-lead record.

- Automatically update a field value when another field on a related record is updated or created.

- Automatically create and assign a task to a Lightning Platform user to notify and instruct them to follow up a record that has been received or has met certain criteria, such as an opportunity sales stage.

- Automatically update a value in an external system when the status of a record changes using an Outbound Message, such as when a contact becomes a member and this is to be set in an external membership system.

Workflow rules are evaluated when a type of change is detected within a record that then triggers actions to be carried out with the following use cases and behaviors:

- **Action types**: The actions that Workflow rules can perform are sending emails, updating records, creating task records, and sending calls to external systems with Outbound Messages.

- **Action behavior**: The resulting actions associated with workflow rules always run in the background.

- **Scheduled actions**: Workflow can be used to schedule one-time actions after a pre-determined or calculated time using time-dependent actions.

- **Process execution**: The actions in a workflow are executed using simple logic with if/then types of statements that are initiated after a change has been detected within a record. The process change or action is limited to a single object or association with a related object that is part of a master-detail relationship.

Let's now consider use cases for Flow.

Use cases for Flow

Flow, in contrast to Workflow, is a more recent introduction to the suite of process automation tools within the Lightning Platform and allows you to build processes that offer the most flexibility using complex logic and functionality. An example of the use of Flow is to update fields in a different object record whenever changes affect a given record, which would run in the background. Flow can also run in the user interface and an example is a scenario whereby a customer service representative can use a script to help guide the conversation during a call with a customer.

Flows can be created as screen flows and run in the background, which then triggers actions to be carried out with the following use cases and behaviors:

- **Action types:** The actions that Flow can perform are creating, updating, and deleting any records, sending emails, posting to Chatter, launching a flow, calling Apex code, sending a custom notification, and submitting records for approval.

- **Action behavior**: The resulting actions associated with Flow can run in the background and also allow user interaction whereby process steps and screens can be presented to users.

- **Scheduled actions**: Flow can be used to schedule highly flexible time-scheduled actions.

- **Process execution**: The actions in a flow are executed using complex logic and statements that are initiated before and after a record is created or updated and changes have been detected within a record. With the manual selection of a button or link, the process change or action is not limited to a single object or association with a related object.

Let's now consider the use cases for Process Builder.

Use cases for Process Builder

Process Builder allows you to build processes that offer more flexibility than Workflow and that use moderately complex logic and functionality. An example of the use of Process Builder is to update fields in a different object record whenever changes affect a given record.

Process Builder runs in the background and offers more actions than either Workflow or Flow that are performed in the background with the following use cases and behaviors:

- **Action types**: The actions that Process Builder can perform are creating, updating, and deleting any records, sending emails, posting to Chatter, launching a flow, invoking a process, and calling Apex code, invoking a quick action (to create a record, update a record, or log a call), sending a custom notification, and submitting records for approval.

- **Action behavior**: The resulting actions associated with Process Builder run in the background.

- **Scheduled actions**: Process Builder can be used to schedule timed actions.

- **Process execution**: The actions in Process Builder are executed using multiple if... then logic and statements that are initiated before and after a record is created or updated and changes have been detected within a record. With the manual selection of a button or link, the process change or action is not limited to a single object or association with a related object.

Let's now compare the specific features and capabilities of the process automation tools in the Lightning Platform.

Comparing Workflow, Flow, and Process Builder features

A comparison of the specific features and capabilities of Workflow, Flow, and Process Builder process automation can be seen in the following summary table:

	Workflow	Flow	Process Builder
Single or multiple steps?	A single step and a single set of results	Multiple steps and different sets of results	Multiple steps and different sets of results
Able to design the logic using a visual interface?	No	Yes	Yes
Can be triggered when a record is changed?	Yes	No	Yes
Can be triggered when a user clicks a custom tab, button, or link?	No	Yes	No
Can be triggered by another process?	No	No	Yes
Can be triggered when Apex is called?	No	Yes	No
Can be triggered when the user accesses pages or tabs: Lightning pages, community pages, Visualforce pages, or a custom tab?	No	Yes	No
Can be triggered when the user accesses an item via the utility bar?	No	Yes	No
Supports time-based actions?	Yes	Yes	Yes
Supports user interaction?	No	Yes	No

Table 7.1 – Comparing the features of Workflows, Flow, and Process Builder

Let's look at the specific actions that can be carried out within the Workflow, Flow, and Process Builder process automation mechanisms.

Comparing Workflow, Flow, and Process Builder actions

For a comparison of the specific actions that can be carried out within Workflow, Flow, and Process Builder process automation, the following table sums it up:

	Workflow	Flow	Process Builder
Able to create records?	Tasks only	Yes	Yes
Able to delete records?	No	Yes	No
Able to update fields?	The initiating record or its parent only	Any record	The initiating or any related record
Able to send email?	Yes	Yes	Yes
Able to send an outbound message?	Yes	No	No
Able to post to Chatter?	No	Yes	Yes
Able to launch a flow?	No (was available as a pilot)	Yes	Yes
Able to invoke a process?	No	No	Yes
Able to call Apex code?	No	Yes	Yes
Able to invoke a quick action (to create a record, update a record, or log a call)?	No	No	Yes
Able to send a custom notification?	No	Yes	Yes
Able to submit an approval process?	No	Yes	Yes

Table 7.2 – Comparing the actions of Workflows, Flow, and Process Builder

> **Deciding which process automation tool to use in the Lightning Platform**
>
> For more information about which process automation tool to use and the recommendations by Salesforce on when to use workflow rules, Flow, Process Builder, and approval processes, refer to the following guide:
>
> ```
> https://help.salesforce.com/
> articleView?id=process_which_tool.htm&type=5
> ```

Let's now look at the types of business requirements that can be commonly identified and the options that exist for meeting these requirements in the Lightning Platform using automation processes.

Translating business requirements into process automation solutions

As an App Builder in the Lightning Platform, you will most likely encounter situations where you are asked to implement solutions that satisfy certain business requirements through the use of process automation.

The need to be able to recommend an appropriate solution for a given business requirement is considered an important skill for an app builder and this competency is tested in the Salesforce Certified Platform App Builder Exam as part of the following test criteria:

Given a set of business requirements, recommend a solution to automate business processes.

When considering the use cases, actions, and decisions that would lead us to choose a particular automation tool, we can consider the following:

- **Approvals**: Allow the creation of approval processes for holiday requests or supporting business processes that require approval by a salesperson from their line manager for opportunity values over a certain amount and so on.

- **Workflow**: Allows simple updates of fields and limited actions such as email and field updates.

- **Flow**: Allows the creation of highly complex logic and routing and the most flexible range of actions, which can run in the background and as a screen flow for data capture.

- **Process Builder**: Allows the creation of complex logic and routing and a somewhat flexible range of actions that can run in the background.

When deciding which process automation tool to use, it is generally considered good practice to have all automation use the same mechanism, wherever possible, and not to have automation processes for the same business requirement initiated and updated using different types of automation mechanisms. This is covered in more detail in the *Configuring automation processes using Process Builder* section.

We will look at how we can build out functionality that satisfies an example set of business requirements for process automation and we'll begin by creating an automation process using Workflow.

Creating an automation process using Workflow

In *Chapter 2*, *Designing and Building a Data Model*, we created a custom object called Location to meet the requirements for our example custom **Lead Assignment** app. We will now use Workflow to create a workflow rule that will be used to set the name of the record to a standardized format whenever new Location records are created or updated.

The purpose of the workflow rule is to set the name of a Location record to a combination of the values that have been selected for the **Country** and **State** picklist field values. This will prevent inconsistent naming information from being captured whenever records are created or updated and will result in better quality and more consistent data.

Let's go ahead and create the workflow rule for the **Location** custom object by following these steps:

1. Navigate to **Setup** and then search for **Workflow rule** in the **Quick Find** search box located at the top of the **Setup** menu on the left sidebar.
2. Click on **Workflow rule** in the **Setup** menu.
3. Click on **New Rule** on the **Workflow Rules Setup** page.
4. On the **Step 1. Select object** page, choose **Location** for the **Object** type.
5. Click on **Next** to continue.
6. On the **Step 2: Configure Workflow Rule** page, enter the following:

    Rule Name: Location: Set Name

    Description: Platform App Builder Certification Guide, Custom Lead Assignment Scenario, Location Set Name Workflow rule

    For the picklist option **Evaluate the rule when a record is.**, select the choice **created, and every time it's edited**.

    For the **Rule Criteria** option, go to **Run this rule if the** and select **formula evaluates to true**.

7. Enter the following in the formula editor:

    ```
    Name <> TEXT(Country__c) + " " + TEXT(State__c)
    ```

The formula editor enables the formula to be entered as shown in the following screenshot:

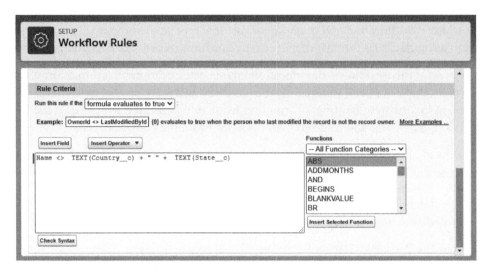

Figure 7.6 – Workflow Rules new field update formula

8. Click on **Save & Next** to continue.

9. On the **Step 3: Specify Workflow Actions** page, click on the **Add Workflow Action** button (to present a list of actions):

10. In the list of actions, click on **New Field Update** as shown in the following screenshot:

Figure 7.7 – Workflow Rules New Field Update

11. On the **New Field Update** page, enter the following:

Name: **Location**: `Set Name`

Unique Name: `Location_Set_Name` (set by default)

Description: `Platform App Builder Certification Guide, Custom Lead Assignment Scenario, Location Set Name Workflow Field Update`

Field to Update: choose **Location Name**

12. In the **Specify New Field Value** section, choose the **Use a formula to set the new value** option.

13. Enter the following in the formula editor:

`TEXT(Country__c) + " " + TEXT(State__c)`

This is shown in the following screenshot:

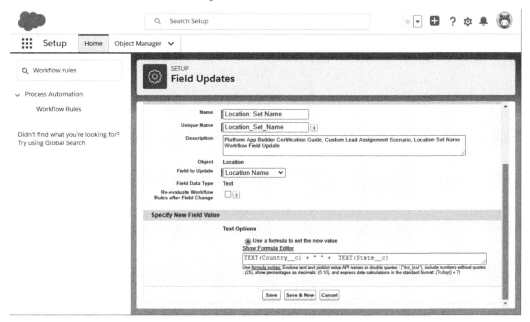

Figure 7.8 – Workflow Rule Details

Click on **Save** to continue.

14. Click on **Done** to complete the creation of the workflow rule as shown in the following screenshot:

Figure 7.9 – Workflow rule saved

Finally, click on **Activate** to activate the workflow rule as shown in the following screenshot:

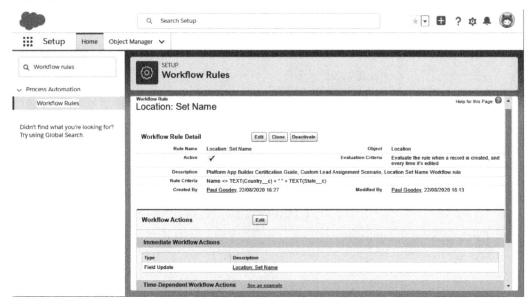

Figure 7.10 – Workflow rule activated

Let's see how this workflow rule helps to reduce inconsistent information from being captured when creating new Location records. Here, we will create a record for Canada with the Country picklist selection and no State value, as shown, by carrying out the following steps:

1. Navigate to the **Locations** list view and click the **New** button as shown in the following screenshot:

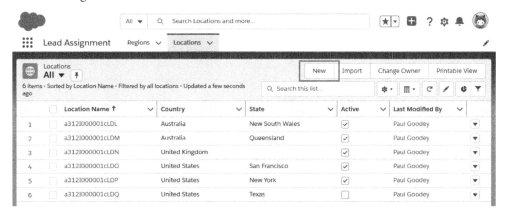

Figure 7.11 – The New button in the Locations list view

2. Enter CAN (a non-consistent value for Canada) in the **Location Name** field and select **Canada** for the **Country** picklist value.

3. Click on **Save** and observe that the name has been set to **Canada** as shown in the following screenshot:

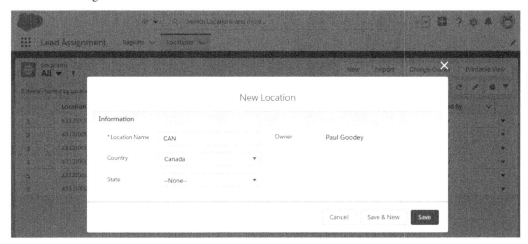

Figure 7.12 – New Location screen

4. After having saved the record, the name has been set to **Canada** as shown:

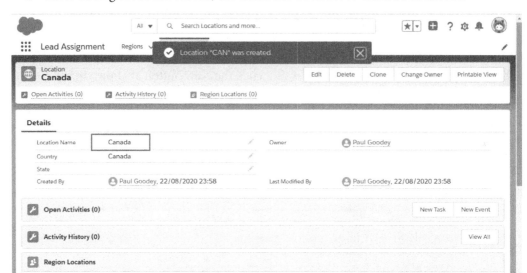

Figure 7.13 – New saved record screen

As a result of creating a workflow rule to set the record name whenever a Location record is created or updated using a formula, the format of the record name is saved in a consistent way and not only improves the data quality of the information for locations but simplifies the task of processing **Location** data.

Let's now implement an automation process using Flow.

Implementing automation processes using Flow

In *Chapter 2, Designing and Building a Data Model*, we were presented with an example scenario to help with the understanding of designing and building a data model. The scenario outlined a business requirement for us to build a custom **Lead Assignment** app and associated functionality. We'll now return to one of the core requirements and build process automation so that leads are automatically assigned to a salesperson based on the organization's sales regions.

We created custom objects called **Region, Location**, and **Region Location** to meet the requirements for the custom Lead Assignment app in *Chapter 2, Designing and Building a Data Model*, and we will now create a flow that will be used to set the salesperson field on a **Lead** record whenever a Lead is created by checking the values of the assignments within the **Region Location** record.

The flow will use the value of the Country and State that is set in the Lead to find the Country and State within the Region Location records and determine the salesperson user record that is set on the parent Location record.

As a reminder, the data model that we built in *Chapter 2, Designing and Building a Data Model,* which will enable this automation to be implemented, is shown in the following screenshot:

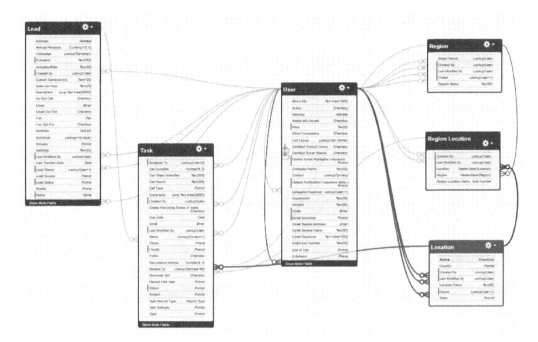

Figure 7.14 – Scenario schema

The purpose of the flow is to retrieve the **Sales Person** field within the Region record that is associated with the Region Location record that matches the Country and State values for the Lead record. Where there is a match, the Lead record is then updated to set the standard **Owner** field.

Before we continue, we must first create a new custom formula field on the **Region Location** object called **Country State** to enable the filtering of records during the retrieval of records with the Get Records operation in the flow. The formula will comprise the following:

```
TRIM(TEXT(Location__r.Country__c) + " " + TEXT(Location__r.
State__c))
```

The completed **Country State** field label should appear as shown in the following screenshot:

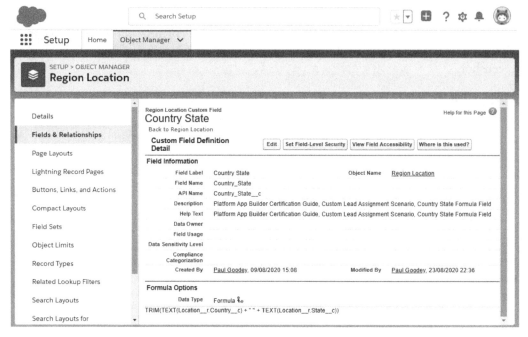

Figure 7.15 – Region Location object: Country State field label

Let's go ahead and implement the flow using Flow Builder by following these steps:

1. Navigate to **Setup** and then search for **Flows** in the Quick Find search box located at the top of the **Setup** menu on the left sidebar.

2. Click on **Flows** in the **Setup** menu.

3. Click on **New Flow** on the **Flows Setup** page.

4. On the **New Flow** option page, choose **Record-Triggered Flow** for the type of flow as shown in the following screenshot:

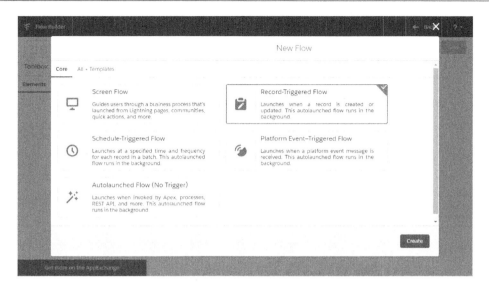

Figure 7.16 – New Flow: Record-Triggered Flow

5. Click on **Create** to continue.

6. In the dialog **How do you want to start building?** choose **Freeform** (at the time of writing, the **Auto-Layout** option enables auto-positioning of the elements when you add them to the Flow canvas).

The flow that we are going to implement will be triggered whenever new lead records are added to the Lightning Platform. The Flow comprises several steps and uses various types of elements to meet the requirement and uses the following features:

- **Get Records**: `GetRegionLocation` using a formula: `fma`
- **Get Records**: `GetRegion`
- **Assignment**: `SetLeadOwnerRegionSalesperson`
- **Update Records**: `UpdateLead`

Let's set up the flow to trigger on changes to the Lead record by carrying out the following steps:

1. In the **Flow** canvas section, locate the **Start** element and click on the **Edit** link.

2. On the **Configure Trigger** dialog screen, verify that the following default values are set:

    Trigger the Flow When: `A record is created`

    Run the Flow: `After the record is saved`

3. Click on either **Cancel** or **Done** (if you needed to amend the values).

4. In the **Start** element, click the **+ Choose Object** link.

5. On the **Choose Object** dialog screen, select the **Lead** record.

6. Set the picklist option **Condition Requirements** to **None**.

7. Click on **Done**.

The completed flow and the steps and elements that we are going to implement can be seen in the following screenshot:

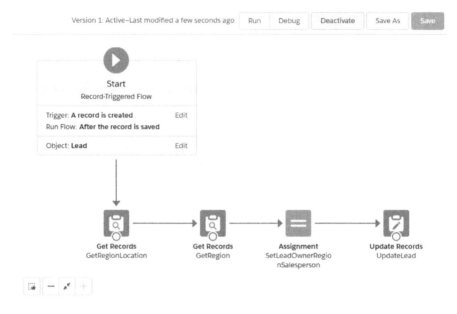

Figure 7.17 – Flow steps and elements

Let's set up the flow to query the data in the Region Location record and match the Country State to the Country State that is set in the Lead record. Note: in order to simplify the matching, we are going to create a formula in the flow that concatenates the lead Country and State field values into one field.

Get Records: GetRegionLocation

Let's implement the functionality for looking for the Country State that is set on the Region Location and create a formula element in the flow by carrying out the following steps:

1. In the **Toolbox** section, within the **Manager** tab, click the **New Resource** button and create a formula (set in the **Resource Type**) with the following values:

    API Name: fmaLeadCountryState

    Description: Platform App Builder Certification Guide, Custom Lead Assignment Scenario, Flow Formula Lead Country State

    Data Type: Text

    Formula:

    TRIM({!$Record.Country} + " " + {!$Record.State})

2. Click on the **Done** button as shown in the following screenshot:

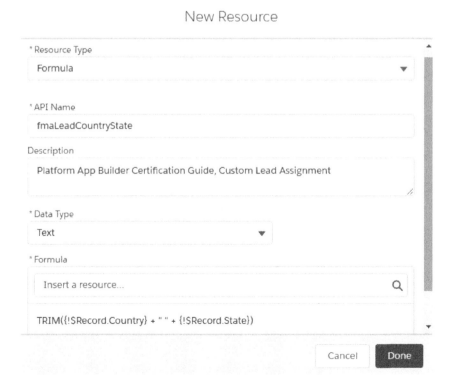

New Resource

* Resource Type

Formula

* API Name

fmaLeadCountryState

Description

Platform App Builder Certification Guide, Custom Lead Assignment

* Data Type

Text

* Formula

Insert a resource...

TRIM({!$Record.Country} + " " + {!$Record.State})

Cancel   Done

Figure 7.18 – Flow formula

3. In the **Toolbox** section, within the **Elements** tab, click the **Get Records** element and drag and drop it onto the **Canvas** section below the **Start** element.

4. On the **New Get Records** dialog screen, enter the following:

    Label: `GetRegionLocation`

    API Name: `GetRegionLocation` (set by default)

    Description: `Platform App Builder Certification Guide, Custom Lead Assignment Scenario, Flow Get Records Region Location`

    Get Records of This Object: `Region Location` (this will present further options to filter records)

    Condition Requirements: `All Conditions Are Met (AND)`

    Field: `Country_State__c`

    Operator: `Equals`

    Value: `{!fmaLeadCountryState}` (the formula we created previously)

    Sort Order: `Ascending`

    Sort By: `Id`

    How Many Records to Store: `Only the first record`

    How to Store Record Data: `Choose fields and let Salesforce do the rest`

    Select Region Location Fields to Store in Variable: `Field: ID and Field: Region__c`

5. Click on the **Done** button as shown in the following screenshot:

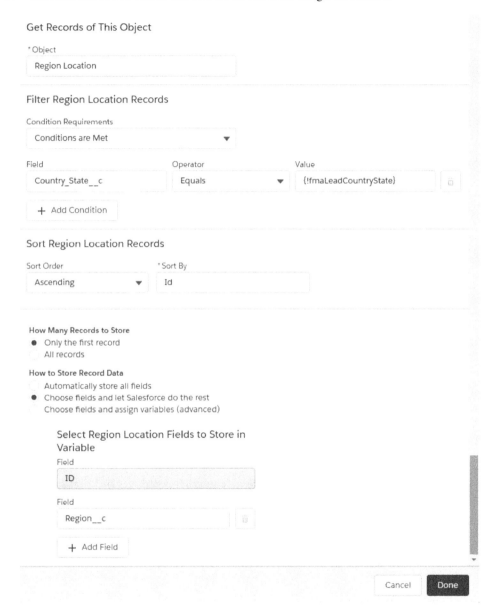

Figure 7.19 – Flow to get Region Location

Now, connect the **Start** element and the new **Get Records** element.

For **Get Records: GetRegion**, we see the following:

1. In the **Toolbox** section, within the **Elements** tab, click the **Get Records** element and drag and drop it onto the **Canvas** section to the right of the **GetRegionLocation** element.

2. On the **New Get Records** dialog screen, enter the following:

Label: GetRegion

API Name: GetRegion (set by default)

Description: Platform App Builder Certification Guide, Custom Lead Assignment Scenario, Flow Get Records Region

Get Records of This Object: Region (this will present further options to filter records)

Condition Requirements: All Conditions Are Met (AND)

Field: Id

Operator: Equals

Value: {!GetRegionLocation.Region__c} (the **Get Records** element we created previously)

Sort Order: Ascending

Sort By: Id

How Many Records to Store: Only the first record

How to Store Record Data: Choose fields and let Salesforce do the rest

Select Region Location Fields to Store in Variable: **Field**: ID and **Field**: Sales_ Person__c

3. Click on the **Done** button as shown in the following screenshot:

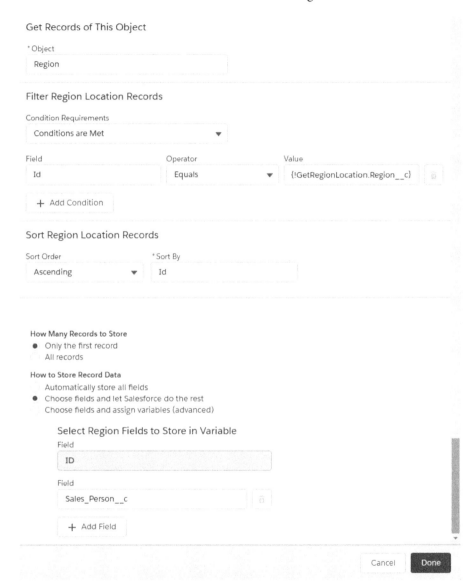

Figure 7.20 – Flow Get Region

Now, connect the **GetRegionLocation** element and the new **Get Records** element.

We are working with the **Assignment: SetLeadOwnerRegionSalesperson**. This is how it goes:

1. In the **Toolbox** section, within the **Elements** tab, click the **Assignment** element and drag and drop it onto the canvas section to the right of the **GetRegion** element.

2. On the **New Assignment** dialog screen, enter the following:

    Label: `SetLeadOwnerRegionSalesperson`

    API Name: `SetLeadOwnerRegionSalesperson` (set by default)

    Description: `Platform App Builder Certification Guide, Custom Lead Assignment Scenario, Flow Assignment Lead Owner Region Salesperson`

    Variable: `{!$Record.OwnerId}`

    Operator: `Equals`

    Value: `{!GetRegion.Sales_Person__c}`

3. Click on the **Done** button as shown in the following screenshot:

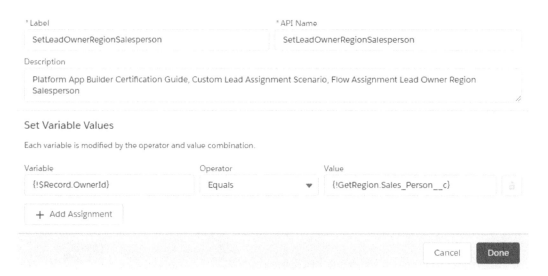

Figure 7.21 – Flow assignment

4. Now, connect the **GetRegion** element and the new **Assignment** element.

We will now configure an element to update a record.

Update Records: UpdateLead

To add an element to update records, carry out the following steps:

1. In the **Toolbox** section, within the **Elements** tab, click the **Update Records** element and drag and drop it onto the canvas section to the right of the **SetLeadOwnerRegionSalesperson** element.

2. On the **New Update Records** dialog screen, enter the following:

   Label: UpdateLead

   API Name: UpdateLead (set by default)

   Description: Platform App Builder Certification Guide, Custom Lead Assignment Scenario, Flow Update Records Lead

   How to Find Records to Update and Set Their Values: Use the IDs and all field values from a record or record collection

3. In the **Select Record(s) to Update** section, enter the following:

   ```
   Record or Record Collection: {!$Record}
   ```

4. Click on the **Done** button as shown in the following screenshot:

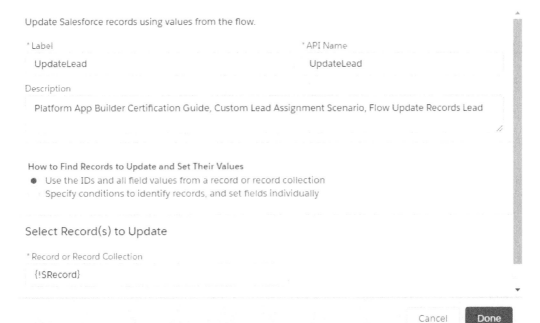

Figure 7.22 – Flow Update Record

5. Now, connect the `SetLeadOwnerRegionSalesperson` element and the new `Update Records` element.

To save the flow, click on the **Save** button to present the **Save the flow** dialog and enter the following:

Flow Label: `Lead Update Owner`

Flow API Name: `Lead_Update_Owner` (set by default)

Description: `Platform App Builder Certification Guide, Custom Lead Assignment Scenario, Flow to Update Lead Owner from Region Salesperson`

6. Click on the **Save** button as shown in the following screenshot:

Figure 7.23 – Save the flow

7. Finally, click on the **Activate** button to activate the flow as shown in the following screenshot:

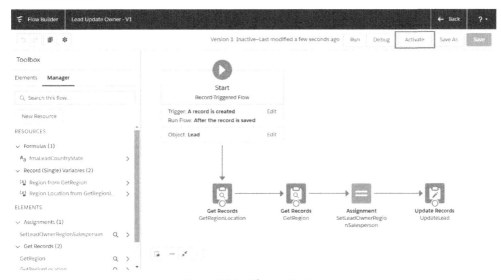

Figure 7.24 – Flow activation

As a result of creating the flow to query the Country and State that is set on the Region Location records based on the Country and State that has been recorded on the lead record, it is possible to identify which salesperson to set as the owner of the lead.

Let's now configure an automation process using Process Builder.

Configuring automation processes using Process Builder

In *Chapter 2*, *Designing and Building a Data Model*, we were presented with an example scenario to help with our understanding of designing and building a data model. The scenario outlined a business requirement for us to build a custom Lead Assignment app and associated functionality.

We'll now return to this requirement for process automation, where leads are automatically assigned to a salesperson based on the organization's sales regions, and for this automation process, we'll configure Process Builder to automatically create a task record whenever lead records are assigned to a salesperson.

We created custom objects called Region, Location, and Region Location to meet the requirements for the custom Lead Assignment app in *Chapter 2*, *Designing and Building a Data Model*, and we will now create a process with Process Builder that will be initiated when the owner of the lead record changes.

Let's go ahead and configure the automation using Process Builder by following these steps:

1. Navigate to **Setup** and then search for **Process Builder** in the Quick Find search box located at the top of the **Setup** menu on the left sidebar.

2. Click on **Process Builder** in the **Setup** menu.

3. Click on **New** on the **My Processes List View Page** page.

4. On the **New Process** dialog screen, enter the following:

    Process Name: Lead Assignment Owner Task

    API Name: Lead_Assignment_Owner_Task (set by default)

    Description: Platform App Builder Certification Guide, Custom Lead Assignment Scenario, Lead Assignment Owner Task Process Builder

    The process starts when: A record changes

5. Click on **Save** to continue as shown in the following screenshot:

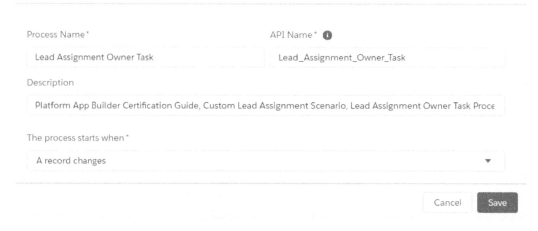

Figure 7.25 – Process Builder New Process dialog

6. In the Process Builder **Canvas** section, click on the **+ Add Object** link to present the **Choose Object and Specify When to Start the Process** section.

7. In the **Choose Object and Specify When to Start the Process** section, enter the following:

Object: **Lead**

Start the process: **when a record is created or edited**

8. In the **Advanced** section, leave the checkbox **Yes** unchecked for the setting **Recursion - Allow process to evaluate a record multiple times in a single save operation**.

9. Click on **Save** to continue as shown in the following screenshot:

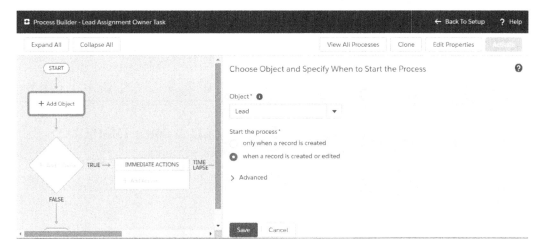

Figure 7.26 – Process Builder: choose when to start

10. Click on + **Add Criteria** to present the **Define Criteria for this Action Group** section.

11. In the **Define Criteria for this Action Group** section, enter the following:

Criteria Name: Create Task for Lead Owner

Criteria for Executing Actions: Formula evaluates to true

Enter the following formula (this checks that the owner is changing and that the new owner is a user and not a queue):

```
AND (
  ISCHANGED ( [Lead].OwnerId ),
  LEFT([Lead].OwnerId,3)= "005"
)
```

12. Click on **Save** to continue as shown in the following screenshot:

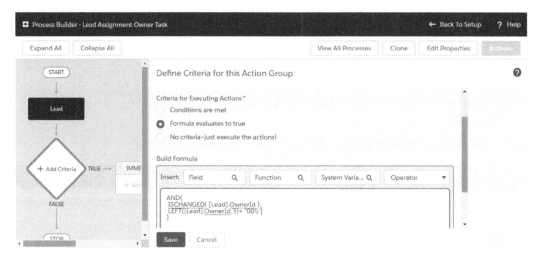

Figure 7.27 – Process Builder criteria

13. In the Process Builder Canvas section, click on **+ Add Action** in **IMMEDIATE ACTIONS** to present the **Select and Define Action** section.

14. In the **Select and Define Action** section, enter the following:

Action Type: Create a Record

Action Name: New Task for Lead Owner

Record Type: **Task**, as shown in the following screenshot:

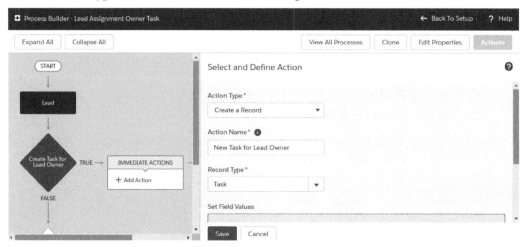

Figure 7.28 – Process Builder Action 1

15. Scroll down to the **Set Field Values** section and enter the following:

Field: `Due Date Only`, **Type**: `Formula`, **Value**: `TODAY() + 7`

Field: `Assigned To ID`, **Type**: `Field Reference`, **Value**: `[Lead].OwnerId`

Field: `Priority`, **Type**: `Picklist`, **Value**: `Normal`

Field: `Status`, **Type**: `Picklist`, **Value**: `Not Started`

Field: **Name ID**, **Type**: `Field Reference`, **Value**: `[Lead].Id`

Although not needed here, if you need to set more field values, you can click on +
Add Row to show more field values.

16. Click on **Save** as shown in the following screenshot:

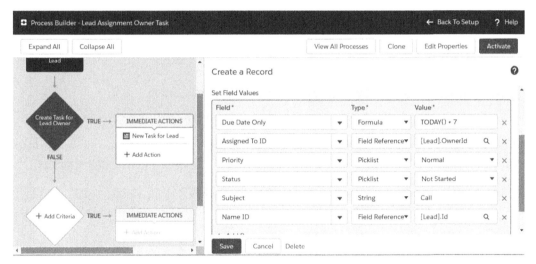

Figure 7.29 – Process Builder Action 2

17. Click on **Activate** as shown in the following screenshot:

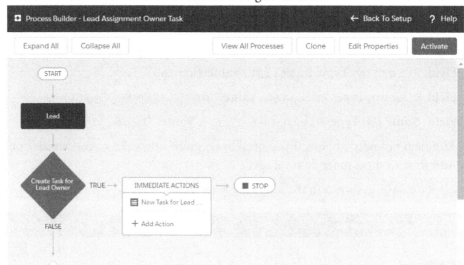

Figure 7.30 – Process Builder: the Activate button

18. Finally, on the **Activate Version** dialog, click **Confirm** to activate Process Builder.

As a result of creating the Process Builder process, a task will be created whenever the lead owner is changed to action the new owner to call the lead 7 days after the date that the lead record was assigned.

In this scenario, a lead called **Smith** is assigned to a new owner as shown in the following screenshot:

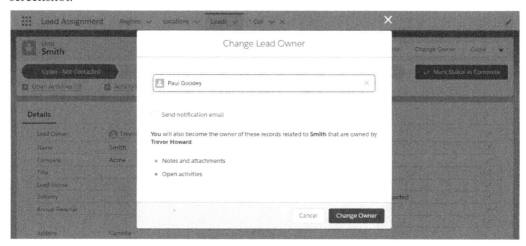

Figure 7.31 – Process Builder Lead Assignment

After selecting the new owner and clicking the **Change Owner** button, the following new task record is created:

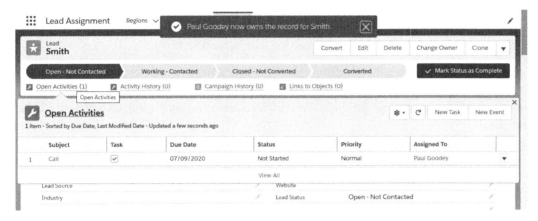

Figure 7.32 – Process Builder lead task created

Let's now look at the implications of auto-updating fields and recursion issues within process automation.

Understanding the implications of auto-updating fields

Earlier in this chapter, we looked at the limits that exist when building process automation processes in the Lightning Platform. We detailed the limits at the org level but noted that the limits also apply at the object level. The process automation limits at the object level see a restriction on the number of active automation processes regardless of which automation tool is needed. This is because there is an underlying impact of auto-updating fields, whether the update is being performed using Workflow, Flow, or Process Builder.

The impact of auto-updating fields can lead to performance issues and also create record update conflicts during the updating of records and is an important concept to consider when building process automation in the Lightning Platform.

We will now look at two areas of concern that affect Workflow when auto-updating fields. These areas of concern are caused by the setting of **re-evaluations of workflow rules** and also by the **non-deterministic** nature of Workflow.

Understanding the re-evaluation of workflow rules

When creating workflow rules, there is an option that can be set to re-evaluate workflow rules after the workflow actions have been triggered.

The action of setting the re-evaluation setting within workflow rules according to Salesforce is as follows:

If the field update changes the field's value, all workflow rules on the associated object are re-evaluated. Any workflow rules whose criteria are met as a result of the field update will be triggered.

The effect of setting the re-evaluation setting within workflow rules according to Salesforce is as follows:

If any of the triggered workflow rules result in another field update that's also enabled for workflow rule re-evaluation, a domino effect occurs, and more workflow rules can be re-evaluated as a result of the newly-triggered field update. This cascade of workflow rule re-evaluation and triggering can happen up to five times after the initial field update that started it.

Salesforce advises that you should do the following:

Make sure that your workflow rules aren't set up to create recursive loops. For example, if a field update for Rule1 triggers Rule2, and a field update for Rule2 triggers Rule1, the recursive triggers may cause your organization to exceed its limit for workflow time triggers per hour.

> **Setting the re-evaluation setting within workflow rules**
>
> For more details about the impacts and mitigations when setting the re-evaluation of workflow rules, refer to the following article:
>
> ```
> https://help.salesforce.com/
> articleView?id=workflow_field_updates_reevalute_
> wf.htm&type=5
> ```

Salesforce describes workflow rules as always being non-deterministic, so let's now consider the non-deterministic nature of Workflow.

Considering the non-deterministic nature of Workflow

When creating workflow rules, there is no option to set the order of execution for each of the workflow rules as workflow rules are always non-deterministic.

> **Workflow rules are always non-deterministic**
>
> For more details about how Salesforce cannot guarantee which order workflow rules will be evaluated in, refer to the following Trailhead guide:
>
> ```
> https://trailhead.salesforce.com/en/content/learn/
> modules/workflow_migration/workflow_migration_
> criteria
> ```

As a result of this non-deterministic behavior of Workflow, Salesforce recommends using Process Builder instead, where there are automation processes that can be triggered and the execution action is available in a process.

This is because Process Builder allows the creation of a single process that is performed on the given object so that all actions can be determined and ordered appropriately. Here, it is important to order the criteria nodes in Process Builder correctly, otherwise, the same issues with the behavior of the non-deterministic workflow will result.

If you create multiple processes for a given object, you risk the same problem as you had with workflow rules. Salesforce therefore recommends setting the process automation for all actions in one process, whenever possible.

So whenever possible, use Process Builder and replace Workflow as described in the following guide.

> **Salesforce recommends the following for Workflow and Process Builder**
>
> The following Trailhead details exist for the recommendation from Salesforce:
>
> *"...it's best practice to avoid mixing processes (from Process Builder) with workflow rules for a given object. Otherwise, you can't guarantee what order the processes and workflow rules are evaluated in. If you want to replace one case workflow rule with a process, we recommend migrating every case workflow rule to Process Builder".*
>
> The URL for this can be found at: ```https://trailhead.salesforce.com/en/content/learn/modules/workflow_migration/workflow_migration_intro```

Let's now look at some questions to test your knowledge of automating business processes in Salesforce Lightning.

Questions to test your knowledge

We'll now present six questions to help assess your knowledge of automating business processes in the Lightning Platform. There are questions about using approvals, Workflow, Flow, and Process Builder, along with recommendations for business requirements and auto-updating fields with recursion issues.

Question 1 – Automating business processes

The new sales director in your organization, who is not familiar with Salesforce, has asked you to notify them, somehow, whenever salespeople indicate giving discounts of over 20% to customers midway through the sales process so that they can chat about the discount with the salesperson. Which automation solution could you recommend that meets this requirement? (Select one)

a) Create a workflow rule of opportunities and filter where the discount is >=20% and opportunity probability=50%, and send a task to the sales director to chat to the salesperson.

b) Create a validation rule on the opportunity for the criteria discounts that are >=20% and opportunity probability=50% to stop the salesperson so they have to chat with the sales director.

c) Create an approval process with the entry criteria discount as >=20% and opportunity probability=50% and allow the salesperson to submit a request for approval from the sales director.

d) Create a scheduled report of opportunities and filter where the discount is >=20% and opportunity probability=50% and send it to the sales director.

Question 2 – Workflow capabilities

Which of the following is not a capability of Workflow? (Select one)

a) Able to update fields on a parent master-detail record

b) Able to send an outbound message

c) Able to create **Event** records

d) Able to send emails

Question 3 – Flow capabilities

Which of the following are capabilities of Flow? (Select two)

a) Able to call Apex code

b) Able to invoke a **Quick Action** (to create a record, update a record, or log a call)

c) Supports user interaction

d) Able to send an outbound message

Question 4 – Process Builder capabilities

Which of the following are capabilities of Process Builder? (Select two)

a) Able to send an outbound message

b) Can be triggered by another process

c) Able to invoke a **Quick Action** (to create a record, update a record, or log a call)

d) Supports user interaction

Question 5 – Recommending a solution for a business requirement

The sales director in your organization has asked you to build an automation process that updates a custom date field on the account record to show the date that the latest won opportunity associated with the parent account was changed, in which the **Stage** was changed to **Closed Won**. There are no other automation processes within the Salesforce org. Which solution has the capability for this requirement and is recommended by Salesforce? (Select one)

a) Workflow

b) Approval process

c) Process Builder

d) Roll-up summary

Question 6 – Re-evaluation of workflow rules

Which of the following statements is not true about the behavior of workflow rules when the re-evaluation of workflow rules is set in the Lightning Platform? (Select one)

a) The limit for workflow time triggers per hour may be exceeded.

b) Up to five workflow triggers can occur after the initial field update.

c) Up to five fields can be updated after the initial field update.

d) Multiple workflow rules can be re-evaluated.

Here are the answers to the six questions:

Answer 1 – Automating business processes

The answer is c):

c) Create an approval process with the entry criteria discount of >=20% and opportunity probability=50% and allow the salesperson to submit a request for approval from the sales director.

The following choices are not correct:

a) Create a workflow rule of opportunities and filter where the discount is >=20% and opportunity probability=50% and send a task to the sales director to chat to the salesperson.

b) Create a validation rule on the opportunity for where the criteria discount is >=20% and opportunity probability=50% to stop the salesperson so they have to chat with the sales director.

d) Create a scheduled report of opportunities and filter where the discount is >=20% and opportunity probability=50% and send to the sales director.

Answer 2 – Workflow capabilities

The answer is c):

c) Able to create Event records

The following choices are not correct:

a) Able to update fields on a parent master-detail record

b) Able to send an outbound message

d) Able to send emails

Answer 3 – Flow capabilities

The answers are a) and c):

a) Able to call Apex code

c) Supports user interaction

The following choices are not correct:

b) Able to invoke a **Quick Action** (to create a record, update a record, or log a call)

d) Able to send an outbound message

Answer 4 – Process Builder capabilities

The answers are b) and c):

b) Can be triggered by another process

c) Able to invoke a **Quick Action** (to create a record, update a record, or log a call)

The following choices are not correct:

a) Able to send an outbound message

d) Supports user interaction

Answer 5 – Recommending a solution for a business requirement

The answer is c):

c) Process Builder

The following choices are not correct:

a) Workflow

b) Approval process

d) Roll-up summary

Answer 6 – Re-evaluation of workflow rules

The answer is c):

c) Up to five fields can be updated after the initial field update.

The following choices are not correct:

a) The limit for workflow time triggers per hour may be exceeded.

b) Up to five workflow triggers can occur after the initial field update.

d) Multiple workflow rules can be re-evaluated.

Summary

In this chapter, you have gained knowledge of the options and capabilities that exist for building process automation in the Lightning Platform.

You have learned how, with the use of approval processes, the mechanisms of approving or rejecting records can be automated from within the Lightning Platform and by responding to email requests.

You understood and learned how to build automation processes for Workflow, Flow, and Process Builder, and the options that are available will equip you with the necessary skills and confidence to configure process automation in the Lightning Platform.

In the next chapter, we will look at this exam objective: Describe the features and capabilities available when creating reports, report types, and dashboards. You will be presented with the features that are available in the Lightning Platform to create analytics with reports and dashboards.

8
Generating Data Analytics with Reports and Dashboards

In this chapter, we will look at the features and capabilities available to generate data analytics in Salesforce Lightning.

You will learn about the options that exist for generating reports and how standard reports can be created using standard report types. You will discover how to configure custom report types, which allow the type of report found in standard report types to be enhanced and extended.

You will discover how you can build dashboards to visually represent the data in your Salesforce organization and learn how dashboards can be scheduled and configured to show the data from the perspective of either a named user or the logged-in user.

Finally, you will be presented with a number of questions about generating data analytics with reports and dashboards in the Lightning Platform that will help reinforce your skills for building reports and dashboards and equip you with the knowledge to take the Certified Platform App exam.

In this chapter, we will cover the following topics:

- Exam objectives: Reporting
- Understanding Salesforce data analytics options
- Creating reports in the Lightning Platform
- Configuring custom report types
- Building dashboards in the Lightning Platform
- Questions to test your knowledge

Exam objectives – Reporting

To complete the *Reporting* section of the Certified Platform App Builder exam, app builders are expected to be able to carry out the following:

Describe the features and capabilities available when creating reports, report types, and dashboards.

> **Reference: Salesforce Certified Platform App Builder Exam Guide**
>
> This guide is published by Salesforce and can be referenced at `https://trailhead.salesforce.com/help?article=Salesforce-Certified-Platform-App-Builder-Exam-Guide`.

In the Salesforce Certified Platform App Builder Exam Guide, the total number of questions is given, along with a percentage breakdown for each of the objectives, and an indication of the number of features/functions that can be expected in each of the objectives.

By analyzing these objectives, percentages, and question counts, we can determine the likely number of questions that will appear in the exam and, for the *Reporting* objective, this is as follows:

> **Reporting: Total number of exam questions**
>
> There are likely to be 3 questions in total.
>
> This is calculated as 5% of 60 total exam questions.

To help reinforce the skills and knowledge for *creating reports and building dashboards*, there is practical work for you to do in Salesforce, so if you do not have a Salesforce environment in which to carry this out, create a free developer org as detailed in *Chapter 1, Core Capabilities of the Lightning Platform*.

We will continue to use an example business scenario that we covered in *Chapter 2, Designing and Building a Data Model*, to demonstrate how the features in the Lightning Platform support the creation of reports, report types, and dashboards.

Let's look at the data analytics options in the Lightning Platform.

Understanding Salesforce data analytics options

In previous chapters, we have covered various mechanisms that involve the use of data such as the design and build of a data model, the importing and exporting of data, and the securing of access to data. The data in the Lightning Platform and Salesforce CRM is a fundamental aspect of the customer relationship management business application. Without data, the Lightning Platform provides very little business benefit.

Data analytics provides the facilities to analyze data that exists or has been generated within a system. By analyzing the data in the Lightning Platform and supporting systems, you can produce reports and dashboards that help to determine metrics, discover hidden insights, and improve business process and overall performance measures.

In the Salesforce suite of data analytics products, there are various options available for carrying out a range of analysis and reporting. These products are either provided out of the box within the Lightning Platform as a standard feature or, for more complex data analytics, are available as an application suite that must be obtained separately to the core features in the Lightning Platform.

Let's first look at the data analytics features that are available out of the box within the Lightning Platform.

Data analytics features in the Lightning Platform

The data analytics features in the Lightning Platform offer facilities to report and visualize data that is accessible from within the platform, and there are various options and capabilities that you as an app builder should be aware of when studying for the Certified Platform App Builder exam.

There are various terms used in relation to data analytics that you will encounter when learning about the features and tools that are available in the Lightning Platform. These are as follows:

- **Lightning Reporting**: Lightning Reporting refers to the mechanism of creating reports using the Lightning report builder, which enables you to analyze data by grouping, filtering, summarizing, and displaying record values in a chart graphic within the Lightning Experience user interface.

- **Classic Reporting**: Classic Reporting refers to the mechanism of creating reports using the report tab within the Salesforce Classic user interface. Classic reporting enables you to analyze data by grouping, filtering, summarizing, and displaying record values in a chart graphic.

- **Lightning Experience dashboard**: Lightning Experience dashboards are used to display a graphical view of report data and are constructed using pre-existing report(s) and show either table, metric, chart, or gauge dashboard components within the Lightning Experience user interface.

- **Salesforce Classic dashboard**: Salesforce Classic dashboards are used to display a graphical view of report data and are built using pre-existing report(s) and show either table, metric, chart, or gauge dashboard components in the Salesforce Classic user interface.

- **Report Types**: Report Types are used with both Lightning reporting and Classic reporting and are used to pre-define which data can be used to create the report. Salesforce provides standard report types and you can also create custom report types.

- **Report Types (standard)**: The standard report types that are provided by Salesforce give access to standard and custom object data standard and appear out of the box for the standard objects and are automatically created when you create custom objects.

- **Custom Report Types**: Custom Report Types refers to the mechanism that enables you to create customized report types with specific criteria not present in the standard report types to control which data is available when creating reports.

The following diagram shows the relationship between the underlying mechanisms of report types, reports, and dashboards:

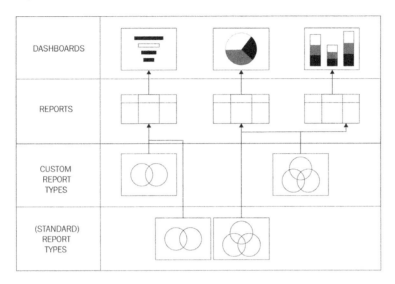

Figure 8.1 – Reporting mechanisms

Now, let's look at other data analytics options that are available by Salesforce.

Other data analytics options by Salesforce

In addition to the out-of-the-box data analytics within the Lightning Platform, there are the following data analytics tools and reporting platforms available from Salesforce:

- **Einstein Analytics**: Einstein Analytics is a cloud-based data analytics platform and provides complex analysis features that offer fast and sophisticated insight using artificial intelligence and natural language analysis features for data that resides in both the Lightning Platform and in external data sources. Einstein Analytics was formerly known as *Wave*.

- **Tableau**: Tableau is an on-premise and cloud-based data analytics platform and provides complex data visualization features that allow for user self-service and statistical analysis for data that resides in various business data sources, including the Lightning Platform.

These other Salesforce products and reporting platforms are not covered in the Certified Platform App Builder exam and are not required knowledge for an app builder.

In this chapter, we will be covering reports and dashboards and the report builder, which are available in the Lightning Platform. Now, let's look at the capabilities of the reporting features in the Lightning Platform.

Creating reports in the Lightning Platform

As an app builder, you will need to know how to create reports and understand the various options that are available to you for the building and formatting of reports in the Lightning Platform.

Reports are used to display one or more fields for the records that are accessible within the platform and you can choose the appropriate report type that allows for the fields of a given object or set of objects to be selected.

You can imagine that the fields that are selected form a table of data for the report details and you can apply various filters to control the breadth and depth of information that is retrieved and displayed. Filters, therefore, are used to determine which results are returned. Using the analogy of a table of data, the results are the rows in the table.

Salesforce recommends that in order to improve the performance and enable reports to run quicker, you only include fields that are strictly necessary to display the information that you require and remove any fields that are not needed.

It is important to understand the following terms for creating reports in the Lightning Platform:

- **Lightning report builder**: The Lightning report builder is a tool with a visual interface that allows you to build reports using point-and-click features to create new reports and edit existing reports within the Lightning Experience user interface. Reports built in Salesforce Classic are compatible in the Lightning report builder.

- **Report builder**: The report builder refers to the Salesforce Classic tool that allows you to build reports using point-and-click features to create new reports and edit existing reports within the Salesforce Classic user interface. Reports built in Lightning report builder are compatible in the Salesforce Classic report builder.

- **Report format**: The report format is used to specify the way in which the report results (rows and columns) are formulated and displayed. The options that are available are tabular, summary, matrix, and joined.

- **Tabular report format**: Tabular reports allow you to create lists that can be thought of as a table of data and are the default report format when you first create a report.

- **Summary report format**: Summary reports allow you to create reports with grouped data using summarized and aggregated information by data rows.

- **Matrix report format**: Matrix reports allow you to create reports with grouped data using summarized and aggregated information that is also aggregated by column as well as by data rows.

- **Joined report format**: Joined reports allow you to create reports that take data from other reports and are associated with key values to visualize information in side-by-side data blocks.

- **Filtering reports**: Filtering of reports allows you to limit the rows of data that are returned in the report results and can be used to extract specific data. The filtering of reports is carried out using **Report Filters** and can also be useful in improving the performance of running reports and allow report data to load quicker.

- **Scheduling and Subscribing to reports**: Scheduling and Subscribing to reports allows you to receive notifications with report information without needing to run the report manually. In Salesforce Classic, in addition to scheduling and subscribing, you can also specify criteria for the report data that can be used to initiate the report notifications.

Let's now look at the features and functions for creating reports in the Lightning report builder.

Creating reports using the Lightning report builder

In the Lightning Platform, there are two tools for creating reports, namely, the Lightning report builder, which uses the **Lightning Experience** user interface, and the earlier tool called the **Report builder**, which makes use of the Salesforce Classic user interface.

You can access the Report builder to build reports using Salesforce Classic features from within the Lightning Experience user interface, but you cannot access the Lightning report builder from within the Salesforce Classic user interface.

The Lightning report builder is a tool with a visual interface that allows you to build reports using point-and-click features to create new reports and edit existing reports within the Lightning Experience user interface and that enables grouping, filtering, and so on, as shown in the following screenshot:

Figure 8.2 – Report Builder UI

As shown in the preceding screenshot, the user interface for the Lightning report builder comprises the following sections:

1. **Filters**: The **Filters** function allows you to limit the rows of data that are returned in the report results and can be used to extract specific data.

2. **Menu Bar**: The functions in the Menu Bar allow you to undo or redo actions, add a chart, save, run the report, and access the report properties.

3. **Groups**: The **Groups** section allows you to group the report by rows and columns.

4. **Fields Pane**: The fields pane allows you to search and select available fields. You can also create aggregate formulas that can be added to summary sections for summarizing values.

5. **Columns**: The **Columns** section allows you to add or remove report columns used in conjunction with the fields pane.

6. **Report Preview Pane**: The report preview pane can be used to show the report rows and columns and is used in conjunction with the fields pane to add fields.

7. **Totals Toggles**: The toggle options allow you to select summary values that include the Row Counts, Detail Rows, Subtotals, and the Grand Total. Within this area, you can also select the **Conditional Formatting** option, which allows you to highlight field values using colors to represent a value range. The **Totals** toggles and **Conditional Formatting** options are only available for summary or matrix reports where there are summarized values or formulas.

Update Preview Automatically Toggle

You can edit reports quicker by switching off the option to update the preview automatically. When **Update Preview Automatically Toggle** is on, the report preview is refreshed after each change you make. Therefore, it can be more time-efficient to switch the toggle on only when you are ready to view the preview.

Let's now look at the practicalities of building reports that satisfy a specific business requirement by implementing a report with the use of the Lightning report builder.

Implementing Lightning reports

In *Chapter 2*, *Designing and Building a Data Model*, we were presented with an example scenario to help with the understanding of designing and building a data model. The scenario outlined a business requirement for us to build a custom lead assignment app and associated functionality. We now return to one of the core requirements, build process automation, so that leads are automatically assigned to a sales person based on the organization's sales regions.

We created custom objects called `Region`, `Location`, and `Region Location` to meet the requirements for the custom `Lead Assignment` app in *Chapter 2*, *Designing and Building a Data Model*, and we will now create a summary report that will be used to display the number of active locations.

The report will use the `Region`, `Location`, and `Region Location` records and, as a reminder, the data model that we built in *Chapter 2, Designing and Building a Data Model*, which will enable this reporting to be implemented, is shown in the following screenshot:

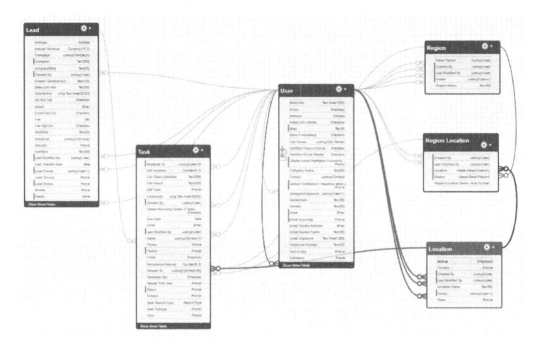

Figure 8.3 – Scenario schema

The purpose of the report is to display the number of active locations that are associated with regions and the name of the salesperson who is to be assigned any lead record for that region.

Let's go ahead and create the **Active Region Locations Report** using the Lightning report builder by following these steps:

1. Optionally add the **Reports** tab to an applicable app (in this example, we have added the **Reports and Dashboard** tabs to the **Lead Assignment** app that we created in *Chapter 5, Setting Up the User Interface*).

2. Click on the **Reports** tab.

3. Click on **New Report** in the **Reports** tab.

4. In the **Choose Report Type** page, search for `Region` and then select the **Regions with Region Locations** and **Locations** report type.

5. Click on **Continue** to continue.

6. In the **GROUP ROWS** section, add the **Region: Region Name** field.

7. In the **Columns** section, add the fields **Location: Location Name**, **Sales Person**, and **Location: Active**, as shown in the following screenshot:

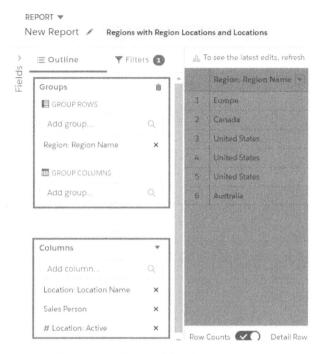

Figure 8.4 – Creating New Report regions

8. Click on the **Save** button in the Menu Bar to save the report.

9. In the **Save Report** dialog, enter the following:

    Report Name: `Regions: Active Region Locations Report`

    Report Unique Name: `Regions_Active_Region_Locations_Report_XYZ` (set by default)

    Description: `Platform App Builder Certification Guide, Custom Lead Assignment Scenario, Regions Active Locations Report`

    Folder: `Private Reports`

10. Finally, click on the **Save** button to save the report, as shown in the following screenshot:

Save Report

* Report Name

Regions: Active Region Locations Report

Report Unique Name ⓘ

Regions_Active_Region_Locations_Report_IsQ

Report Description

Platform App Builder Certification Guide, Custom Lead Assignment Scenario, Regions Active Locations Report

Folder

Private Reports   Select Folder ▼

Cancel   Save

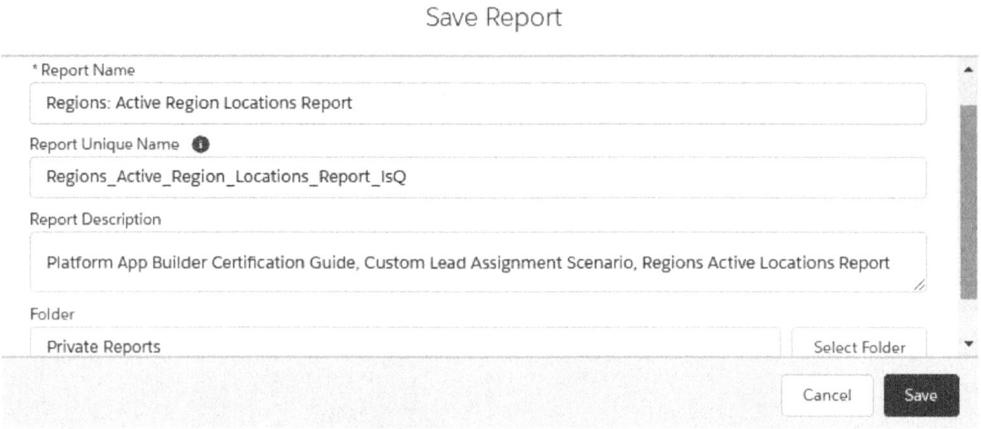

Figure 8.5 – Create a new report and save it

Upon saving the report, preview the resulting rows and columns that have been grouped by the **Region** name. In addition, the summary values have been included to display the row counts, detail rows, subtotals, and the grand total, as shown in the following screenshot:

Figure 8.6 – Creating a new saved report

When creating reports, there are various considerations that you need to be aware of that may limit the types and amount of information that can be reported on, which we will cover now.

Considering limits and allocations for reporting

There are a number of limits and allocations applied by Salesforce to restrict the number of report elements that can be created in total. There are also limits that restrict the number of report elements that can be processed per person and per hour.

The following limits apply to reporting in the Lightning Platform:

- **Total number of custom report types per org (Unlimited/Performance Edition)**: 2,000

- **Total number of custom report types per org (Enterprise Edition)**: 200

- **Total number of scheduled reports per hour (Unlimited/Performance Edition)**: 2

- **Total number of scheduled reports per hour (Enterprise Edition)**: 1

- **Total number of subscriptions to reports per person**: 5 reports

> **Report limits, limitations, and allocations in the Lightning Platform**
>
> For more details about the limits for reports, refer to the following article:
>
> ```
> https://help.salesforce.com/articleView?id=rd_
> reports_dashboards_limits.htm&type=5
> ```

Let's now configure a custom report type to extend the standard report types in the Lightning Platform.

Configuring custom report types

As an app builder, you will need to understand how to build and use custom report types in the Lightning Platform.

When we created the report earlier in this chapter, we selected a standard report type that associated the `Region`, `Region Location`, and `Location` custom objects and allowed the custom fields to be accessed in our report. Standard report types cannot be modified and if we wanted to associate another object with our source report type or hide any of the fields to prevent them from being selected by users, we can create a custom report type.

Custom report types allow the extension of standard and custom objects and field relationships that allow up to four related objects to be used as the source for new reports. Within the custom report type, you can include up to 1,000 fields.

We could configure a custom report type that associates the custom `Location` object with the standard `Task` activity object, which would be useful as a way of reporting any tasks that were linked to any `Location` records. A practical use case for this would be if we chose to create a task record whenever an approval was submitted for a new location to be used.

Let's go ahead and configure a custom report type that associates the custom `Location` object with the standard `Task` activity object by following these steps:

1. Navigate to **Setup** and then search for `Report Types` in the **Quick Find** search box located at the top of the **Setup** menu on the left side bar.

2. Click on **Report Types** in the **Setup** menu.

3. Click on **New Custom Report Type** in the **All Custom Report Types** page.

4. In the **Step 1. Define the Custom Report Type** dialog screen, enter the following:

    Primary Object: `Locations`

    Report Type Label: `Locations with Activities`

    Report Type Name: `Locations_with_Activities` (set by default)

    Description: `Platform App Builder Certification Guide, Custom Lead Assignment Scenario, Locations with Activities Custom Report Type`

    Store in Category: `Other Reports`

    Deployment Status: `Deployed`

5. Click on **Next**.

6. In the **Step 2. Define Report Records Set** dialog screen, select the following:

    A: Primary Object: `Locations`

    B: A to B Relationship: `Each "A" record must have at least one related "B" record`

    C: B to C Relationship: `"B" records may or may not have related "C" records`

7.   Click on **Save**, as shown in the following screenshot:

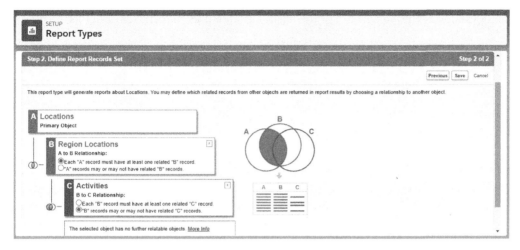

Figure 8.7 – New custom report type

Upon saving the custom report type, you can then choose which fields to make available when users select the custom report type when they create new reports and also configure a page layout in which you can create sections to group together the fields.

Only the fields that you specify on the page layout will be available in any resulting reports based on the custom record type. If you delete a custom report type, all reports that were created using that custom report type are deleted.

The saved custom report allows the fields and resulting rows and columns to be set on the custom record type page layout, as shown in the following screenshot:

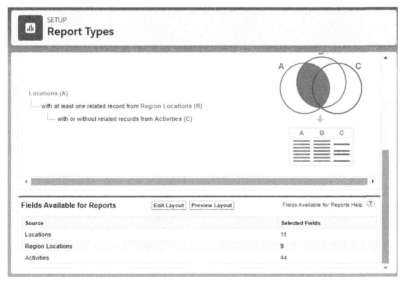

Figure 8.8 – New custom report type page layout

Now, let's look at the capabilities of the dashboard features in the Lightning Platform.

Building dashboards in the Lightning Platform

Dashboards are used to visualize underlying report data and can help users to more easily understand how business information is changing and data trends are being impacted. The core elements of dashboards consist of source reports, dashboard filters, and dashboard components.

The source reports that are used to feed dashboards are the same reports that we covered earlier in this chapter and these source reports provide the data that is visualized in the dashboard components and each dashboard component has a single source report.

Although each dashboard component has a single source report, you can reuse reports in more than one dashboard component.

As an app builder, you will need to understand the building of dashboards in the Lightning Platform and, for the Certified Platform App Builder exam, it is important to understand the following terms:

- **Dashboard filters**: Dashboard filters allow you to generate multiple visualizations of data using the same dashboard to enable different users to view the filtered information that is most appropriate for them.

- **Dashboard running user**: Dashboard has the concept of a running user. The data that is made available to the dashboard is run under the security context of the running user. Therefore, anyone viewing the dashboard can see the data as determined by the explicit and implicit data security settings for that particular user.

- **Dynamic dashboards**: Dynamic dashboards simply describe any dashboards that have been configured with the running user set as the logged-in user. By using this setting, the data security of the underlying report data is always determined by the permissions that the logged-in user who is viewing the dashboard has.

- **Dashboard Components**: Dashboard Components are the graphical elements within a dashboard and are visualized as chart, gauge, metric, or a table.

- **Subscribe to or Schedule Dashboards**: Subscribe to or Schedule Dashboards allows you to configure the data feed to the dashboard to be automatically refreshed. Here, you can set up dashboard refreshes to email the data visualization using email according to a schedule that you can specify. Let's look at the restrictions that exist for creating dashboards in the Lightning report builder.

Considering limits and allocations for dashboards

There are a number of limits and allocations applied by Salesforce to restrict the number of dashboard elements that can be created in total. There are also limits for the number of elements per person and per hour.

The following limits apply to dashboards in the Lightning Platform:

- **Total number of Dynamic dashboards per org (Unlimited/Performance Edition)**: 10

- **Total number of Dynamic dashboards per org (Enterprise Edition)**: 5 dashboards

- **Total number of values for dashboard filters**: 50 values

- **Total number of dashboard components per dashboard**: 20 components

- **Total number of subscriptions to dashboards per person**: 5 dashboards

- **Total number of minutes between dashboard refreshes**: 1 minute (at least)

Report limits, limitations, and allocations in the Lightning Platform

For more details about the limits for dashboards, refer to the following article:

```
https://help.salesforce.com/articleView?id=rd_
reports_dashboards_limits.htm&type=5
```

There are sample dashboards that can be used as a starting point available on the Salesforce AppExchange that have been produced by Salesforce Labs.

Using sample dashboards from the AppExchange

Salesforce CRM Dashboards by Salesforce Labs is a great dashboard pack to get you started. Your one-stop shop for good example dashboards. It includes dashboards for executives, reps, sales, support and more. This app is located at the following link:

```
https://appexchange.salesforce.com/
appxListingDetail?listingId=a0N30000004g316EAA
```

Let's now consider some questions to help test your knowledge of creating reports and building dashboards in the Lightning Platform.

Questions to test your knowledge

We now present *three* questions to help assess your knowledge of data analytics in the Lightning Platform. Here, there are questions regarding the use and capabilities of reports, custom report types, and dashboards in the Lightning Platform.

Question 1 – Reports in the Lightning Platform

A sales representative in your organization would like guidance on how they could create a report that shows them the total number of won opportunities for each of their accounts. Which report type would you recommend that meets this requirement? (Select one)

a) Tabular

b) Total Won

c) Joined

d) Summary

e) Matrix

Question 2 – Custom record type capabilities

Which of the following is a capability of a custom record type? (Select one)

a) Up to 1,000 object relationships can be included in a custom report type.

b) If you delete a custom report type, all reports that were created using that custom report type are deleted.

c) You can change the primary object in a custom report type at any time.

d) If new custom fields are created for a given object, then the new field is automatically added to any custom report type that uses that object.

Question 3 – Dashboard capabilities

What is the maximum number of components that can be included within a dashboard? (Select one)

a) 12

b) 16

c) 20

d) 25

Here are the answers to the *three* questions.

Answer 1 – Reports in the Lightning Platform

The answer is: d) Summary.

The following choices are incorrect:

a) Tabular, b) Total Won, c) Joined, and e) Matrix

Answer 2 – Custom record type capabilities

The answer is: b).

b) If you delete a custom report type, all reports that were created using that custom report type are deleted.

The following choices are incorrect:

a) Up to 1,000 object relationships can be included in a custom report type.

c) You can change the primary object in a custom report type at any time.

d) If new custom fields are created for a given object, then the new field is automatically added to any custom report type that uses that object.

Answer 3 – Dashboard capabilities

The answer is: c) 20.

The following choices are incorrect: a) 12, b) 16, and d) 25.

Summary

In this chapter, you have gained knowledge of the options and capabilities for data analytics in the Lightning Platform.

You have learned, with the help of reports and custom report types, how field values and record information can be reported on and can be used to provide a visual overview of the data within the Lightning Platform.

You learned about the features that are available within the dashboard building tool that enables the building of dashboards that use reports as the underlying data analytics tool and the features that can secure data, refresh, subscribe to, and schedule dashboard information.

In the next chapter, we will learn about the Salesforce mobile features for apps and how they are configured. Here, we will look at the exam objective: Configuring the mobile features, where you will be presented with the features that are available in the Lightning Platform to create user interfaces for use in a mobile context.

Section 3: A Step Closer to the Exam

This section of the book will help you prepare for the final step of the exam. Here, we will cover the mobile and social features as well as look in detail at application life cycle management, which is used to manage the building of apps, and then we will look in detail at how to study for the Salesforce Certified Platform App Builder exam.

This section has the following chapters:

- *Chapter 9, Configuring the Mobile Features*
- *Chapter 10, Understanding the Social Features*
- *Chapter 11, Managing the App Building Process*
- *Chapter 12, Studying for the Certified Platform App Builder Exam*

9
Configuring the Mobile Features

In this chapter, you will acquire the knowledge to be able to configure the Salesforce Mobile App using declarative customization and actions in the Salesforce Lightning platform.

Within this chapter, you will learn about features that are available to customize the Salesforce mobile application user interface.

You will be able to configure actions and action layouts and optimize the Salesforce Mobile App user experience for users accessing the Lightning Platform on the go.

Finally, you will be presented with a number of questions about configuring mobile features with declarative customization and actions in the Lightning Platform.

In this chapter, we will cover the following topics:

- Exam objectives – Mobile apps
- Installing the Salesforce Mobile App
- Configuring the Salesforce mobile application user interface
- Building global and object-specific actions and action layouts
- Questions to test your knowledge

Exam objectives – Mobile apps

To complete the Mobile section of the Certified Platform App Builder exam, app builders are expected to be able to carry out the following tasks:

- Describe the declarative customization options available for the Salesforce mobile application user interface.

- Given a set of requirements, determine the appropriate global and object-specific actions and action layouts to optimize the Salesforce mobile application user experience.

> **Reference – Salesforce Certified Platform App Builder Exam Guide**
>
> This guide is published by Salesforce and can be referenced at `https://trailhead.salesforce.com/help?article=Salesforce-Certified-Platform-App-Builder-Exam-Guide`.

In the Salesforce Certified Platform App Builder Exam Guide, the total number of questions is given, along with a percentage breakdown for each of the objectives, and an indication of the number of features/functions that can be expected in each of the objectives.

By analyzing these objectives, percentages, and question counts, we can determine the likely number of questions that will appear in the exam, and for the Mobile objective, this is as follows:

> **Mobile – Total number of exam questions**
>
> There are likely to be three questions in total.
>
> This is calculated as 5% of 60 total exam questions.

To help reinforce the skills and knowledge required to create reports and build dashboards, there is some practical work for you to do in Salesforce, so if you do not have a Salesforce environment in which to carry this out, create a free developer org as detailed in *Chapter 1, Core Capabilities of the Lightning Platform*.

We will continue to use the example business scenario that we covered in *Chapter 2, Designing and Building a Data Model*, to demonstrate how the features in the Lightning Platform support the configuration of mobile using declarative customization and actions.

The options and capabilities of the mobile features will be covered in this chapter and you will learn how mobile features enable you to design an appropriate user interface on the mobile platform and optimize the user experience.

Let's now look at the Salesforce Mobile App and learn how to set up the app on mobile devices.

Installing the Salesforce Mobile App

Mobile phones and devices are ubiquitous within both our private lives and the business environment. In the current climate of mixing work from the office, the home, remotely, and on the move, organizations of all sizes have realized the benefits of using mobile devices to access business applications in today's mobile-first world.

Mobile app development, however, is not always cost-effective, as the final product can be expensive to build or does not meet user requirements. Not all developments of mobile apps pass the test for usability and often apps built for mobile devices provide a lack of functionality and poor user experience. New mobile apps or migrations of desktop apps to mobile sometimes fail as they are simply mobile screen overlays that are not fit for purpose and result in poor user adoption, the root cause of which can be identified by tracing back to an underlying platform or mobile government that is poorly integrated and not fit for purpose.

The Salesforce Mobile App differs in its approach as it is built within the Lightning Platform and configurations carried in the desktop are fully integrated and reflected in the mobile app. The mobile offering that is provided with the Lightning Platform provides a common security model, and a common set of configuration features that provide an innovative, responsive, and easy-to-use mobile experience for users.

The Salesforce mobile web browser is no longer available

Prior to the Summer 2020 release, there were two options for accessing Salesforce mobile features using a mobile device. The first option was the downloadable Salesforce Mobile App and there was a second option, the Salesforce mobile web browser app, which did not require any software installation and used the web browser on mobile devices.

Starting from the Summer 2020 release, the Salesforce mobile web browser app is no longer available and users must use the downloadable Salesforce Mobile App to access the mobile features on mobile devices, as detailed in the following article:

```
https://help.salesforce.com/
articleView?id=000349471&language=en_
US&type=1&mode=1
```

The Salesforce Mobile App includes many of the customizations that have been configured within the desktop version of your organization and are therefore already partly tailored out of the box to deliver your mobile application requirements.

Let's now look at which mobile devices are supported for use with the Salesforce Mobile App.

Supported mobile devices for the Salesforce Mobile App

The Salesforce Mmobile App is accessible from most Salesforce edition types of user license and is supported for use with the following two operating systems and versions: Apple iOS version 12.0 or later, and Android version 7.0 or later.

Salesforce conducts ongoing tests using various mobile phones and tablets to verify that the Salesforce Mobile App operated correctly with the stated platform.

At the time of writing, Salesforce has identified the following mobile phones that are supported for use with the Apple iOS platform:

- iPhone 11 Pro and Pro Max
- iPhone 11
- iPhone XR
- iPhone XS and XS Max
- iPhone X
- iPhone 8 and 8 Plus
- iPhone 7 and 7 Plus
- iPhone SE
- iPhone 6S
- iPhone 6

Salesforce has identified the following tablets as being supported for use with the Apple iOS platform:

- iPad Pro 10.5 inch
- iPad Air 2
- iPad Mini 4

At the time of writing, Salesforce has identified the following mobile phones as being supported for use with the Android platform:

- Google Pixel 4 XL

- Google Pixel 3

- Samsung Galaxy S10 and S10+

- Samsung Galaxy S9 and S9+

- Samsung Galaxy S8 and S8+

- Samsung Galaxy S7

- Samsung Galaxy Note 10+

- Samsung Galaxy Note 9

- Samsung Galaxy Note 8

> **Salesforce Mobile App-supported devices and minimum platform requirements**
>
> Salesforce may, at any time, change the list of supported devices and minimum platform requirements for the Salesforce Mobile App. The latest set of supported devices and minimum platform requirements can be accessed from the following article:
>
> ```
> https://help.salesforce.com/
> articleView?id=salesforce_app_requirements.
> htm&type=5
> ```

We will now look at how to set up the Salesforce Mobile App on a supported mobile device.

Setting up the Salesforce Mobile App

The Salesforce Mobile App is available from the App Store for mobile devices that are running on the iOS platform and from Google Play for mobile devices that are running on the Android platform.

We will step through the process of setting up the Salesforce Mobile App on an iOS device. The set up process is similar for an Android device, although there may be some minor variations.

To access the installation links for the Salesforce Mobile App on an iOS device, perform the following steps:

1. Navigate to the **Getting started with the Salesforce Mobile App** page by browsing to the web URL located at `https://www.salesforce.com/solutions/ mobile/getting-started/`, as shown in the following screenshot:

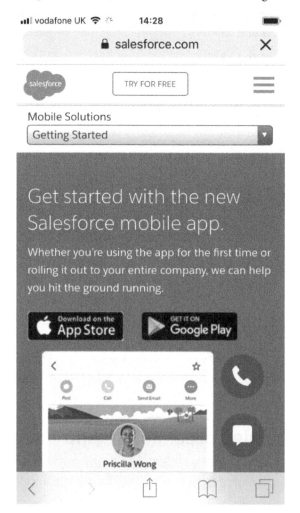

Figure 9.1 – Getting Started

In this setup, we will install the Salesforce Mobile App on an Apple iPhone that runs under the iOS platform, so here we'll select the App Store option.

2. Click on **Download on the App Store** within the **Getting Started** screen to navigate to the Salesforce App Store menu, as shown in the following screenshot:

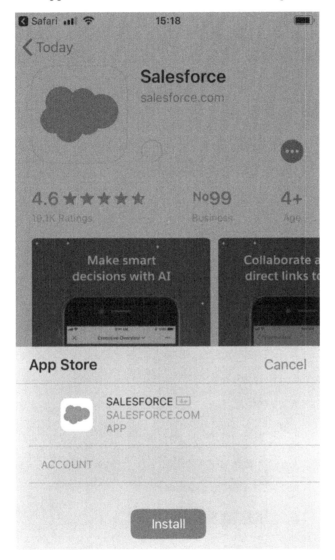

Figure 9.2 – Salesforce on the App Store

3. Click on **Install** in the **App Store**.

4. Wait for a few moments for the installation to complete and the screen will then change to present an option to open the Salesforce Mobile App, as shown in the following screenshot:

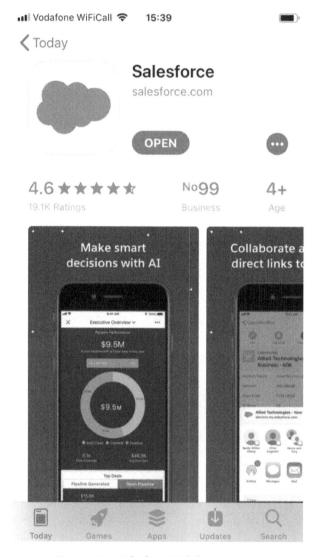

Figure 9.3 – Salesforce Mobile App open

5. Click on **Open** in the Salesforce Mobile App and this action will (upon navigation to the Salesforce Mobile App for the first time) present the **Allow Access** screen, as shown in the following screenshot:

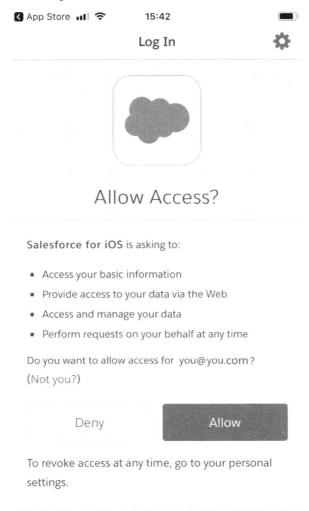

Figure 9.4 – Salesforce Mobile App access permissions

6. Click on **Allow** to permit the Salesforce Mobile App to gain access to your Salesforce organization, whereby the screen will then change to the **Welcome to the Salesforce Mobile App** screen, as shown in the following screenshot:

Figure 9.5 – The Salesforce Mobile App welcome screen

7. Finally, click on **Get Started** to navigate to the Salesforce Mobile App menu, as shown in the following screenshot:

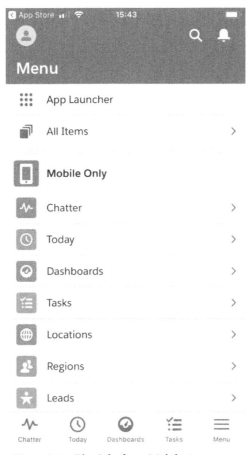

Figure 9.6 – The Salesforce Mobile App menu

> **More information about setting up the Salesforce Mobile App**
>
> To find out more information about setting up the Salesforce Mobile App, refer to the following article:
>
> `https://help.salesforce.com/`
> `articleView?id=salesforce_app_set_up.htm&type=5`

This will set up the mobile app. Now let's look at the mobile app user interface options in the Lightning Platform.

Configuring the Salesforce mobile application user interface

The options and capabilities of the Salesforce Mobile App are not the same as the full Lightning Platform application, and there are many differences within the Salesforce Mobile App, in particular, concerning the ways in which data is entered, screens are presented, and navigation is carried out between screens.

Salesforce has built mobile-friendly alternatives to the way information is captured, and navigation takes place accordingly to cater for the much smaller screen real estate and the reduced capability of a mobile device to display functions and features to a user.

> **Differences between the full Lightning Experience app and the Salesforce Mobile App**
>
> For more detailed information about the features that are not available in the Salesforce Mobile App when compared to the full Lightning Experience app, refer to the following article:
>
> ```
> https://help.salesforce.com/articleView?id=limits_
> mobile_sf1_parent.htm&type=5
> ```

The features and capabilities that are available to you in order to configure the Salesforce Mobile App user interface are as follows:

- **Lightning** App Navigation Menu: The Lightning app navigation menu can be changed by users who have permission to personalize the desktop navigation bar. This also allows a user who has permission to edit the desktop navigation bar, for a given app, to reorder items in the navigation menu within the Salesforce Mobile App, for that particular app.

- **Mobile Only** Default Navigation Menu: The Mobile Only app allows you to create navigation items that become the default set of items within the Salesforce Mobile App.

- **Mobile** App Branding: This provides the facilities to configure the way in which the app appears.

- **Global** Quick **actions**: These actions in the Lightning Platform can be thought of as shortcuts that appear within the user interface. A given global quick action is available in both the desktop and mobile apps and can be used to create records, log calls, and so on.

- **Object-specific Quick actions**: In the same way as global quick actions, object-specific quick actions can be thought of as shortcuts that appear within the user interface. They are also available in both the desktop and mobile apps, but are associated with a specific Lightning Platform object type and can be used to update as well as create records, log calls, and so on.

> **Customization options in the Salesforce Mobile App**
>
> For more information about customizing the Salesforce Mobile App, refer to the following article:
>
> ```
> https://help.salesforce.com/
> articleView?id=salesforce_app_customize.htm&type=5
> ```

Having looked at the ways in which to configure the user interface, let's now look at how the changes are reflected when personalizing the Lightning app menu in the Salesforce Mobile App.

Customizing a Lightning app navigation menu in the Salesforce mobile app

The Lightning app navigation menu can be personalized by any user who has permission to modify the navigation bar whereby they are able to add, remove (only for items that they have added), rename, and reorder items.

The modifications to the navigation bar are also applied to the navigation menu and navigation bar for the specific Lightning app within the Salesforce Mobile App, as shown in the following screenshot:

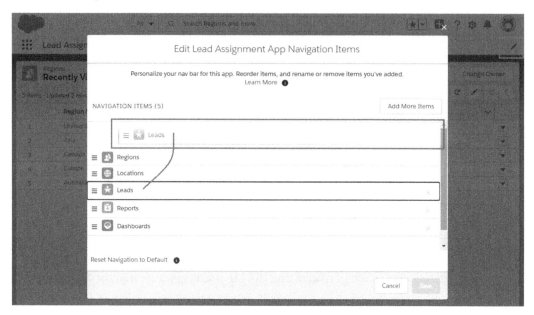

Figure 9.7 – The Lightning app navigation menu

The preceding screenshot demonstrates reordering by placing the **Leads** tab to appear as the first item that is reflected in the Salesforce mobile app, as shown in the following screenshot:

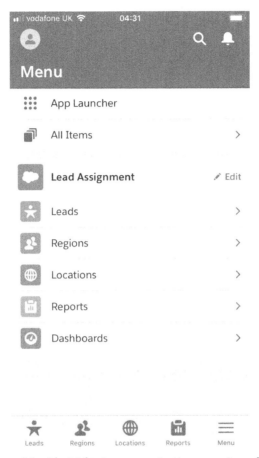

Figure 9.8 – The Lightning app navigation menu in mobile

Having identified how the Lightning app navigation menu can be personalized, let's now look at the Mobile Only default navigation menu in the Salesforce mobile app.

Customizing the Mobile Only default navigation menu in the Salesforce Mobile App

The Mobile Only default navigation menu can only be configured by users with system administrator permission and is used to create navigation items that become the default set of items within the Salesforce mobile app.

By configuring the items that are presented to users, you can include Lightning pages, Visualforce pages, Lightning components, and so on in the default navigation menu and navigation bar of the Salesforce mobile app.

Modification of the navigation bar for the Mobile Only default navigation menu can be carried out by performing the following steps:

1. Navigate to **SETUP** and then search for `Salesforce Navigation` in the **Quick Find** search box located at the top of the **Setup** menu on the left side bar.

2. Click on **Salesforce Navigation** in the **SETUP** menu.

3. In the **Salesforce Navigation** setup screen, choose the items from the **Available** list and move them to the **Selected** list, as shown in the following screenshot:

Figure 9.9 – The Mobile Only default navigation menu

4. Finally, click on **Save**.

    The **Mobile Only** default option shows the selected items in the Salesforce mobile app, as shown in the following screenshot:

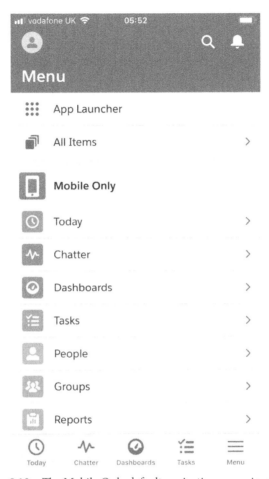

Figure 9.10 – The Mobile Only default navigation menu in mobile

---

Customization options in the Mobile Only default navigation menu

For more information about customizing the Mobile Only default navigation menu, refer to the following article:

```
https://help.salesforce.com/
articleView?id=salesforce_app_customize.htm&type=5
```

We will now look at the mechanism for setting branding for the Salesforce mobile app.

Mobile app branding

Mobile app branding provides the facilities to configure the way in which the app appears. Here, the features that can be configured are the loading page logo, the loading background color, and the header background color.

Mobile app branding modifications can be carried out by performing the following steps:

1. Navigate to **SETUP** and then search for `Branding` in the **Quick Find** search box located at the top of the **SETUP** menu on the left side bar.

2. Click on **Salesforce Branding** in the **SETUP** menu.

3. In the **Salesforce Branding** setup screen, click on **Edit**.

4. In the **Salesforce Branding** edit page, choose the colors for **Brand Color** and **Loading Page Color**, and then choose a **Loading Page Logo**, as shown in the following screenshot:

Figure 9.11 – Mobile app branding

The loading page color and loading page logo appear within the Salesforce mobile app, as shown in the following screenshot:

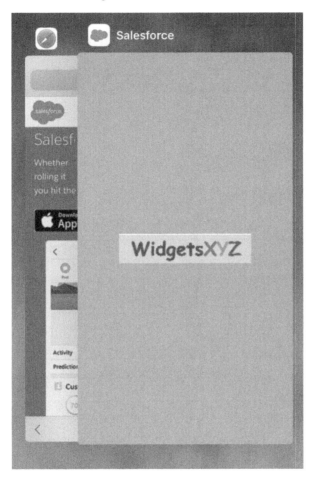

Figure 9.12 – Mobile app branding on a mobile device

The brand color appears within the Salesforce mobile app, as shown in the following screenshot:

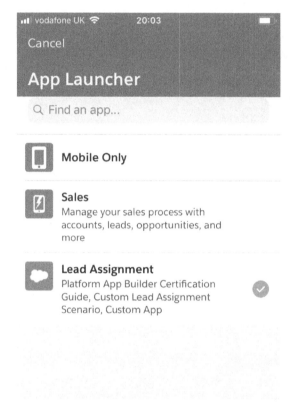

Figure 9.13 – Mobile app branding in a mobile device

We will now look at the mechanism for building global and object-specific actions and action layouts in the Lightning Platform.

Building global and object-specific actions and action layouts

Global and object-specific quick actions in the Lightning Platform can be thought of as shortcuts that appear within the user interface. They are two forms of what is known as a quick action, which are available in both the desktop and mobile apps and can be used to create records, update records, log calls, and so on.

In the Salesforce mobile app, global and object-specific quick actions offer a quick way to access functions that launch a specific action or custom process automation that exists in the Lightning Platform.

In addition to the custom actions that are tailored to your business processes, the Salesforce Mobile App comes with standard pre-built actions. The quick actions are located within the action bar and the action menu that appear at the top of the screen of the mobile device.

Quick actions that are used to capture data input have their own type of page layout called an **action layout** and allow you to reduce the number of fields to ensure that only those that are absolutely essential are presented to the mobile user.

In addition to presenting a limited set of fields for data capture, you can also set fields with given values, which are shown on the page layout, to save the user time when there are records that have common values that are to be entered. This feature is called **prepopulate fields** and is available in both the desktop and the Salesforce Mobile Apps.

As an app builder, you will need to understand how to build global and object-specific actions and action layouts in the Lightning Platform and understand the following key differences.

Global quick actions can be used to create records that are not associated with any other record (that is, there is no option to set an object relationship field). They are called global quick actions because they can be placed anywhere within the Lightning Platform where actions are supported such as the **Home** page, the **Chatter** tab, object pages, and custom Lightning app pages.

Global quick actions

For more information about the actions that can be carried out using global quick actions, refer to the following article:

```
https://help.salesforce.com/
articleView?id=actions_overview_global.htm&type=5
```

Object-specific actions, on the other hand, can be used to create and also update records as they operate in the context of a given Lightning Platform object type. Within the Salesforce mobile app, object-specific quick actions can be placed on record detail pages. So, for example, an action associated with the lead object is only available when viewing a lead record.

> **Object-specific actions**
>
> For more information about the actions that can be carried out using object-specific actions, refer to the following article:
>
> ```
> https://help.salesforce.com/
> articleView?id=actions_overview_object_specific.
> htm&type=5
> ```

Let's look at how to create global quick actions in the Lightning Platform.

Creating global quick actions

In this example, we will add a **New Lead** action to global layouts that will allow mobile users to create lead record details from within a **Chatter** thread.

Let's go ahead and configure a global quick action by performing the following steps:

1. Navigate to **SETUP** and then search for `Actions` in the **Quick Find** search box located at the top of the **SETUP** menu on the left side bar.
2. Click on **Global Actions** in the **SETUP** menu.
3. Click on **New Action** in the **Global Actions** setup page.
4. In the **Enter Action Information** dialog screen, enter the following:

- **Action Type**: `Create a Record`
- **Target Object**: `Lead`
- **Standard Label Type**: --None--
- **Label**: `New Lead (Global Action)`
- **Name**: `New_Lead_Global_Action`
- **Description**: `Platform App Builder Certification Guide, Custom Lead Assignment Scenario, Global Action New Lead`
- **Create Feed Item**: `Enabled` (when enabled, a feed item is created along with the action. The compact layout for the target object sets the fields for the feed item.)
- **Success Message**: `Lead Created`
- **Icon**: `Accept the default lead icon for the Lead` (icons change according to the target object.)

5. Finally, click on the **Save** button to save the global action, as shown in the following screenshot:

Figure 9.14 – Global actions

The options for the action types are as follows:

- **Create a Record**
- **Send Email**
- **Log a Call**
- **Custom Visualforce**
- **Custom Canvas**
- **Lightning Component**

Upon saving the global action, the layout setup screen appears as shown in the following screenshot:

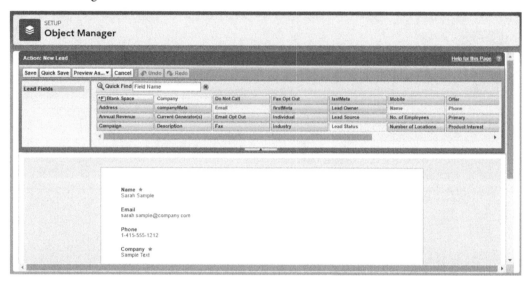

Figure 9.15 – Global actions layout

The following fields are added as default: **Name**, **Email**, **Phone**, **Company**, **Title**, and **Lead Status**. The **Name**, **Company**, and **Lead Status** fields marked with a red asterisk are mandatory fields and cannot be removed from the page layout.

6. Remove the following fields, **Phone** and **Title**, by clicking on the **Remove** icon, as shown in the following screenshot:

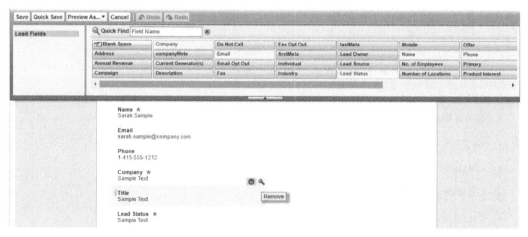

Figure 9.16 – Global actions – removing layout

7. Add the following fields by dragging and dropping the field section, as shown in the following screenshot:

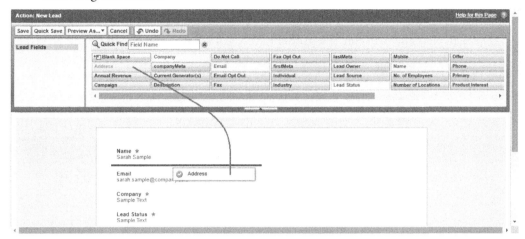

Figure 9.17 – Global actions – adding layout

8. Finally, click on the **Save** button to save the global action layout.

> **Limiting the number of fields on an action layout**
>
> Salesforce recommends including fewer than five and observing a maximum number of eight fields on an action layout, as referenced in the following article:
>
> ```
> https://trailhead.salesforce.com/en/content/learn/
> modules/salesforce1_mobile_app/salesforce1_mobile_
> app_actions_global
> ```

To present the **New Lead** global action as an option in the user interface, we now need to add the global action to a publisher layout. We can create custom publisher layouts. However, there is a standard layout that we will use called the **Global Publisher** layout. You may need to check that this layout is included within the profiles within the **Publisher Layout Assignment** if you have already made any changes to the **Global Publisher** layout.

Let's now go ahead and add the global action to the global publisher layout by performing the following steps:

1. Navigate to **SETUP** and then search for Publisher in the **Quick Find** search box located at the top of the **SETUP** menu on the left side bar.

2.   Click on **Publisher Layouts** in the **SETUP** menu.

3.   Click on **Edit** for the standard **Global Publisher** layout.

4.   If you are editing **Global Publisher** for mobile actions for the first time, you will need to click the **override the predefined actions** link, as shown in the following screenshot:

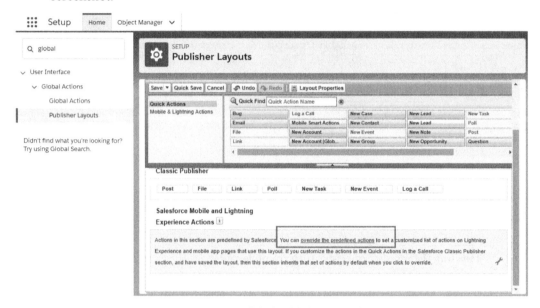

Figure 9.18 – Global Publisher override

5.   Optionally, click on **override the predefined actions** in the **Global Publisher** layout.

6. Ensure that **New Lead (Global Action)** is included within **Salesforce Mobile and Lightning Experience Actions**, as shown in the following screenshot:

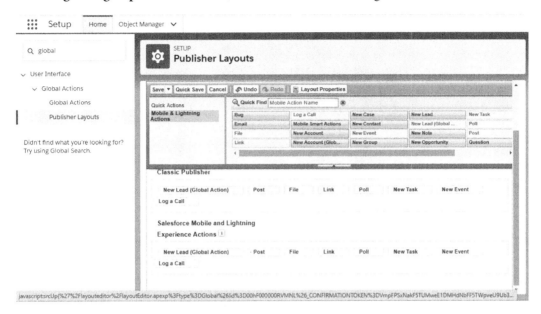

Figure 9.19 – Global Publisher layout

7. Finally, click on the **Save** button to save the publisher layout.

Let's now see how this looks in the Salesforce Mobile App by navigating to the **Chatter** item (this can be found in the **Mobile Only** app). **The New Lead (Global Action)** option will be presented, as shown in the following screenshot:

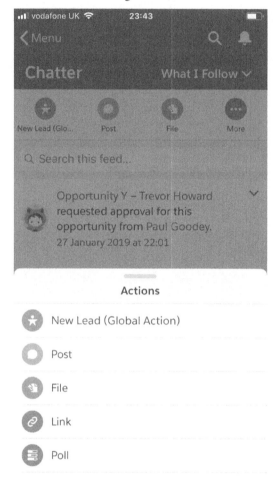

Figure 9.20 – Global Publisher layout mobile

Let's now look at the practicalities of building reports that satisfy a specific business requirement by implementing a report with the use of the Lightning report builder.

Configuring object-specific actions

In this example, we will add a **Deactivate** action to the location records that will allow mobile users to easily mark the location as inactive from within a location record.

Let's go ahead and configure an object-specific quick action by performing the following steps:

1. Navigate to **SETUP** and then search for `Object Manager` in the **Quick Find** search box located at the top of the **SETUP** menu on the left side bar.

2. Click on **Object Manager** in the **SETUP** menu.

3. In the **Object Manager** setup screen, search for the **Location** object.

4. Click on **Location** in **Object Manager** in the **SETUP** menu.

5. In the **Location** object manager setup screen, click on **Buttons, Links, and Actions** from within the **Location** object setup menu on the left side bar.

6. In the **Buttons, Links, and Actions** section, click on **New Action**.

7. In the **Enter Action Information** dialog screen, enter the following information:

- **Action Type**: `Update a Record`
- **Standard Label Type**: --None--
- **Label**: `Deactivate Location`
- **Name**: `Deactivate_Location`
- **Description**: `Platform App Builder Certification Guide, Custom Lead Assignment Scenario, Object-specific Action Deactivate Location`
- **Success Message**: `Location Deactivated`
- **Icon**: `Accept the default icon`

8. Finally, click on the **Save** button to save the global action, as shown in the following screenshot:

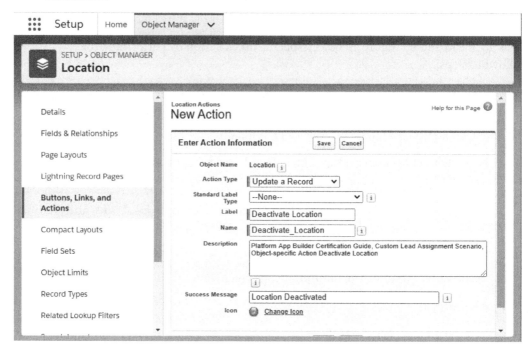

Figure 9.21 – Object-specific actions

The options for **Action Types** are as follows:

- **Create a Record**
- **Send Email**
- **Log a Call**
- **Custom Visualforce**
- **Update a Record**
- **Lightning Component**
- **Flow**

Upon saving the global action, the layout setup screen appears as shown in the following screenshot:

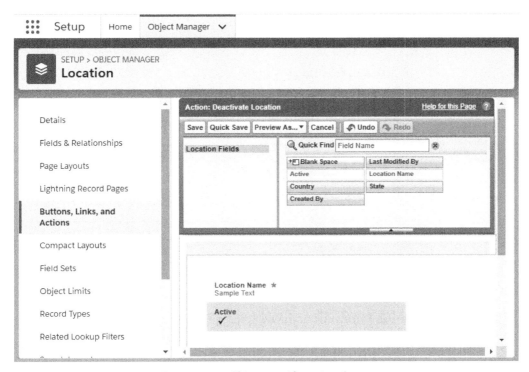

Figure 9.22 – Object-specific actions layout

The following field, **Location Name**, is added by default and is marked with a red asterisk to show it is a mandatory field and cannot be removed from the page layout.

1. Add the **Active** field to the action layout.
2. Click on the **Save** button to save the action layout.

3. Upon saving the action layout, click on **New** in the **Predefined Field Values** section, as shown in the following screenshot:

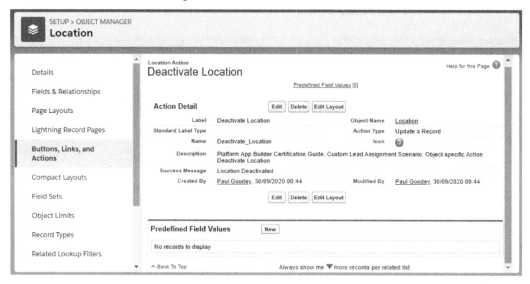

Figure 9.23 – Object-specific action predefined

4. In the **Enter Action Information** dialog screen, enter the following information:

- **Field Name**: **Active**

- **Specify New Field Value: Formula Value (Checkbox)**: **FALSE**

5. Click on the **Save** button to save the **Predefined Field Value**, as shown in the following screenshot:

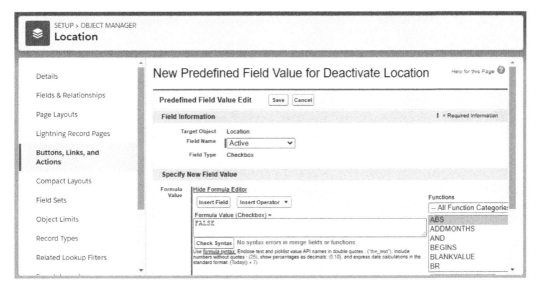

Figure 9.24 – Object-specific predefined action saved

Let's now add the object-specific action to the **Location** page layout by performing the following steps:

6. In the **Location** object manager setup screen, click on **Page Layout** from within the **Location** object setup menu on the left side bar.

7. Click on the **Location Layout** page layout.

8.   Drag the **Deactivate Location** action to the **Salesforce Mobile and Lightning Experience Actions** section of the page layout, as shown the following screenshot:

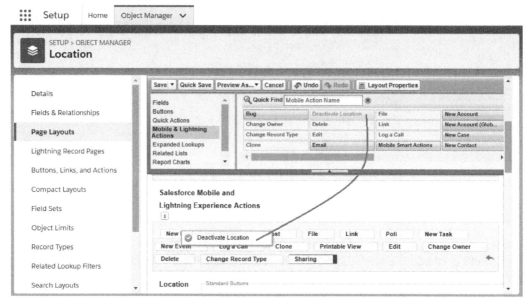

Figure 9.25 – Object-specific action page layout

9.   Finally, click on the **Save** button to save the page layout.

Let's now see how this looks in the Salesforce Mobile App by navigating to the **Chatter** item (this can be found in the **Mobile Only** app). The **New Lead (Global Action)** option will be presented, as shown in the following screenshot:

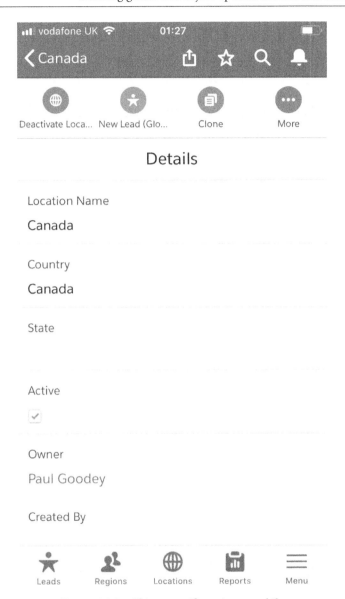

Figure 9.26 – Object-specific action – mobile

Having looked at how to configure object-specific actions, let's now consider some questions to help test your knowledge of the Salesforce mobile app.

Questions to test your knowledge

We now present three questions to help assess your knowledge of the Salesforce mobile app. Here, there are questions about configuring mobile features with declarative customization and actions in the Lightning Platform.

Question 1 – Mobile Only default navigation menu

Which of the following statements is true concerning the use and capability of the Mobile Only default navigation menu? (Select one)

a) Any user can configure the items that appear in the Mobile Only default navigation menu.

b) The Mobile Only default navigation menu can include Lightning pages, Lightning components, and others, but not Visualforce pages.

c) The Mobile Only default navigation menu is used to create navigation items that become the default set of items within the Salesforce mobile app.

d) The Mobile Only default navigation menu and included items can be accessed in mobile and desktop apps.

Question 2 – Mobile app branding

Which of the following features can be configured as part of mobile app branding? (Select three)

a) The loading page logo

b) The actions background color

c) The header background color

d) The loading background color

e) The background page logo

Question 3 – Mobile quick actions

Which of the following statements is true concerning the use and capability of quick actions in the Lightning Platform? (Select one)

a) Global quick actions can be used within both the desktop and the mobile interface.

b) Object-specific quick actions can only be used within the mobile interface.

c) Global and object-specific quick actions can be used to update object records.

d) Object-specific quick actions can update records, but cannot create new records.

Here are the answers to the three questions.

Answer 1 – Mobile Only default navigation menu

The answer is: c) The Mobile Only default navigation menu is used to create navigation items that become the default set of items within the Salesforce mobile app.

The following choices are incorrect:

a) Any user can configure the items that appear in the Mobile Only default navigation menu.

b) The Mobile Only default navigation menu can include Lightning pages, Lightning components, and others, but not Visualforce pages.

d) The Mobile Only default navigation menu and included items can be accessed in the mobile and desktop apps.

Answer 2 – Mobile app branding

The answers are the following:

a) The loading page logo

c) The header background color

d) The loading background color

The following choices are incorrect:

b) The actions background color

e) The background page logo

Answer 3 – Mobile quick actions

The answer is: a) Global quick actions can be used within both the desktop and the mobile interfaces.

The following choices are incorrect:

b) Object-specific quick actions can only be used within the mobile interface.

c) Global and object-specific quick actions can be used to update object records.

d) Object-specific quick actions can update records, but cannot create new records.

Summary

In this chapter, we have looked at the features and capabilities available to configure mobile using declarative customization and actions in the Salesforce Lightning Platform.

You have learned about the setup and installation of the Salesforce Mobile App and about the features that are available to customize the Salesforce mobile application user interface.

You have gained the knowledge to be able to configure quick actions within the Salesforce Mobile App that can be used to implement global quick actions, object-specific actions, and action layouts to optimize the Salesforce mobile application user experience.

In the next chapter, we will look at exam objective – Understanding the social features. Here, you will discover the capabilities of the social networking features in the Lightning Platform.

10
Understanding the Social Features

In this chapter, we will look at the capabilities of the social networking features of the Lightning Platform.

You will learn how to set up, configure, and authorize a social network and the way in which accounts, leads, and contacts can be linked to social networks.

You will also learn about the settings for the social features and find out how to associate account, lead, and contact records with social networking profiles.

Finally, you will be presented with a number of questions about the capabilities of and use cases for social features in the Lightning Platform.

In this chapter, we will cover the following:

- Exam objectives – Social features
- Setting up social accounts, leads, and contacts
- Configuring the social features by users
- Linking accounts, leads, and contacts to social networks
- Questions to test your knowledge

Exam objectives – Social features

To complete the **social features** section of the Certified Platform App Builder exam, app builders are expected to be able to carry out the following:

Understand the capabilities of and use cases for social features.

Reference: Salesforce Certified Platform App Builder Exam Guide

This guide is published by Salesforce and can be found at `https://trailhead.salesforce.com/help?article=Salesforce-Certified-Platform-App-Builder-Exam-Guide`.

In the Salesforce Certified Platform App Builder Exam Guide, the total number of questions is given, along with a percentage breakdown for each of the objectives and an indication of the number of features/functions that can be expected in each of the objectives.

By analyzing these objectives, percentages, and question counts we can determine the likely number of questions that will appear in the exam, and for the mobile use case objective this is as follows:

Social features: Total number of exam questions

There are likely to be 1 or 2 questions in total.

This is calculated as 3% of 60 total exam questions.

To help reinforce the skills and knowledge required to create reports and build dashboards, there is practical work for you to do in Salesforce. So, if you do not have a Salesforce environment to carry this out, create a free developer org as detailed in *Chapter 1*, *Core Capabilities of the Lightning Platform*.

We will create account, lead, and contact records to demonstrate how the features in the Lightning Platform support the configuration of the social features.

Let's look at the social features and begin by setting up social accounts, leads, and contacts.

Setting up social accounts, leads, and contacts

Social accounts, leads, and contacts in the Lightning Platform enable the users in your organization to access the social network profiles of individuals. Having social networking information within the records in Salesforce allows users to improve communication and improves the interaction with customers and prospects.

Depending upon which user interface in the Lightning Platform you are using in your organization, you can connect with social networking information from Twitter and YouTube. From within the Lightning Experience user interface, you can access Twitter and from within the Salesforce Classic user interface, you can access Twitter and YouTube. The Salesforce mobile app supports social networking information from Twitter only.

Salesforce mobile app supported devices and minimum platform requirements

Salesforce may, at any time, need to change the list of available social networks. This is because the integration between the Lightning Platform and a social network uses a public API that Salesforce has no direct control of, and that can be changed or stopped at any time.

LinkedIn, Facebook, and Klout used to be available social networks, but LinkedIn integration was terminated as of the Winter '16 release. Facebook and Klout integrations were terminated in May 2018.

For the latest information about the social networks that are available, refer to the following article:

```
https://help.salesforce.com/
articleView?id=salesforce_app_requirements.
htm&type=5
```

To enable social accounts, leads, and contacts in the Lightning Platform and to specify which of the available social networks are accessible by the users in your organization, follow these steps:

1. Navigate to **Setup** and then search for `Social Accounts` in the **Quick Find** search box located at the top of the **Setup** menu in the left sidebar.

2. Click on **Social Accounts and Contacts Settings** in the **Setup** menu.

3. In the **Social Accounts and Contacts Settings Setup** screen, enable the **Enable Social Accounts, Contacts, and Leads** checkbox. When this is enabled, the social network options appear in the **Social Networks** section.

4. In the **Social Networks** section, enable the social networks that the users in your organization are permitted to access, as shown in the following screenshot:

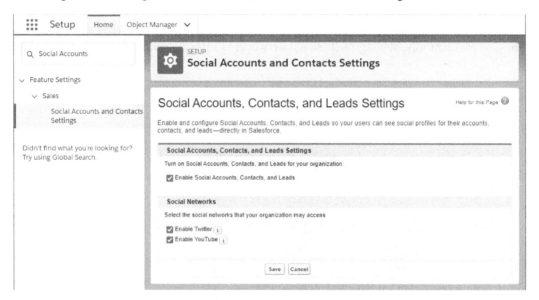

Figure 10.1 – Enabling social accounts

5. Finally, click **Save**.

Having set up the feature for social accounts, leads, and contacts in the Lightning Platform, users can choose whether to show or hide the social features. They can specify whether to show all types of social networks or choose a specific social network depending on which user interface they are using.

Let's now look at the way users can configure the visibility of social networking features.

Configuring social features by users

Users can choose whether they want to hide or show social networking features and choose which social network, depending on which user interface they are using, to display for the social accounts, leads, and contacts. Users can only choose to show or hide the social networking features for their user account; they cannot affect whether other users' can view social networking information.

User can enable social accounts, leads, and contacts for themselves and specify which of the available social networks are visible by following these steps:

1. Navigate to the **Personal Settings** options by clicking on your profile image and then clicking on **Settings**, as shown in the following screenshot:

Figure 10.2 – Personal settings

2. Search for **Social Accounts** in the **Quick Find** search box located at the top of the **Personal Settings** menu in the left sidebar.

3. Click on **My Social Accounts and Contacts** in the **Personal Settings** menu.

4. In the **Social Accounts and Contacts Settings Setup** screen, enable the **Use Social Accounts and Contacts** checkbox. When this is enabled, the choice of social networks appears in the **Social Networks** section.

5. In the **Social Networks** section, enable the social networks that the users in your organization are permitted to access, as shown in the following screenshot:

Figure 10.3 – Enabling social accounts

6. Finally, click **Save**.

Now that we have enabled the social features, let's look at how we can link account, lead, and contact records to social networks and choose the profile to associate with the records in Salesforce.

Linking accounts, leads, and contacts to social networks

To link account, lead, and contact records to social networking profiles, users must be signed up to the respective social network. So, to associate Twitter information to a lead record, say, a user must have a Twitter account.

After the social features have been enabled and the desired social network has been chosen, users will be able to link the account, lead, and contact records within the Lightning Platform by following these steps:

1. Logging into their social networking account.

2. Clicking on either an account, lead, or a contact record and navigating to the social network option, which will be either a section on the account page or the **News** tab on a lead or contact record page.

3. Clicking on the **Sign in** option.

4. Authorizing the Salesforce social account feature to access their social networking account.

5. Finally, linking the account, lead, or contact record to a specific profile within the social network.

Let's look at the process of signing into a social networking account using the example of Twitter; we'll see how Twitter presents the screen to authorize access to the social network features in the Lightning Platform.

Signing into and authorizing access to social networking accounts

Users will be asked to sign into their social networking account in order to associate account, lead, and contact records with their profiles on the social network.

In the following example, using Twitter, we will carry out one-off actions for signing in and authorizing, which will then grant ongoing communication between the social network and the Lightning Platform. Follow these steps:

1. Navigate to an account, lead, or contact record. In this example, we'll navigate to a lead record called **John Smith**.

2. Click on the **News** tab.

3. Click on **Sign in with Twitter**, as shown in the following screenshot:

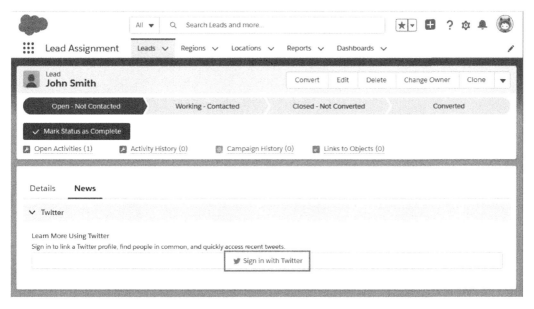

Figure 10.4 – Social network sign-in

Upon clicking the **Sign in with Twitter** option, users will be presented with the authorization screen, as shown in the following screenshot:

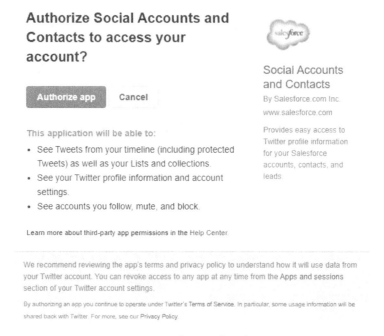

Figure 10.5 – Social network authorization

The Lightning Platform uses the security of the OAuth protocol when users sign into their social networking accounts. Users' login information and credentials are not accessible within the Lightning Platform and passwords are not stored.

Now that the signing into and authorization of the social network has been carried out, users can start to link social network profiles to the records in the Lightning Platform.

Linking accounts to social networks

For accounts within the Lightning Experience user interface, the method of linking the Twitter social network information is to click **Link Twitter Account**, which is within the **Twitter** section, as shown in the following screenshot:

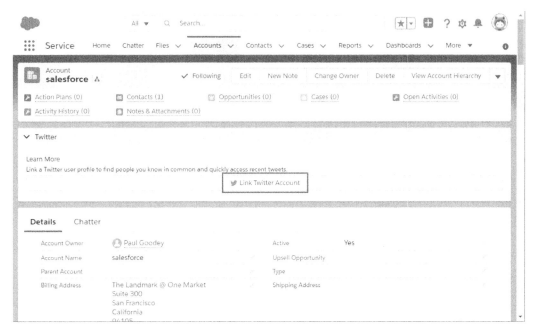

Figure 10.6 – Social Accounts in Salesforce Lightning

If the **Twitter** section is not shown on the page you may need to add it by clicking the gear icon in the top-right corner of the page and then clicking **Edit Page**. From within the Lightning page you can drag and drop the Twitter component onto the page canvas, as shown in the following screenshot:

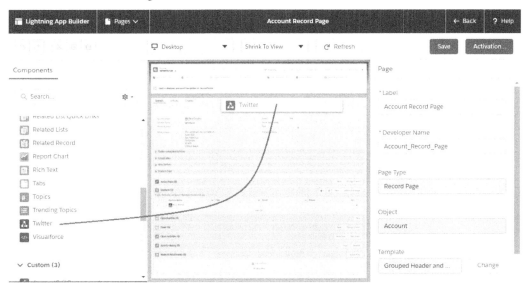

Figure 10.7 – Social accounts Twitter component

For accounts within the Salesforce Classic user interface, the method of linking and accessing social network information is to click the social network icon, which is below the account name for the Lightning Experience user interface, as shown in the following screenshot:

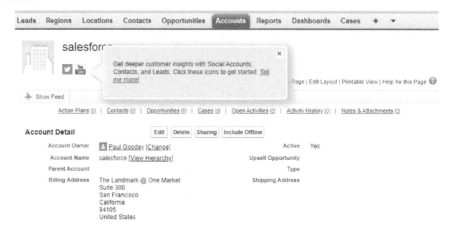

Figure 10.8 – Social accounts in the Classic platform

This will enable the linking of account records to social network profiles. Now let's look at how to link lead and contact records to social network profiles in the Lightning Platform.

Linking leads and contacts to social networks

As with leads and contacts within the Salesforce Classic user interface, the method of linking and accessing social network information is to click the social network icon that is below the lead or contact name for the Lightning Experience user interface, as shown in the following screenshot for a lead record:

Figure 10.9 – Social Accounts Lead present in Salesforce Classic

For leads and contacts within the Lightning Experience user interface, the method of linking the Twitter social network information is to click **Link Twitter Account**, which is within the Twitter section, as shown in the following screenshot:

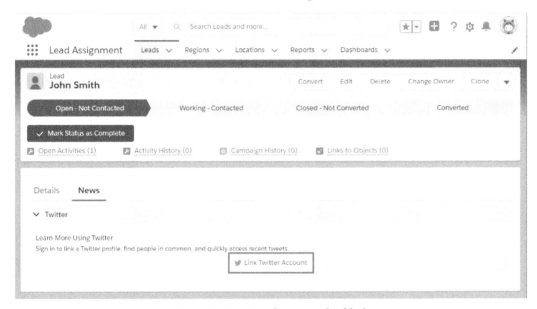

Figure 10.10 – Social accounts lead link

Upon clicking the **Link to Twitter Account** link, users will be presented with the option to select an appropriate profile with which to link the record with the social network, as shown in the following screenshot:

Figure 10.11 – Social accounts lead link profile page

Upon selecting a social network profile, the association between the record in the Lightning Platform and the social network profile is made and users can start to see the social networking information within the Salesforce record detail page, as shown in the following screenshot:

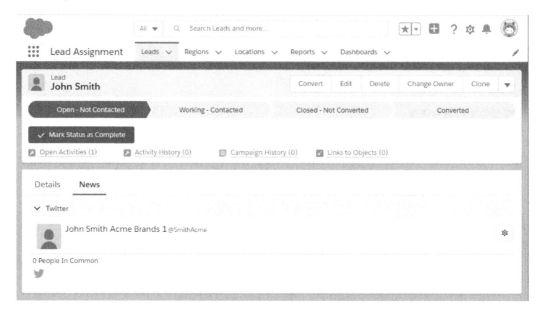

Figure 10.12 – Social accounts lead linked profile page

The Lightning Platform does not extract or store any social network information. When users select a particular social profile or access a YouTube video, the information is retrieved directly from the social networking site so that users see the latest information associated with the account, lead, or contact record.

When linking a record in the Lightning Platform with a social networking profile, there is no activity reflected within the social network as the association is strictly read-only from the Lightning Platform. Furthermore, for Twitter linking, users are not set to become a follower of that particular profile and the Lightning Platform will not make any posts to the social network site.

Let's now consider some questions to help test your knowledge of the Salesforce mobile app.

Questions to test your knowledge

We now present two questions to help assess your knowledge of the social features. We have questions about configuring and linking records in the Lightning Platform with social networks.

Question 1 – Capabilities of and use cases for social features

Which of the following statements is true concerning the capabilities of and use cases for social features in the Lightning Experience user interface? (Select one)

a) The social features in the Lightning Platform enable the connection of Twitter and Facebook social networking information to account, lead, and contact records.

b) The social features in the Lightning Platform enable the connection of Twitter and YouTube social networking information to account, lead, and contact records.

c) The social features in the Lightning Platform enable the connection of Twitter, Facebook, and YouTube social networking information to account, lead, and contact records.

d) The social features in the Lightning Platform enable the connection of Twitter social networking information to account, lead, and contact records.

Question 2 – Linking Salesforce records to social networks

The Lightning Platform can use its social features to associate social networking profiles with which of the following? (Select one)

a) Account, lead, and contact records

b) Account, contact, and user records

c) Account, contact, and social records

d) Account, lead, and user records

Here are the answers to the two questions.

Answer 1 – Capabilities of and use cases for social features

The answer is: d) The social features in the Lightning Platform enable the connection of Twitter social networking information to account, lead, and contact records.

The following choices are not correct:

a) The social features in the Lightning Platform enable the connection of Twitter and Facebook social networking information to account, lead, and contact records.

b) The social features in the Lightning Platform enable the connection of Twitter and YouTube social networking information to account, lead, and contact records.

c) The social features in the Lightning Platform enable the connection of Twitter, Facebook, and YouTube social networking information to account, lead, and contact records.

Answer 2 – Linking Salesforce records to social networks

The answer is: a) Account, lead, and contact records

The following choices are not correct:

b) Account, contact, and user records

c) Account, contact, and social records

d) Account, lead, and user records

Summary

In this chapter, we have looked at the social features in the Salesforce Lightning Platform.

You have learned about the mechanisms of social network setup, configuration, and authorization and the way in which accounts, leads, and contacts can be linked to social network profiles.

You have learned how to configure social features and how to choose which social networking sites can be linked by users in the org. You have also gained the skills to authorize access to a social networking site and link account, lead, and contact records within the Lightning Platform.

In the next chapter, we will look at the exam objectives for managing the app-building process. We will be identifying the tasks and issues we encounter when managing the application life cycle and determining appropriate deployment options for given scenarios. We will look at the types of sandboxes, understand the capabilities and issues when using change sets, and examine the options for using unmanaged packages.

11
Managing the App Building Process

In this chapter, we will look at the processes and steps for managing the application life cycle when building apps using the Lightning Platform and identify the tasks and issues that can be encountered during the app building process.

You will learn about the different types of Salesforce environment and the capabilities of sandboxes, which are available to help orchestrate change management during the building of apps.

An overview of development models is covered, where you will learn in detail about the capabilities and considerations of using the change sets development approach for the migration of changes between Salesforce environments.

You will also discover scenarios that warrant the use of unmanaged packages to deploy changes, and you will learn about the various deployment strategies that help to determine the appropriate strategy for a given scenario.

Finally, you will be presented with a number of questions about managing the app building process.

In this chapter, we will cover the following:

- Exam objectives: App Development

- Managing the application life cycle

- Understanding the types of sandboxes

- Using change sets for app deployment

- Discovering the capabilities and options for using unmanaged packages

- Determining deployment options for given scenarios

Exam objectives: App Development

To complete the App Development section of the Certified Platform App Builder exam, app builders are expected to be able to carry out the following:

- Describe the key milestones and considerations when managing the application life cycle.

- Describe the differences between and considerations when using the various types of sandboxes.

- Describe the capabilities of and considerations when using change sets.

- Describe the use cases of and considerations when using unmanaged packages.

- Given a scenario, determine the appropriate deployment plan.

Reference: Salesforce Certified Platform App Builder Exam Guide

This guide is published by Salesforce and can be found at `https://trailhead.salesforce.com/help?article=Salesforce-Certified-Platform-App-Builder-Exam-Guide`.

In the *Salesforce Certified Platform App Builder Exam Guide*, the total number of questions is given, as is a percentage breakdown for each of the objectives and an indication of the number of features/functions that can be expected in each of the objectives.

By analyzing these objectives, percentages, and question counts, we can determine the possible amount of questions that will appear in the exam; for the App Development objective, this is as follows.

> **App Development: Total number of exam questions**
>
> There are likely to be four or five questions in total.
>
> This is calculated as 8% of 60 total exam questions, which equates to 4.8 questions; therefore, possibly up to five questions will appear.

Using these figures for the App Development objective and the number of items that may be assessed, we can determine that there will most likely be one or two questions for each of the following concepts: application life cycle management, sandboxes, change sets, unmanaged packages, and deployment options for given scenarios.

Let's now look at the processes and steps for managing the application life cycle on the Lightning Platform.

Managing the application life cycle

By adopting an **Application Life Cycle Management (ALM)** approach when building changes for systems, there are several benefits, such as improved planning and change management, improved testing process, and improved project communications. ALM helps to avoid issues such as managing versions of change items and failures through a lack of testing after deploying changes, as well as reducing risk and providing an improved approach to the building of apps.

Using an organized approach to building apps and having processes and policies that support the various steps of the processes within the Lightning Platform helps to ensure that apps can be built more smoothly and, hence, more quickly. By adopting certain policies, a more robust way of building apps can be carried out that helps to ensure that functions change as expected and avoids breaking existing functionality.

Although the use of the supporting apps and tools for the management of the application life cycle can vary, the overarching key milestones and considerations for the application life cycle remain the same.

Let's now look at the key milestones that Salesforce specifies as part of their ALM process, specifically the six steps that make up the Salesforce ALM framework, shown in the following diagram:

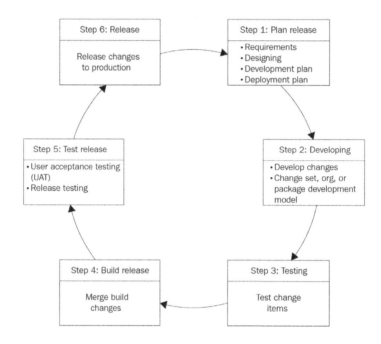

Figure 11.1 – Salesforce ALM

Let's learn about the preceding steps of this ALM cycle in the following sections.

Step 1 – Plan release

The first step of ALM is concerned with the planning of the change. By planning the list of processes and actions that are necessary for the building of apps, the items that are needed can be identified, monitored, and implemented. Salesforce suggests that you write down the plan for release so that stakeholders know what is happening, to avoid confusion, and to help identify all the known tasks and uncover any issues.

By creating and communicating the written plan, it becomes easier to understand the specific items and responsibilities and list them in concrete terms rather than in an abstract hypothetical manner. This means the decision and milestones that have to be achieved become more obvious, and it also uncovers the specifics that need attention, such as task assignment, development team availability, test plans, milestones, and more.

The plan will ultimately help you communicate with all who are involved in the project, to carry out the tasks in the correct order. The planning will help to identify the key resources, both manpower- and system-wise, such as detailing which development and testing environment to use in each ALM step. Finally, you'll understand when and how the project is to be signed off as complete.

However, it should be considered that usually, whenever building new functionality, there will be some element of risk, and this can raise issues that cause planning items to change during the plan release step. The initial plan, therefore, cannot be set in stone, and everyone should be prepared for revisions to the plan throughout the release as risks, issues, and new details surface.

During the plan release step, the following actions are carried out in order to determine an appropriate plan:

1. **Requirements gathering**: Requirements gathering involves the gathering of requirements and requirement analysis. During this time, stakeholders and user requirements are identified and the resultant use case and user stories are produced, which detail which items of functionality should be built.

2. **Designing**: The designing stage makes use of the results of the requirements-gathering activity to design the detailed instructions needed in order to proceed with the project's functional items. The results of the designing activity are either the creation of a design specification or because of the use of working models and prototypes.

3. **Development and test planning**: The stage that entails planning for the development makes use of the results of the designing stage to determine the way in which the functionality is to be built. It also makes use of the results of the requirements-gathering stage to list the checks that need to be carried out to ensure that the completed work conforms to what was required. Both the planning for development and for testing need to be tailored to the available resources. Here, the resources can be to do with either the individuals that are available to work on the project or the availability of systems such as development and test environments.

4. **Deployment planning**: This stage makes use of the results of the designing stage to determine an approximation of size and estimated length of time of the deployment. Deployment planning also needs to take into account resources both in terms of the number of person hours and the proposed deployment approach. Here, the deployment approach is tied in with the development model, which is covered in more detail later in this section (see *Step 2 – Develop*), as it presents different ways to migrate changes from the development environment into the production instance.

It may initially seem that the use of ALM adds to the overhead of building functionality within the Lightning Platform, if you have previously managed changes using a less structured approach. However, the results of having a proven ALM process adds significant benefits, such as improving planning and communications, helping to eliminate risk by making changes in a separate development environment, and ensuring adequate testing. This ultimately helps to ensure that changes do not cause issues after deploying into your production org.

> **Plan for changes to your org**
>
> For more information about this step when using the change set development model, refer to the following Trailhead resource:
>
> `https://trailhead.salesforce.com/en/content/learn/`
> `modules/declarative-change-set-development/plan-`
> `for-changes-to-your-org`

Once the planning activities have been completed and communicated to the business, you can start the implementation and enter the development step of the ALM cycle, which we will now look at.

Step 2 – Developing

The second step of ALM focuses on development. The development phase can also be termed the build or implementation phase, where people such as app builders, system administrators, developers, and so on develop changes to meet the requirements according to the design specification, prototype, or working model.

From the perspective of an app builder, the aim of the development step using the Lightning Platform is to build new solutions or modify existing functionality using declarative tools. The completed declarative changes consist of an appropriate combination of declarative tools and functionality using tools such as the custom object UI, Schema Builder, process automation, page layouts, Lightning pages, validation rules, and so on.

For developers, the development step involves the use of programmatic tools and functionality such as **source code editors** and the **developer console** for producing Apex code, Lightning components, Visualforce pages, and so on. For system administrators, the development step may involve the use of configuration tools and functionality such as roles and profiles, reports and dashboards, and so on.

In accordance with ALM and regardless of whether the change is being carried out using tools and functionality for app builders, developers, or system administrators, the work should be carried out in an environment that mirrors the production org and should not be performed directly in the production org.

One of the biggest strengths of the Lightning Platform is the capability to create and expose new functionality to users in an immediate and agile manner. However, this also presents potential risks when certain changes are applied directly to the production org. Furthermore, Salesforce does not recommend building new functionality directly in the production instance and instead advocates the use of sandboxes in accordance with ALM. There are, however, some changes, such as those to reports and dashboards, list views, email templates, and so on, that can be carried out directly in the production org.

Understand what is appropriate to change directly in production

For more information about the build step and to learn about what is fine to change directly in the production org, refer to the *What's Safe to Change In Production?* section of the following Trailhead resource:

```
https://trailhead.salesforce.com/en/content/learn/
modules/application-lifecycle-and-development-
models/understand-what-application-lifecycle-
management-is
```

Having an environment that is a reflection of the production setup is possible within the Lightning Platform by the use of a refreshed sandbox. Here, we can use a developer sandbox for both the declarative and programmatic changes, as well as the system administrator configurations, prior to deploying to the production org.

Furthermore, within the development step, there is a choice of development models available for both declarative and programmatic changes that offer capabilities to meet varying levels of requirement complexity. There are three development models that place a different emphasis on how the source of the change is stored and differ regarding the tools that are used to access the source repository. They are as follows:

- **Change set development**: The source of truth in the change set development model is, as the name suggests, within change sets, and this approach is useful for managing changes at an individual change item level or a solution level. The tool that the user employs is the **change set** feature, within the Lightning Platform, to create the release artifacts. These release artifacts are metadata changes that differ from the base production instance and are migrated between environments to go through the ALM process. In this chapter, we will look in more detail at the use of change sets, which enable the application of the change set development model.

- **Org development**: The source of truth in the org development model is within a separate source repository known as a **version control system** (**VCS**). Rather than using change sets and environments to track changes against the base production instance, users' changes can be implemented within personal environments and then merged in the VCS. Similar to change sets, the release artifacts are metadata changes that differ from the base production instance. However, where there are multiple users and projects, the use of separate repositories for changes at the org level makes it easier to track, deploy, and manage things, and hence to stay in sync. In this book, this is as far as we go with our coverage of the org development model.

- **Package development**: The source of truth in the package development model is within a package. Rather than using change sets or migrating from VCS, the package contains the related code and customization that forms the release artifact. A VCS is also key to the use of the package development model and multiple users or development teams can implement and own particular packages. Development teams can therefore develop in separate workstreams and deliver a release of a particular package, rather than a release based on changes for the org. In this book, this is as far as we go with our coverage of the package development model.

Although there are multiple development models and variation in the tools that are used to support, track, and manage the development models, the steps in the ALM cycle apply to any Salesforce development project.

We will look at the use of sandboxes in the Lightning Platform in more detail in the *Using change sets for app deployment* section, which comes later in this chapter.

Once the development step has been completed, the changes should be tested and verified before they are allowed to be migrated to the production org. We will now look at the activities involved in the testing step of ALM.

Step 3 – Testing

The third step of the ALM is concerned with the system testing of the change items. By conducting appropriate testing, we can check that the specific changes that have been developed work in accordance with the design specification, working models, or prototypes that were produced during the designing step.

The purpose of the testing in this testing step is to check that the changes made by the various app builders, system administrators, developers, and so on work as intended before these individuals merge them with other developers' changes. This testing should be done in the same type of environment as was used in the development step, but the actual development and integrated testing environments should remain separate from other users' environments.

Salesforce recommends that at this point in the testing, the focus should be on the validation of the specific changes and not on achieving full testing, which verifies the full functionality of the new functional requirement, nor should the aim be to validate how everyone's changes function alongside other parts of the solution release or the solution as a whole.

Step 4 – Build release

The fourth step of ALM focuses on the building of the release. In this step, all contributors to the release add their changes into a single release artifact, which is the set of configurations, customizations, and code that makes up the project.

Each member of the build and development teams migrates the build and customization changes from their specific developer sandboxes to a common developer environment so that all changes can be merged. The developer sandbox does not contain any production data, but it should be populated with test data that reflects the data within the production instance.

In some organizations, where there are a large number of changes and a larger team of app builders, system administrators, developers, and so on, an individual within the development team assumes the role of the release manager (or they may already be a release manager) and assumes responsibility for migrating the changes to production.

Step 5 – Test release

The fifth step of ALM is concerned with the building of the test release. In this step, testing should be carried out in an environment that mirrors the production org, and all changes should be tested, verified, and approved before they are migrated to the production org. The testing in this step checks both the release artifacts and the functional changes.

The testing in this step differs from the type of testing that is done by the builders and developers of the changes and has to be performed by experienced functional experts or the end users who ideally will be involved in using the system when it is deployed into the production environment. During **user acceptance testing** (**UAT**), the use cases and user stories that may have been produced in the requirements-gathering step can be used to verify that the solution or change functions as intended.

The test release step also enables the release artifact and deployment process to be tested prior to actually performing the release to the production instance. Here, you can identify whether there are any missing or dependent change artifacts and make sure that they are included before attempting to apply the release to the production environment.

When testing has been completed and approved by the stakeholders, you can release the changes to production.

Step 6 – Release

The sixth step of ALM focuses on releasing the changes to the production environment. In this step, all contributors to the release will have completed their part of the project.

For the release, there should be no need for anyone that has developed the changes to carry out the release; instead, it is the release manager, or someone assuming that role, who is responsible for the final release step.

There are several types of mechanisms and tools that can be used to deploy changes to a Salesforce production environment, and these include Salesforce change sets, managed packages, and third-party deployment tools.

In addition, there are various options available for migrating metadata, code, and resources between Salesforce orgs using sandboxes. We will now look at the setting up and use of sandboxes on the Lightning Platform.

Understanding the types of sandboxes

As mentioned in an earlier section, we have some options when it comes to sandboxes. Sandboxes are separate Lightning Platform environments that can contain declarative configuration, programmatic code, and in some instances data that reflects the entities that are contained in the production org. Sandboxes are separate and isolated from the Salesforce production organization, so changes to settings, configurations, and code that are performed in a sandbox do not affect the Lightning Platform production environment, and vice versa.

To view and manage your existing sandboxes or create new ones on the Lightning Platform, you need to log into your production org, as this is where the option for maintaining sandboxes is located. Sandboxes are not available from within the Developer Edition, so if you do not have access to a licensed production edition, you will not be able to get to the sandbox setup screen.

Access to the sandbox setup screen within a Lightning Platform production org can be achieved by following these steps:

1. Navigate to **Setup** and then search for `sandboxes` in the **Quick Find** search box located at the top of the **Setup** menu in the left sidebar.

2. Clicking on **Sandboxes** takes you to the following screen:

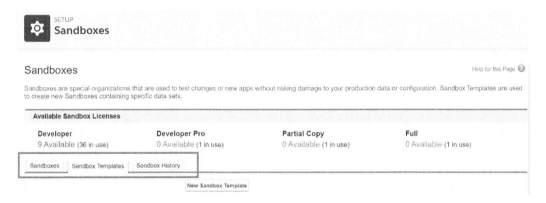

Figure 11.2 – List of sandboxes in the production org

Here, there are three tabs: **Sandboxes**, **Sandbox Templates**, and **Sandbox History**. The first tab is **Sandboxes**, and this tab presents a list of sandboxes for the production org. Within the list, you can view existing sandboxes that have been created, and by clicking on a sandbox name, you can view further details about the sandbox, such as when it was created.

In the sandbox list, you can see the informative fields such as **Name**, **Type**, **Status**, **Location**, **Current Org Id**, **Completed On**, and **Description**. You can also carry out actions such as **Clone**, **Delete**, and **Refresh**, as well as being able to navigate to the sandbox with the **Log In** option.

> **Available Sandbox Licenses**
>
> You will notice that there is a section labeled **Available Sandbox Licenses**. Here, the list and quantity of available sandboxes is determined by the type of Salesforce edition and other factors related to the license agreement, so this may vary from what is shown in the values displayed in our example sandbox setup screen.

On the **Sandboxes** screen, you can see the following sandbox types: **Developer**, **Developer Pro**, **Partial Copy**, and **Full**. These will depend upon your Salesforce license type. The **Sandboxes** tab is shown by default when you navigate to the setup page, as shown in the following screenshot:

Figure 11.3 – Sandbox list

Let's now consider the features and capabilities of the available types of sandboxes:

- **Developer**: A **Developer** sandbox can be used for app building, programmatic coding, and configuring, and it contains a copy of all the metadata and settings from the production instance. Developer sandboxes, when created, do not contain any production data. Developer sandboxes provide a maximum of 200 MB of data storage and 200 MB of file storage, and they can be refreshed once per day.

- **Developer Pro**: A **Developer Pro** sandbox can be used for the same activities as a Developer sandbox, and they can also be used for limited testing and user training as they contain more storage. Developer Pro sandboxes contain a copy of all the metadata and settings from the production instance, and when created, they do not contain any production data. Developer Pro sandboxes provide a maximum of 1 GB of data storage and 1 GB of file storage, and they can be refreshed once per day.

- **Partial Copy**: A **Partial Copy** sandbox can be used as a test or training environment and contains a copy of all the metadata and settings from the production instance. Unlike the Developer and Developer Pro sandboxes, a Partial Copy sandbox can be configured, when being created, with a sample of the production instance data. The type of data that is automatically created is defined using a sandbox template; Partial Copy sandboxes can be refreshed once every 5 days.

- **Full**: A **Full** sandbox can be used as a **UAT** or training environment and contains a complete copy of the metadata and settings from the production instance, as well as all the data. Full sandboxes have the same storage limit as the production organization and can also be used for data volume testing. Because the data is also copied over during a refresh, the limit on refreshing a Full sandbox is once every 29 days.

Let's look at some additional capabilities and considerations for sandboxes:

- **Users' email addresses will be modified**: With the exception of the user that creates or refreshes a sandbox, all other users have their email modified with a suffix of .invalid after a sandbox refresh; for example, john.smith123456@gmail.com becomes john.smith123456@gmail.com.invalid after a sandbox refresh. This is used to keep access to the sandbox secure and only allow users access to the sandbox when it's actively requested.

- **The Sandbox Templates tab**: Templates are applied when Partial Copy sandboxes are created or refreshed to specify the type of data to be created. There is a maximum of 5 GB of data storage and 5 GB of file storage that can be stored, and for each selected object in the sandbox template, up to 10,000 records are copied from the production instance. This tab displays the details for the templates as shown in the following screenshot:

Figure 11.4 – The Sandbox Templates tab

- • **The Sandbox History tab**: This tab displays the details of when a sandbox was last refreshed and by whom, as shown in the following screenshot:

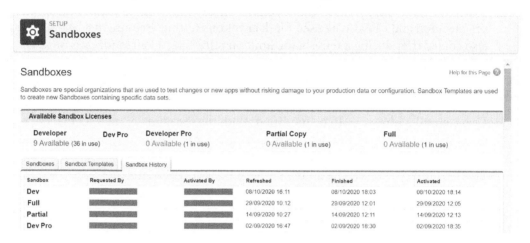

Figure 11.5 – The Sandbox History tab

> **Sandbox feature quick reference**
>
> Information about sandbox licenses and the latest storage limits can be obtained by referring to the following article:
>
> ```
> https://help.salesforce.com/articleView?id=data_
> sandbox_environments.htm&type=5
> ```

Sandboxes help to ensure that the process of deploying changes is carried out in a structured and controlled way, and they reduce the risk that the deployment of new items of functionality or modifications to existing functionality will cause any issues.

Now that we have looked at the types of sandboxes, let's now look at the use and capabilities of change sets, which are used to deploy changes between Lightning Platform environments.

Using change sets for app deployment

Earlier in this chapter, we looked at ALM and discovered that the sixth and final step involves the release of changes to the production org.

We also learned about various development models, and in particular the change set development model, which is enacted using the setup UI. Here, the change set feature enables the grouping of change items into change sets within a development environment, which can then be migrated between environments during ALM steps.

A change set comprises a set of changes that are either new or modified metadata items of the production environment. Multiple change sets can be created, and they contain metadata that reflects the configuration, declarative customization, and programmatic code for the build.

The process of using change sets to migrate changes between environments on the Lightning Platform is as follows:

1. **Creating a deployment connection**: A deployment connection allows change sets to be uploaded between two environments. To upload changes from one org – say, org A – to another org, org B, you must set the deployment connection in org B to allow incoming change sets from org A. Deployment connections can only be created between orgs that have been created from the same production org. For example, a production org and a sandbox, or two sandboxes created using the same production org, can have an associated deployment connection.

2. **Creating an outbound change set**: An outbound change set contains a set of new or modified metadata items, which can be uploaded from the current org to one or more orgs that are associated with a common production org.

3. **Uploading the outbound change set**: An outbound change set can be uploaded from the current org to one or more orgs that are associated with a common production org – for example, a production org, or a sandbox that has been created from the same production org. After the outbound change set has been uploaded, the set of changes appears within the receiving org as an inbound change set.

4. **Validating the inbound change set**: An inbound change set can be validated prior to deployment to check that it will deploy successfully in the receiving org. The validation carries out all the checks that would be made when deploying, but no actual changes are made.

5. **Deploying the inbound change set**: An inbound change set can be deployed in the receiving org, at which time validation is carried out to ensure that the change set contains all dependent changes and that there is no conflict with the environment in which the changes are being made.

Enabling change sets to be uploaded between two environments requires creating deployment connections, which is done by following these steps:

1. Navigate to **Setup** and then search for `Deployment Settings` in the **Quick Find** search box located at the top of the **Setup** menu in the left sidebar.

2. Click on **Deployment Settings** in the **Setup** menu.

3. On the **Deployment Settings** setup screen, the options for deployment connections are available, as shown in the following screenshot:

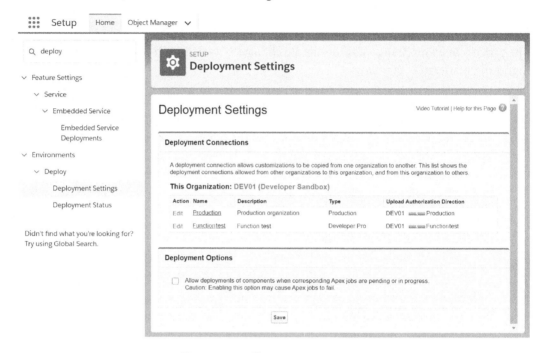

Figure 11.6 – Change set connections

The deployment connections must be set for the destination Lightning Platform environment, to allow inbound change sets, and for the source environment, to enable outbound change sets.

An outbound change set can be created, within a Lightning Platform sandbox or production org, by carrying out the following steps:

1. Navigate to **Setup** and then search for Change Sets in the **Quick Find** search box located at the top of the **Setup** menu on the left sidebar.

2. Click on **Outbound Change Sets** in the **Setup** menu.

3. On the **Outbound Change Sets** setup screen, the options for creating new outbound change sets and viewing the history of previous change sets is available as shown in the following screenshot:

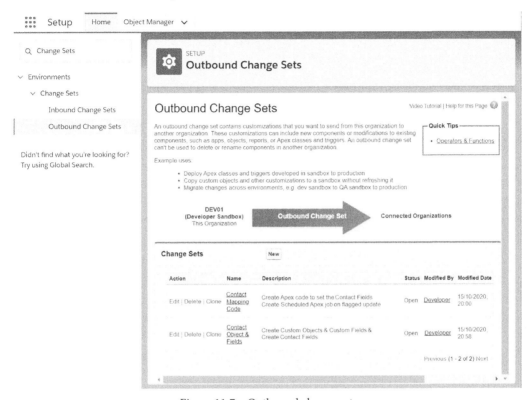

Figure 11.7 – Outbound change sets

Change sets provide an easy method of deploying metadata changes between Lightning Platform environments that are associated with a common production instance. They help to show and monitor the changes within outbound and inbound change set histories and offer a simple set of options using the setup UI to enable a declarative method of deployment.

Let's now look at the use cases for unmanaged packages, which can be used to deploy changes into a Lightning Platform environment.

Identifying the options for using unmanaged packages

Unmanaged packages are a feature of the Lightning Platform that enables you to create packages that contain a set of metadata items that can be uploaded from the current org to one or more Lightning Platform orgs that are not associated with a common production org.

The typical use case for unmanaged packages is building a private template app or a set of change items that can be later modified, or distributing a public free metadata source to provide Lightning App developers with a framework or proof of concept from which to build an app or solution.

After an unmanaged package has been deployed to a Lightning Platform org, the metadata items that are included in the package can be modified and extended within the org where they have been installed. Unlike managed packages, which are used to create public apps for Salesforce AppExchange, which we looked at in *Chapter 1, Core Capabilities of the Lightning Platform*, unmanaged packages do not obfuscate the details of the change items within a package.

By not obfuscating or hiding the details within an unmanaged package, the change items can be viewed and modified. The author and intellectual copyright owner of the changes, therefore, has no control over the installed components, and cannot change them or automatically upgrade them as can be done with managed packages.

> **Do not release changes using unmanaged packages**
>
> Salesforce recommends that you do not use unmanaged packages to migrate changes from a development or testing sandbox to a production instance. For more information about unmanaged packages, refer to the following article:
>
> ```
> https://help.salesforce.com/
> articleView?id=sharing_apps.htm&type=5
> ```

Viewing and creating unmanaged packages can be carried out by following these steps:

1. Navigate to **Setup** and then search for `Package` in the **Quick Find** search box located at the top of the **Setup** menu on the left sidebar.

2. Click on **Package Manager** in the **Setup** menu.

On the **Package Manager Setup** screen, there are two sections, namely **Developer Settings** and **Packages**. The options that are available in the first section, **Developer Settings**, are dependent on which Salesforce edition you are using; the settings are limited for the Developer Edition:

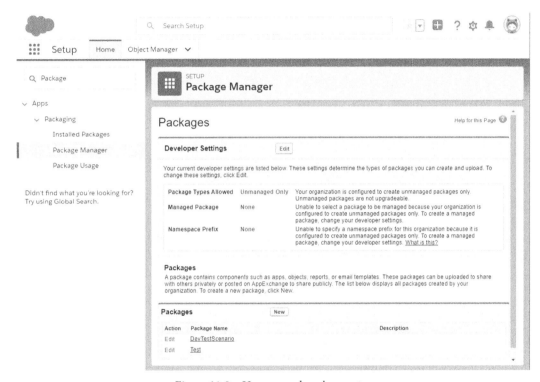

Figure 11.8 – Unmanaged package setup

The second section allows you to create an unmanaged package, as shown in the preceding screenshot. Let's now look at the various deployment options and scenarios when using change sets to deploy changes.

Determining deployment options for given scenarios

When deploying changes between Lightning Platform environments, there are various deployment options and scenarios that you should consider when using change sets.

In particular, when migrating changes to a production instance, there are additional requirements for programmatic Apex code that mean Apex test classes need to be written and executed to test that the lines of code function as expected.

There is a minimum acceptable percentage of tested code lines before a change set is permitted to be deployed to a production instance. These tests are required to prevent code from causing errors that would have an impact on the production org. During the running of all tests in the org, the code coverage must be at least 75%.

The deployment options are determined by the type of metadata changes within the change sets; the following should be considered:

- **Apex code test classes**: When Apex code is included in a change set, extra time is needed to run to the test classes, which must be present before the code can be deployed.

- **Quick deploy**: When Apex code is included in a change set and you have successfully validated and run the associated test classes, you have a time limit of 10 days to carry out a quick deploy, which completes the deployment without re-running the tests. This reduces the amount of time it takes to migrate changes for Apex code and is useful when you want to prepare a change set in readiness for an agreed deployment time.

- **Manual deployment**: There are some metadata components that cannot be included and deployed using change sets because they are not currently supported. These includes the account team, lead settings, mobile administration, sales processes, standard picklist values, web-to-lead configuration settings, and others.

- **Deployment status**: When inbound change sets are deployed and completed, their status is set to either **Failed** or **Succeeded** within the change set history. No changes are made to the inbound org if the status is set to **Failed**, which might occur if dependent items are missing, components have errors, Apex tests are failing, or the deployment is canceled.

Let's now consider some questions to help test your knowledge of managing the application life cycle on the Lightning Platform.

Questions to test your knowledge

We now present five questions to help assess your knowledge of managing the application life cycle. Here, there are questions about the key milestones within the application life cycle, the various types of sandboxes, the capabilities and considerations of change sets, and the use of unmanaged packages to deploy changes on the Lightning Platform.

Question 1 – ALM

What are the steps of ALM? (Select one.)

a) i) Plan release, ii) Requirements, iii) Test, iv) Build release, v) Test release, and vi) Release

b) i) Design, ii) Develop, iii) Test, iv) Build release, v) Test release, and vi) Release

c) i) Plan release, ii) Requirements, iii) Test, iv) Build release, v) Test release, and vi) Release

d) i) Plan release, ii) Develop, iii) Test, iv) Build release, v) Test release, and vi) Release

Question 2 – The plan release step

What actions are carried out during the plan release step of ALM? (Select one.)

a) Designing, change set development, and planning for development, testing, and deployment

b) Requirements gathering, designing, and planning for development, testing, and deployment

c) Requirements gathering, designing, and planning for change set development

d) Designing and planning for development, testing, and deployment

Question 3 – Sandboxes

Which type of sandbox would be appropriate for carrying out a full data load of migrated data that will be later loaded into production? (Select one.)

a) Developer sandbox

b) Partial Copy sandbox

c) Full sandbox

d) Developer Pro sandbox

Question 4 – Change sets

As the app builder in your company, you have been receiving an increasing amount of new change requests and projects and have engaged an external Salesforce consultant to help cope with all the new work. You have also looked at the use of change sets to help improve the way changes are deployed by everyone involved in these new projects. What benefits do change sets provide? (Select two.)

a) They provide a simple set of options using the setup UI to enable a declarative method of deployment.

b) They separate workstreams and deliver changes within a package that can be deployed to any Lightning Platform.

c) They track changes using a separate source repository known as a version control system.

d) They're an easy method to deploy metadata changes.

Question 5 – Change sets – sequence of events

What is the correct sequence of events that you should perform when deploying changes to a Salesforce org with change sets? (Select one.)

a) Deploy, validate, and then upload.

b) Validate, upload, and then deploy.

c) Upload, validate, and then deploy.

d) The sequence does not matter.

Here are the answers to the five questions.

Answer 1 – ALM

The answer is d) i) Plan release, ii) Develop, iii) Test, iv) Build release, v) Test release, and vi) Release.

The following choices are not correct:

a) i) Plan release, ii) Requirements, iii) Test, iv) Build release, v) Test release, and vi) Release

b) i) Design, ii) Develop, iii) Test, iv) Build release, v) Test release, and vi) Release

c) i) Plan release, ii) Requirements, iii) Test, iv) Build release, v) Test release, and vi) Release

Answer 2 – The plan release step

The answer is b) Requirements gathering, designing, and planning for development, testing, and deployment.

The following choices are not correct:

a) Designing, change set development, and planning for development, testing, and deployment

c) Requirements gathering, designing, and planning for change set development

d) Designing and planning for development, testing, and deployment

Answer 3 – Sandboxes

The answer is c) Full sandbox.

The following choices are not correct:

a) Developer sandbox

b) Partial Copy sandbox

d) Developer Pro sandbox

Answer 4 – Change sets

The answers are these:

a) They provide a simple set of options using the setup UI to enable a declarative method of deployment.

d) They're an easy method to deploy metadata changes.

The following choices are not correct:

b) They separate workstreams and deliver changes within a package that can be deployed to any Lightning Platform.

c) They track changes using a separate source repository known as a version control system.

Answer 5 – Change sets – sequence of events

The answer is c) Upload, validate, and then deploy.

The following choices are not correct:

a) Deploy, validate, and then upload.

b) Validate, upload, and then deploy.

d) The sequence does not matter.

Summary

In this chapter, we have looked at the features available for managing the application life cycle on the Salesforce Lightning Platform.

You have learned about the processes and steps for managing the application life cycle when building apps on the Lightning Platform. You were presented with an overview of the development models and the benefits and considerations of using the change sets development approach to migrate changes between Salesforce environments.

You have gained the knowledge needed to be able to configure different types of Salesforce environment and have examined the capabilities of the sandboxes that are available to help orchestrate change management during the building of apps.

You also discovered the use cases and capabilities of unmanaged packages and learned about the various deployment strategies that help to determine an appropriate strategy for a given scenario.

In the next chapter, we will take a detailed look at the Certified Platform App Builder exam and identify further resources and strategies, as well as offering more insights into the process of planning for and completing the exam.

12
Studying for the Certified Platform App Builder Exam

In this chapter, we will look at the Salesforce Certified Platform App Builder exam, which is a Salesforce credential for individuals seeking a certification path in either a Salesforce administrator or Salesforce developer role. The Salesforce Platform App Builder exam is used to measure individuals' ability to design, build, and deploy custom applications using the declarative features within the Lightning Platform.

Before taking the Salesforce Certified Platform App Builder exam, you should have experience of using the declarative customization capabilities and also an awareness of the programmatic capabilities of the Lightning Platform.

Within this chapter, we will review the study guide for the Salesforce Certified Platform App Builder exam and you will discover various resources that will help you to study for the exam. You will learn about the resources available from Salesforce and other channels that aim to improve your understanding of the knowledge and functionality that is tested in the Salesforce Platform App Builder exam.

We will also look at the process of planning, booking, and attending the exam, and offer some insight into the types of questions that may appear, along with advice for handling the questions during the exam.

In this chapter, we will look in detail at the Salesforce Certified Platform App Builder exam and will cover the following:

- Using the Salesforce Platform App Builder exam study guide
- Understanding the format of the exam
- Carrying out a self-assessment for the exam
- Identifying resources available for studying
- Registering for the exam
- Taking and passing the exam

Let's now look at the study guide that Salesforce provides for the Platform App Builder exam.

Using the Platform App Builder exam study guide

Salesforce provides a study guide for the Salesforce Certified Platform App Builder exam, which gives you a good summary of the purpose of the exam and some guidelines on what topics to be familiar with. You should refer to the study guide as it contains the latest information about the number of questions, topics, and so on, as these can change over time.

The exam guide is particularly useful as it outlines the features and functions that a candidate with hands-on experience would need to demonstrate in order to pass. The exam guide also shows the weighting of the features and functions that are applied to the Salesforce Platform App Builder exam. By looking at the weighting, it is possible to determine the approximate number of questions that may appear, to help you focus on the topics with the greatest number of questions.

> Trailhead: **Salesforce Certified Platform App Builder exam guide**
>
> The Salesforce Certified Platform App Builder exam guide is, at the time of writing, located within Trailhead and can be referenced from the following article: `https://trailhead.salesforce.com/en/help?article=Salesforce-Certified-Platform-App-Builder-Exam-Guide`.

The following summarizes the content that you will find in the Salesforce Platform App Builder exam study guide:

- Information about the Salesforce Platform App Builder credential

- Audience description: Salesforce Platform App Builder

- Purpose of the exam guide

- About the exam

- Recommended training and references

- Exam outline

- Maintaining your certification

The following section provides information about the format of the exam as outlined in the study guide.

Understanding the format of the exam

The Salesforce Platform App Builder exam consists of *60 multiple-choice (or single-choice) questions* and the maximum time allowed is *105 minutes*.

There is no mandatory prerequisite training, qualification, or experience; however, Salesforce highly recommends that candidates have a combination of real-world experience, have attended a suitable training course, have completed Trailhead trails, and have completed a period of self-study to improve their chances of passing the exam.

The percentage score for passing the Salesforce Platform App Builder exam is *63%*, which equates to successfully answering a minimum of *38 correct answers* out of a total of 60 questions.

> **Cost of the Salesforce Platform App Builder exam**
>
> At the time of writing, the cost of registering for the exam is *$200 USD* and in the event of an unsuccessful attempt, the cost to retake the exam is *$100 USD*.

During the exam, no written or online resource may be referenced, and when you submit the exam, you are presented with your exam result immediately.

After you have passed the Salesforce Platform App Builder exam, each year you must complete a Platform App Builder Certification Maintenance module. Salesforce Certification maintenance modules are managed within Trailhead and are used to ensure that you have up-to-date knowledge of any new and modified features of the Lightning Platform as new releases become available.

> **Certification maintenance schedule**
>
> To find out more information about the maintenance module and learn more about the Salesforce maintenance requirements, refer to the following: `https://trailhead.salesforce.com/en/help?article=Certification-Release-Maintenance-Schedule`.

It is important to be up to date about when the latest maintenance module is available for the Platform App Builder exam, otherwise you risk losing your certification if you do not complete the maintenance requirements by the published deadline.

> **Cost of the Salesforce Platform App Builder maintenance test**
>
> At the time of writing, it is free to maintain your Salesforce App Builder certification using the App Builder Certification Maintenance module in Trailhead.

Now that you have an understanding of the format of the Salesforce Platform App Builder exam, you should carry out an assessment of the areas of study, along with your own knowledge of these topics, by carrying out a self-assessment for the exam.

Carrying out a self-assessment for the exam

Before deciding when to take the Salesforce Platform App Builder exam, it is a good idea to assess how much knowledge and experience you currently have with building custom applications in the Lightning Platform.

The purpose of the Salesforce Platform App Builder exam is to test that you have the knowledge and level of understanding to use declarative tools to build apps. You should understand how the Lightning Platform can be used for the creation, management, and modification of data models. You should know which features can be used to implement application security. You should be able to make use of declarative functionality to implement business logic and develop process automation. Finally, you should understand the process and options that enable the deployment of changes.

The Salesforce Platform App Builder exam contains questions that cover the features and functionalities that we have included in this book. The features and functionalities are grouped into topics that contribute to the overall score in the exam, with the following number of questions and percentage weightings:

- **Salesforce Fundamentals**: **5 questions** and an exam weighting of **8%**

- **Data Modeling and Management**: **12 questions** and an exam weighting of **20%**

- **Security**: **6 questions** and an exam weighting of **10%**

- **Business Logic and Process Automation**: **16 questions** and an exam weighting of **27%**

- **Social**: **2 questions** and an exam weighting of **3%**

- **User Interface**: **8 questions** and an exam weighting of **14%**

- **Reporting**: **3 questions** and an exam weighting of **5%**

- **Mobile**: **3 questions** and an exam weighting of **5%**

- **App Development**: **5 questions** and an exam weighting of **8%**

The features and functionalities that are listed are taken from the Salesforce Platform App Builder exam *Study Guide*, and have different weightings according to the numbers of questions. The topics therefore constitute different percentages of the exam and can be represented as shown in the following pie chart:

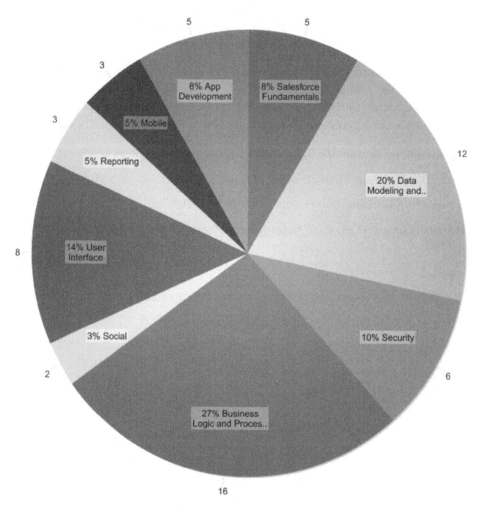

Figure 12.1 – Exam weighting

One strategy that candidates may find useful, especially when they have a limited amount of time for studying, is to focus their study on the features and functionalities that carry the highest numbers of questions. As an example, there could be as many as 17 questions (or 27% of the exam) in the exam covering *Business Logic and Process Automation*, or as few as 2 questions (or 3% exam coverage) for *Social*.

Given these numbers, a good approach is to focus more of the time that is available for study on the topics that make up the largest number of questions. Nonetheless, even if time is less of an issue and you are seeking to gain the maximum number of correct answers, you should still aim to plan your study and review the features and functionalities within the Salesforce Platform App Builder exam and assess how much knowledge and what skills you currently possess.

By reviewing the topics and the percentage weightings, you can reduce the amount of study for the areas of strength and conversely concentrate more on the areas you are less familiar with, and then tailor your study plan and the amount of studying for these areas accordingly.

By going through the list of features and functionalities and self-assessing your current knowledge, you can determine the specific areas where you may need to study more. Even highly seasoned Salesforce professionals may not have experience in all of the areas that are likely to be covered in the exam, so there may be some need to spend a lot of time studying the topics that you are less familiar with.

Identifying resources available for studying

There are many resources available to help you with the process of studying for the Salesforce Platform App Builder exam. The resources that will be outlined in this section include official Salesforce resources and third-party resources that have been provided by the wider Salesforce community. There are resources that you have to pay for and others that are free with both the official and third-party resources.

If you are fortunate enough to be currently working with the Lightning Platform for a Salesforce customer or partner and have system administrator permissions, then you should be able to gain valuable on-the-job experience and will be able to gain much of the knowledge of the features and functionalities required while carrying out your day job.

For individuals that may not currently be full-time app builders in their companies, but work for organizations with a training budget and a desire to train them to carry out the building of custom apps in the Lightning Platform, these individuals can take advantage of the instructor-led training courses that are produced by Salesforce. Also, individuals who are able to pay for their own training can attend these official instructor-led Salesforce training courses.

Salesforce recommends carrying out on-the-job experience, attending training courses, and carrying out self-study to help improve an individual's chances of passing the Salesforce Platform App Builder exam.

The official Salesforce resources for training and studying for the Salesforce Platform App Builder exam are as follows:

- Signing up for classroom-based and online training courses
- Creating a free personal Developer Edition org
- Learning with Trailhead
- Accessing official online and social networking channels
- Using third-party study resources

Let's now look at these resources for training and studying for the Salesforce Platform App Builder exam.

Signing up for classroom-based and online training courses

Some people find it more convenient and easier to learn in a classroom-based environment where they are guided through an agenda of topics relating to the building of apps in the Lightning Platform.

In this type of class, students can carry out practical tasks while under the supervision of a skilled training professional with Salesforce certification skills. Students can ask various questions to help gain a better understanding and knowledge of building apps in the Lightning Platform.

> **Limited availability of classroom-based in-person training**
>
> At the time of writing, due to COVID-19, there is limited availability for the classroom-based in-person training offered by Salesforce and their authorized training center partners. Therefore, you may find more options for virtual training courses.

The following instructor-led training courses for building apps with declarative development are available from Salesforce or an authorized training center:

- **DEX403**: The DEX403 course is called **Declarative Development for Platform App Builders in Lightning Experience**. This course is delivered in person over 5 days and as a virtual course over 5 days. The cost of the course is $4,500.

- **DEX403E**: The DEX403E course is called **Declarative Development for Platform App Builders in Lightning - Extended**. This course is an extended version of the DEX403 course and is delivered with 4 hours of virtual learning a day that is spread over 2 weeks. The cost of the course is $4,500.

- **CRT403**: The CRT403 course is called **Certification Preparation for Platform App Builder**. This course is delivered as a virtual course over 5 days. The cost of the course is $900.

- **TVB403**: The TVB403 course is called **Trailhead Virtual Bootcamp for Platform App Builder**. This course is delivered as a virtual expert-led training course that uses a 30-day blended learning program. The cost of the course is $900.

Salesforce offers these courses in a variety of delivery formats, namely conventional classroom-based teaching, but also virtual learning.

Trailhead Academy: In-person and virtual learning

To find out more information about the instructor-led training courses that are delivered through in-person and virtual learning from the Salesforce Trailhead Academy, refer to the following: `https://trailhead.salesforce.com/en/academy`.

The following free webinar is also available from Salesforce: **CDW-402**. The CDW-402 webinar's full title is **Free Webinar: Preparation for the Platform App Builder Certification**. The webinar is free.

Salesforce certification days

Salesforce certification days are free, half-day webinars that are available to help you prepare for the App Builder exam. For more information about the certification days, refer to the following: `https://trailhead.salesforce.com/credentials/cert-days`.

Creating a free personal Developer Edition org

It can be assumed that if you have read this far into the book, you have already signed up for or had access to a Salesforce instance. If you have been using your company's org either within the production instance or a sandbox, it can be useful to sign up for your own developer org.

You can create a free personal Salesforce Developer Edition org by carrying out the following:

1. Navigate to the web URL: `https://developer.salesforce.com/`.
2. Click on the **Sign Up** button on the page.
3. Enter your details into the **Sign Up** form.
4. Click on the **Sign me up** button.
5. You should then receive a **Welcome to Salesforce** email.
6. Finally, click the **Verify Account** link in the **Welcome to Salesforce** email and you will have created your new Salesforce Developer Edition account features.

It can be beneficial to set up a developer org by using a personal email address; this allows you to try out changes and switch on or off functionality without affecting others in your company organization. This means that you retain access to the developer org even if you are no longer associated with the company that you were working with.

It can be easier to retain the concepts and new information that you will learn by experimenting and practically carrying out changes, rather than trying to memorize the options and configuration screens.

You can also use your personal Developer Edition org to link to a Trailhead login. Here, multiple orgs can be linked and used to carry out hands-on activities during learning trails and challenges, which we will now look at.

Learning with Trailhead

Trailhead is a free interactive online learning tool developed and supported by Salesforce that provides useful training resources for administrators and developers at various levels of experience.

The Salesforce App Builder training content in Trailhead is arranged into trails, modules, and units that can be used to help guide you through the features and function of Salesforce app building and configuration.

Trailhead offers the following set of self-paced training courses, which is delivered online and provides a training experience where you can learn on demand. Here, you can select the features and functionalities that will assist in preparing you for the Salesforce Certified App Builder exam.

> **Trailhead learning**
>
> To find out more information about the trails that are available from the Salesforce Trailhead Platform, refer to the following: `https://trailhead.salesforce.com`.

Trailhead also allows you to gain award points and badges that show that you have applied the Trailhead modules to your Salesforce instance and have been successful in the completion of the Salesforce App Builder units and modules. The badges that have been achieved during the course of a trail can be displayed on your user profile, so you are recognized for your experience and achievements.

Accessing official online and social networking channels

Salesforce has a number of official online and social networking channels that provide videos, files, forums, and guidance for individuals looking for resources to help them study for the Salesforce Certified App Builder exam. These online and social networking channels can be found on YouTube, Twitter, LinkedIn, and the Salesforce Success Community.

> **Salesforce YouTube channel**
>
> To access the Salesforce YouTube channel, navigate to the following: `https://www.youtube.com/user/salesforce`.

The Salesforce YouTube channel contains videos of various Salesforce features and functionalities that are very useful for training Salesforce professionals at all levels of knowledge and experience.

Using third-party study resources

There are a number of resources that are not endorsed by Salesforce but that may be useful. A word of caution though; they are not sanctioned or endorsed by Salesforce, so you need to be very careful when using these types of material.

It is essential that you carry out due diligence to ensure that the information is accurate and that the facts shown are valid for the current version of the Salesforce Lightning Platform.

The following types of resources are not official Salesforce resources and are not endorsed by Salesforce but may or may not be useful to help identify further information for studying for the Salesforce Certified App Builder exam:

- Paid practice exam questions
- Paid study guides
- Salesforce study groups
- Blogs
- Forums
- Online tests
- Flash cards
- Google

Be wary of third-party resources that present questions and answers, as they are often outdated, no longer valid, or in some cases, incorrect and misleading. For the online tests and flash cards, verify first that they are correct for the current release of the Salesforce Lightning Platform.

It is recommended not to use these resources without carrying out due diligence to ensure the questions that are presented are accurate.

Registering for the exam

To register and sign up to take the Salesforce Certified Platform App Builder exam, you must first register your details with **Webassessor**. Webassessor, operated by Kryterion Inc, is a secure, online testing tool used by Salesforce and other organizations to manage and process certification exams.

> **Salesforce Webassessor exam registration page**
> To access the Salesforce Webassessor exam registration page, navigate to
> `https://www.webassessor.com/salesforce`.

Once you have registered and created an account, you can register for a new exam by clicking on the **Register For An Exam** tab at the top of the Webassessor screen. To register for the Salesforce Platform App Builder exam, scroll down to the **App Builder Exams** section, as shown in the following screenshot:

Figure 12.2 – Register

Lightning Platform release versions

When booking the Salesforce Certified Platform App Builder exam, you will notice that there are different versions of the exam, for example, WI22 (Winter 22), SP23 (Spring 23), SU23 (Summer 23), and so on.

Having registered your details with Webassessor, let's now look at booking the exam.

Booking the exam

When you book the exam, you have the choice to take the exam at a testing center or to use online proctoring which allows you to take the exam remotely using a non-test center computer. Online proctored exams are delivered through secure software that allows the exam to be monitored through a webcam. You will need to have administrator access rights for the computer so that you can install the secure software supplied by Webassessor.

> **COVID-19 and the Salesforce certification program FAQ**
>
> At the time of writing, many exam testing centers around the world are closed or have reduced capacity so online proctored exams are in demand. Refer to the following article about the impacts of the outbreak on the Salesforce certification program: `https://trailhead.salesforce.com/help?article=Testing-Center-Closures-Due-to-Coronavirus-COVID-19`.

You will need to check the latest information about online proctored exams such as availability and technical requirements. You'll also need to make sure that your environment and equipment satisfy the hardware and software requirements and comply with the stipulated testing environment mentioned in the Trailhead online proctoring article.

If you choose to take the exam in person and a suitable testing center is available, you will first select the test center in Webassessor. You will then be presented with a calendar showing available dates from which you can select a suitable date and time.

Should you need to, you can change the date and time for both online proctored and testing center exam dates, which we will now consider.

Rescheduling the exam

If you are unable to take the test at the date and time that was scheduled, or you feel that you are not ready to take it, you must reschedule the exam with at least 72 hours' notice or you will be charged a rescheduling fee.

> **Book the exam now!**
>
> You may be tempted to leave the booking of the exam until some future date, perhaps when you feel that you have studied in enough detail to answer every question correctly. This may not always be the best approach as you can book the exam and reschedule multiple times until you are ready.

You will notice that the booked exam shows a version of the exam, for example, **WI22** (**winter 22**), **SP23** (**spring 23**), **SU23** (**summer 23**). If you book your exam in an earlier period but take your test after rescheduling the exam, the exam will automatically be set to the latest version. For example, you register for the exam during **SU21** (**summer 21**) but reschedule after, say, November, which results in your exam falling into the **WI22** (**winter 22**) exam period.

Taking and passing the exam

When taking the exam at a testing center, you need to arrive 15 minutes prior to the start of the examination and will not be able to sit the exam if you are late. Do not bring too much baggage into the testing center as you may only have a small locker in which to store all your personal belongings.

You will need to take two forms of identity documents, which could be your passport and driving license, for example. In addition, you need to either print the email that you received when you registered for the exam or show the test code to the examination room proctor as they will need the code to start the exam. Alternatively, show the exam proctor the code on your smartphone.

For the online proctored exam, you can start several minutes early, which can be useful to check that your remote test environment and computer settings are working correctly. For example, it is necessary at the start of the exam for a photo to be taken of you using your computer webcam, in accordance with biometric security requirements.

> **Online proctored exams**
>
> Refer to the following article for more information about completing your exam remotely: `https://trailhead.salesforce.com/en/help?article=Online-Proctoring-Completing-Your-Exam-Remotely`.

Let's look at what to expect during the exam.

During the exam

During the exam, you may find that a question that you are currently answering has provided a clue for a question you encountered earlier in the exam but did not know at the time, and so is currently set as **Marked for Review**.

In general, there are two main formats for the questions, as follows:

- **Fact-based**: The fact-based format questions can be quicker to answer since the questions are fact-based and present one or a multiple of correct answers. Here, the simplest example of this format is where there is only one correct answer, but even where there is more than one correct answer you will either know the fact or you can make an estimated guess.

- **Scenario-based**: Scenario-based questions can be more time consuming as there is more detail within the question that you must read carefully to understand. This might be, as an example, *You are the App Builder in your organizations and your Sales Director has asked you to build X that allows Y. How would you approach this request and what solution would you use?*. Often you can rule out one or two options quite easily and you may have even seen clues in other questions that would help you to deduce an appropriate solution.

Do not panic if you find yourself spending too long on one question and are unable to proceed, either because of the complexity of the exam question or you do not know the answer with total confidence.

Mark the question for review and then come back to it later, but be mindful of the 105-minute time limit, as it is easy for the time to burn down quickly during the exam. The remaining time is shown in the upper-left of the screen.

You can review the questions that have been marked for review by clicking **Review Exam**. The screen shows the questions that have been marked for review indicated by an asterisk.

After the exam

After you have clicked the **Finish** exam button, you will be first asked a final question to provide feedback for the exam where you can leave a comment, and once this is submitted, you will be presented with your result.

Here, the result is either **Pass** or **Fail**, and there is a **Section-Level Scoring** area of the test result that shows a percentage result for each section within the exam; these result details are also emailed to you.

It may take a short time for the confirmation email showing your result to be received. I have personally sat an exam at 10:30 in the morning at a test center and did not get the result until later that evening. In this scenario, by logging into the Webassessor site after the exam, I was able to see my results before receiving them by email.

Finally, you can show that you have successfully gained the Salesforce Certified Platform App Builder credential by agreeing to show your details on the Webassessor site. When this is done, people can navigate to the certification verification page and search and select your name to display the types of certification that you hold.

> **Salesforce certification verification page**
>
> To access the certification verification page, navigate to `http://certification.salesforce.com/verification`.

Summary

In this final chapter, we have looked in detail at the *Study Guide* for the Salesforce Certified Platform App Builder exam and have identified the various resources to help you study for the exam that are available from Salesforce, which are either free or available at an additional cost.

You will have discovered how to sign up for and book the exam, and how to use the *Study Guide* and resources to plan for successfully passing. You have learned what to expect during the exam and gained insight into the types of questions that may be presented in the exam.

We then concluded the chapter by looking at what happens after the exam and at the requirements for maintaining your Salesforce professional credentials.

At the end, I would like to say that regardless of whether you have passed or failed, you have undertaken a great challenge and while it can be disappointing to fail, you should try to consider it as a part of a learning curve. It can be a challenge taking Salesforce exams, but each time you take one, you become more comfortable with the exam format, the style of questions, and therefore, it will be somewhat easier next time.

Good luck with your Salesforce Certified Platform App Builder exam!

Other Books You May Enjoy

If you enjoyed this book, you may be interested in these other books by Packt:

Salesforce for Beginners

Sharif Shaalan

ISBN: 978-1-83898-609-4

- Understand the difference between Salesforce Lightning and Salesforce Classic
- Create and manage leads in Salesforce
- Explore business development with accounts and contacts in Salesforce
- Find out how stages and sales processes help you manage your opportunity pipeline
- Achieve marketing goals using Salesforce campaigns
- Perform business analysis using reports and dashboards
- Gain a high-level overview of the items in the administration section
- Grasp the different aspects needed to build an effective and flexible Salesforce security model

Hands-On Low-Code Application Development with Salesforce

Enrico Murru

ISBN: 978-1-80020-977-0

- Get to grips with the fundamentals of data modeling to enhance data quality

- Deliver dynamic configuration capabilities using custom settings and metadata types

- Secure your data by implementing the Salesforce security model

- Customize Salesforce applications with Lightning App Builder

- Create impressive pages for your community using Experience Builder

- Use Data Loader to import and export data without writing any code

- Embrace the Salesforce Ohana culture to share knowledge and learn from the global Salesforce community

Leave a review - let other readers know what you think

Please share your thoughts on this book with others by leaving a review on the site that you bought it from. If you purchased the book from Amazon, please leave us an honest review on this book's Amazon page. This is vital so that other potential readers can see and use your unbiased opinion to make purchasing decisions, we can understand what our customers think about our products, and our authors can see your feedback on the title that they have worked with Packt to create. It will only take a few minutes of your time, but is valuable to other potential customers, our authors, and Packt. Thank you!

Index

Made in United States
North Haven, CT
10 January 2022

14467966R00226